Haskell Programming

From Basics to Expert Proficiency

Contents

Introduction

Haskell, a statically typed, purely functional programming language, occupies a unique place in the landscape of programming languages. It is designed with strong emphasis on correctness, stability, and performance, which makes it an ideal choice for a range of applications from academic research to industry-grade software systems. This book, *Haskell Programming: From Basics to Expert Proficiency*, aims to equip readers with a thorough understanding of Haskell, taking them from foundational concepts to advanced topics.

The origins of Haskell can be traced back to a collective effort by a group of researchers in the late 1980s. Their goal was to create a standard for functional programming languages, leading to the development of Haskell. Named after the logician Haskell Curry, the language has since evolved, incorporating features that promote robust software design and efficient execution.

Learning Haskell offers numerous benefits. Firstly, it encourages a disciplined approach to programming, where functions are first-class citizens and immutable values are the norm. These principles result in code that is easier to reason about, refactor, and test. Secondly, Haskell's type system, with its advanced features such as type classes and algebraic data types, empowers developers to catch errors at compile time, thus reducing runtime failures. Lastly, Haskell's lazy evaluation model allows for the definition of infinite data structures and the efficient manipulation of large datasets.

Before embarking on this learning journey, it is essential to set up an appropriate Haskell environment. This involves installing the Glasgow Haskell Compiler (GHC) and related tools such as Cabal or Stack for managing Haskell projects. A thorough step-by-step guide for setting up these tools on various operating systems will be provided to ensure a smooth start.

The first step in programming with Haskell is writing a simple "Hello, World!" program. This exercise introduces the basic structure of a Haskell program, including modules, the main function, and how to compile and run Haskell code. Understanding the compilation process is crucial as it provides insights into how Haskell code is translated into efficient machine code. Additionally, GHCi, Haskell's interactive environment, offers a powerful tool for experimenting with code snippets, testing functions, and debugging.

As you delve deeper into Haskell, you will encounter its distinct syntax and key features. These include pattern matching, list comprehensions, and a syntax that emphasizes expressiveness and clarity. Haskell's syntax might initially seem unconventional for those accustomed to imperative languages, but it is designed to reflect the underlying principles of functional programming.

Throughout this book, numerous resources will be referenced to aid in learning Haskell. These include official documentation, online tutorials, and Haskell communities that provide support and foster discussion. Leveraging these resources can enhance your understanding and proficiency with the language.

In summary, Haskell represents a powerful paradigm in the world of programming languages. By emphasizing pure functions, strong typing, and lazy evaluation, it fosters the development of robust, maintainable, and efficient software. This book is structured to provide a comprehensive introduction to Haskell, gradually building up from basic concepts to more advanced topics, thus equipping you with the knowledge and skills to master this elegant language.

Chapter 1

Introduction to Haskell

This chapter provides a foundational understanding of Haskell, covering its origins, key features, and benefits for programmers. It guides the reader through setting up a Haskell development environment, introduces basic Haskell syntax with a first program, and explains the compilation process using GHC and GHCi. The chapter also highlights important resources for learning Haskell effectively.

1.1 What is Haskell?

Haskell is a purely functional programming language named after the mathematician Haskell Curry. It is known for its strong static typing, immutability, and elegant syntax that encourages a declarative programming style. Haskell allows developers to write concise and efficient code by focusing on what to solve rather than how to solve it, thus promoting code readability and maintainability.

One of the key attributes of Haskell is its emphasis on purity. In Haskell, functions are pure, meaning they do not have side effects and their outputs depend solely on their inputs. This purity facilitates reasoning about code and ensures that functions can be tested in isolation. Consequently, Haskell programs are often more reliable and less prone to bugs compared to programs written in imperative languages.

Haskell employs lazy evaluation, a technique where expressions are not evaluated until their values are needed. This allows for the construction of infinite data structures and supports powerful patterns of computation. For instance, consider the infinite list of natural numbers. In Haskell, you can define it as follows:

```
naturals :: [Integer]
naturals = [0..]
```

With lazy evaluation, the list naturals will generate values only as they are required, making it feasible to work with theoretically infinite structures.

Haskell's type system is another cornerstone of its design. It uses a sophisticated type inference mechanism that enables the compiler to deduce the types of expressions automatically, reducing the need for explicit type annotations. The strong static typing and type inference combined help catch errors at compile-time, thereby avoiding many potential run-time issues.

A simple example of type inference can be demonstrated with the following function:

```
add :: Num a => a -> a -> a
add x y = x + y
```

Here, Haskell infers that the function add takes two arguments of the same numeric type and returns a result of that type. In the type signature, Num a => denotes that the type a must be an instance of the Num type class.

Haskell also supports higher-order functions, which are functions that take other functions as arguments or return them as results. This feature enables a high level of abstraction and code reuse. Consider the function map, which applies a given function to each element of a list:

```
map :: (a -> b) -> [a] -> [b]
map _ [] = []
map f (x:xs) = f x : map f xs
```

In this definition, map takes a function f and a list, then applies f to every element of the list, returning a new list with the results.

Haskell's expressive power is further enhanced by its support for algebraic data types and pattern matching. Algebraic data types allow developers to define complex data structures in a clean and intuitive way. For example:

```
data Maybe a = Nothing | Just a
```

This defines a type Maybe which can represent optional values, a pattern often used to handle missing data without resorting to null references, which are common sources of runtime errors in other languages.

Pattern matching provides a concise and readable way to deconstruct data types and work with their components. For example, handling the Maybe type:

```
safeDiv :: Int -> Int -> Maybe Int
safeDiv _ 0 = Nothing
safeDiv x y = Just (x `div` y)
```

Here, the function safeDiv performs safe division by returning Nothing if the denominator is zero and wrapping the result in a Just otherwise.

Haskell also facilitates concurrency and parallelism, making it well-suited for modern applications that require efficient multitasking. The language's abstractions for concurrent programming, such as Software Transactional Memory (STM), streamline the development process for concurrent tasks, while ensuring reliability and simplicity.

Lastly, Haskell's ecosystem includes the Glasgow Haskell Compiler (GHC), which is renowned for its performance and advanced optimization capabilities. GHC is actively developed and maintained by a vibrant community, ensuring that Haskell remains at the forefront of functional programming.

By understanding these core aspects of Haskell, programmers can leverage its features to write robust, efficient, and elegant code that stands the test of time.

1.2 History of Haskell

Haskell is a purely functional programming language named after Haskell Brooks Curry, an American mathematician and logician known for his work in combinatory logic. The development of Haskell began in the late 1980s, during a period when numerous functional programming languages were being created and explored, each with its own unique attributes and paradigms. The proliferation of these languages was driven by the increasing recognition of the advantages provided by functional programming principles in creating robust, maintainable, and abstractly powerful software.

In September 1987, a meeting took place in Portland, Oregon, where several prominent researchers in the field of functional programming convened. The key attendees included Simon Peyton Jones, Paul Hudak, Philip Wadler, John Hughes, and many others. They recognized that the functional programming community would benefit from a consolidated effort to create a standard functional language. This recognition led to the formation of the Haskell committee, which embarked on the creation of a new language that would embody the best features of existing functional programming languages while offering new insights and capabilities.

The primary design goals for Haskell were:

- **Purity**: The language would emphasize pure functions, where the output value of a function depends only on the arguments that are input to the function, and there are no side effects.
- **Lazy Evaluation**: Haskell would adopt lazy evaluation, ensuring that computations are performed only when necessary, thus enabling better control over resource management and allowing the definition of efficient infinite data structures.
- **Type System**: Haskell would incorporate a strong static type system, facilitating early detection of errors during compilation and promoting robust code.
- **Modularity and Reusability**: The language would support a high degree of modularity, allowing reusable code libraries and facilitating easier maintenance and extension of code bases.
- **Interoperability**: Haskell was designed to interface seamlessly with other languages and systems, thereby enabling integration into existing technology stacks and leveraging existing software infrastructure.

The first version of the Haskell Report was published in April 1990. Haskell 1.0 specified the foundational syntax, semantics, and libraries of the language. The initial specification was followed by several iterations, each introducing refinements and enhancements to the language:

- **Haskell 1.1 to 1.4 (1991-1997)**: These versions involved numerous clarifications, bug fixes, and incremental additions to the standard libraries, further improving the language's robustness and utility.

- **Haskell 98 (1998)**: This release aimed to provide a stable, minimal, and portable version of the language that could act as a solid foundation for future developments and educational efforts. Haskell 98 became widely accepted and was used in many educational and industrial applications.

- **Haskell 2010 (2010)**: Building on Haskell 98, Haskell 2010 incorporated several language extensions and features that had gained widespread acceptance in the community, such as hierarchical module namespaces, the Foreign Function Interface (FFI), and relaxed restrictions on polymorphic types.

The ongoing evolution of Haskell is driven by the Haskell Prime committee, which oversees the language's development and ensures that it continues to meet the needs of both academic research and practical software development. They manage proposed language extensions, ensuring backward compatibility while integrating innovative features that enhance the expressiveness and efficiency of the language.

Haskell's influence extends beyond its own ecosystem, inspiring the development of numerous other functional languages and programming paradigms. Concepts pioneered in Haskell, such as monads, have been adopted in languages like Scala, F#, and even JavaScript. Additionally, the language has found successful applications in various domains, including financial analysis, telecommunications, and formal verification.

The rich history of Haskell reflects the collaborative and open nature of its development process, combining insights from academic research and real-world programming experiences. Through iterative refinement and community engagement, Haskell has become a cornerstone of functional programming, admired for its theoretical elegance and practical potency.

1.3 Why Learn Haskell?

Haskell offers a wide array of advantages and unique features that make it an attractive programming language for both beginner and experienced programmers. Understanding these benefits provides a compelling rationale for learning Haskell and leveraging its capabilities in various domains.

First and foremost, Haskell is a *purely functional programming* (FP) language. It treats computation as the evaluation of mathematical functions and avoids changing-state and mutable data. This approach leads to several advantages:

- **Immutability:** By default, variables in Haskell are immutable. Once a variable is bound to a value, it cannot be altered. This immutability eliminates a whole class of bugs related to state changes and side effects, resulting in more predictable and reliable code.
- **Referential Transparency:** Haskell functions are referentially transparent, meaning that an expression can be replaced by its value without changing the program's behavior. This property simplifies reasoning about code and allows for more powerful optimizations by the compiler.

Haskell's type system is another significant advantage. It uses a strong, static type system with type inference, enforcing that errors are caught at compile time rather than runtime. This type safety is enhanced by features such as:

- **Algebraic Data Types (ADTs):** Haskell supports the creation of custom data types using ADTs. This allows for more expressive code and can enforce invariants and constraints directly in the type system.
- **Pattern Matching:** The ability to match patterns against data structures provides a concise and readable way to decompose data and handle various cases in functions.

Furthermore, Haskell encourages a *declarative programming style*. Instead of describing how to perform computations, Haskell allows programmers to specify what computations should be performed. This style emphasizes expressing computation logic without explicitly describing control flow, making code more abstract and concise.

The language boasts a powerful module system, promoting code reuse and modularity. Haskell programs can be composed of multiple modules, each encapsulating related functionality. This modularity aids in maintaining and scaling large codebases.

Concurrency and parallelism are other domains where Haskell excels. The language's design, particularly its pure functions and immutability, makes it easier to write concurrent and parallel code. Notable features include:

- **Software Transactional Memory (STM):** This abstraction simplifies writing thread-safe concurrent code. It allows for composable memory transactions, avoiding many pitfalls of traditional locking mechanisms.

- **Lightweight Threads:** Haskell supports a large number of lightweight threads through its runtime system. This makes concurrent programming efficient and scalable.

Haskell's lazy evaluation strategy also sets it apart from many other programming languages. Instead of evaluating expressions immediately, Haskell delays computation until the results are required. This can lead to performance benefits and allows for the definition of potentially infinite data structures, such as streams.

```
-- Defines an infinite list of Fibonacci numbers
fibonacci :: [Integer]
fibonacci = 0 : 1 : zipWith (+) fibonacci (tail fibonacci)

-- Takes the first 10 elements of the infinite Fibonacci list
take 10 fibonacci
```

```
Output:
[0,1,1,2,3,5,8,13,21,34]
```

Another significant value of learning Haskell is the community and ecosystem. Haskell has a vibrant and supportive community that contributes to a rich ecosystem of libraries and tools. The Haskell package repository, Hackage, contains thousands of libraries covering a wide range of functionality, from web development to data analysis.

The language's design also makes it suitable for high-assurance systems, where correctness and reliability are paramount. Industries such as finance, aerospace, and telecommunications leverage Haskell for developing software where failure is not an option.

Lastly, learning Haskell can significantly improve one's understanding of programming paradigms. The concepts and patterns learned in Haskell, such as pure functions, immutability, and higher-order functions, can be transferable to other languages and paradigms. This enriches a programmer's skill set and enhances their ability to solve problems in more diverse and effective ways.

1.4 Setting Up Your Haskell Environment

In order to begin programming in Haskell, you need to correctly set up your development environment. This section guides you through the installation and configuration process on various operating systems including Windows, macOS, and Linux. A correctly configured environment is essential for writing, compiling, and debugging Haskell programs efficiently.

Installation of GHC and GHCi

The Glasgow Haskell Compiler (GHC) is the foremost Haskell compiler, and GHCi is its interactive environment. Both are crucial for Haskell development.

- **Windows:**
  1. Download the Haskell Platform from its official site at https://www.haskell.org/platform/.
  2. Run the installer and follow the instructions, accepting the default options.
  3. After the installation is complete, verify it by opening the Command Prompt and typing:

     ```
     > ghc --version
     > ghci --version
     ```

     The commands should output the installed versions of GHC and GHCi, respectively.
- **macOS:**
  1. Install Homebrew if it is not already available. Homebrew is a package manager that simplifies the installation of software on macOS.
  2. Open the Terminal and install Homebrew by running:

     ```
     /bin/bash -c "$(curl -fsSL https://raw.githubusercontent.com/
         Homebrew/install/HEAD/install.sh)"
     ```
  3. Once Homebrew is installed, use it to install GHC and GHCi:

     ```
     brew install ghc
     ```

4. Verify the installation by typing:

```
ghc --version
ghci --version
```

The installed versions of GHC and GHCi should be displayed.

- **Linux:**

1. Use the package manager specific to your Linux distribution.
2. For Debian-based distributions (like Ubuntu), open the Terminal and type:

```
sudo apt-get update
sudo apt-get install ghc
```

3. For Red Hat-based distributions (like Fedora), use:

```
sudo dnf install ghc
```

4. Verify the installation with:

```
ghc --version
ghci --version
```

The respective versions of GHC and GHCi should be displayed.

Setting Up an Integrated Development Environment (IDE)

While it is possible to write Haskell programs using a simple text editor, using an Integrated Development Environment (IDE) enhances productivity by providing syntax highlighting, code completion, and error detection.

- **Visual Studio Code:**

1. Download and install Visual Studio Code from https://code.visualstudio.com/.
2. Install the Haskell extension by opening Visual Studio Code and navigating to the Extensions view by clicking the Extensions icon in the Activity Bar on the side of the window.
3. Search for "Haskell" and install the extension provided by the Haskell team.

4. Enable the extension and restart Visual Studio Code if necessary.
5. Verify that the Haskell extension is working by creating a new Haskell file with the .hs extension and typing some sample Haskell code. The IDE should provide syntax highlighting and basic error checking.

- **Atom:**
  1. Download and install Atom from https://atom.io/.
  2. Open Atom and go to File > Settings > Install. Search for Haskell and install the ide-haskell and language-haskell packages.
  3. To enhance the experience further, you can also install haskell-ghc-mod, which provides additional GHC functionality.
  4. Restart Atom and open a Haskell file to ensure that syntax highlighting and other features are enabled.

- **Sublime Text:**
  1. Download and install Sublime Text from https://www.sublimetext.com/.
  2. Open Sublime Text and install Package Control by following the instructions at https://packagecontrol.io/installation.
  3. Use Package Control to install the Haskell-Sublime-Package and SublimeHaskell.
  4. Open a Haskell file to verify that the Haskell support features are active.

Validating the Environment Setup

After installing GHC, GHCi, and your chosen IDE, it is important to ensure that the environment is set up correctly before diving into writing complex Haskell programs.

- Create a new file named Hello.hs with the following content:

```
main = putStrLn "Hello, Haskell!"
```

- Open your command line interface and navigate to the directory containing Hello.hs.
- Compile the program using GHC:

```
ghc -o hello Hello.hs
```

- Run the executable:

```
./hello
```

  The output should be:

```
Hello, Haskell!
```

- Open the GHCi interactive environment by typing ghci and then load the Hello.hs file:

```
:load Hello.hs
```

  Execute the main function:

```
main
```

  The output should again be:

```
Hello, Haskell!
```

This comprehensive setup process ensures that you have all the necessary tools and configurations to start developing in Haskell efficiently.

1.5 Your First Haskell Program

A critical step towards mastering Haskell is writing and understanding your first program. Haskell, a statically-typed, pure functional programming language, emphasizes immutability and mathematical functions. This section will walk through the creation of a simple Haskell program, explaining each component thoroughly.

Before writing your first Haskell program, ensure you have set up the Haskell development environment and have access to the GHC (Glasgow Haskell Compiler) or GHCi (the interactive environment of GHC). The process was covered in the "Setting Up Your Haskell Environment" section.

```
-- MyFirstProgram.hs

-- The main function is the entry point of a Haskell program
main :: IO ()
main = do
  -- Printing "Hello, World!" to the console
  putStrLn "Hello, World!"
```

The above listing shows a minimal Haskell program saved in a file named MyFirstProgram.hs. Let's break down the components:

- – MyFirstProgram.hs: This is a comment in Haskell. Comments are initiated with two hyphens and extend to the end of the line. This line is used to annotate the filename.
- main :: IO (): This line declares the type of the main function. In Haskell, functions and expressions have types, and :: is the type annotation operator. IO () indicates that main is an Input/Output action that returns no meaningful value (indicated by ()).
- main = do: The main function definition begins here. The do notation allows for sequencing of IO actions.
- putStrLn "Hello, World!": This is an IO action that prints the string "Hello, World!" to the console. putStrLn is a standard library function in Haskell for outputting a string followed by a newline.

After writing the program, you need to compile and run it. Open your terminal and navigate to the directory containing MyFirstProgram.hs. Compile the program using the following command:

```
ghc -o myfirstprogram MyFirstProgram.hs
```

Here, -o myfirstprogram specifies the name of the output executable. After successful compilation, you can execute your program with:

```
./myfirstprogram
```

The output will be:

```
Hello, World!
```

Haskell programs can also be run interactively using GHCi. Load MyFirstProgram.hs by running:

```
ghci MyFirstProgram.hs
```

In the GHCi prompt, execute the main function:

```
*Main> main
```

The output will be the same:

```
Hello, World!
```

This simple program demonstrates the structure of a Haskell program, including function definition, type annotations, and basic IO operations. Understanding these fundamental aspects is crucial for progressing with more complex Haskell applications.

1.6 Understanding Haskell Compilation

Understanding the compilation process in Haskell is fundamental for any programmer aiming to write efficient and effectively managed Haskell code. Haskell, being a statically typed, compiled language, involves a comprehensive compilation sequence to transform the high-level code into executable binaries.

The primary tool for Haskell compilation is the Glasgow Haskell Compiler (GHC). GHC is an open-source native code compiler which supports Haskell 98 and Haskell 2010 standards, with many extensions.

GHC Compilation Stages:

To compile a Haskell program, GHC follows several stages. These stages ensure the code is correctly parsed, checked, and optimized before it is converted to an executable form. Below are the primary stages of GHC's compilation process:

- Parsing - The Haskell source code is read, and a syntax tree is constructed.
- Renaming - The compiler resolves variable bindings and ensures every variable is bound.
- Type Checking - The code is checked for type correctness based on Haskell's type system.
- Desugaring - High-level syntactic sugar is translated into a more primitive core representation.
- Core-to-Core Transformations - The intermediate representation known as "Core" undergoes a series of optimization transformations.

- Code Generation - The optimized Core is translated into intermediate C– code or directly to assembly, depending on back-end options.
- Linking - The generated machine code is linked with necessary libraries to create the final executable.

Basic GHC Commands:

The most common way to compile a Haskell program is using the ghc command followed by various flags and the source file name. Below is an example Haskell program and the corresponding GHC compilation command:

```
-- Example.hs
module Main where

main :: IO ()
main = putStrLn "Hello, Haskell!"
```

To compile this program, one can use the following command in the terminal:

```
ghc -o Example Example.hs
```

This command invokes GHC to compile Example.hs, and the -o Example flag specifies the name of the output executable.

Compilation Options and Flags:

GHC provides a plethora of options and flags to control various aspects of the compilation process. Some useful options include:

- -O0, -O1, -O2 - These flags control the optimization level. Higher levels (-O2) enable more aggressive optimizations.
- -Wall - This flag enables comprehensive warnings which help in identifying potential issues in the code.
- -prof - Enables profiling support, useful for performance analysis.
- -threaded - Enables support for multithreading in the generated executable.

GHCi - The Interactive Compiler:

GHCi is the interactive environment provided by GHC. It allows for rapid testing and development by executing Haskell expressions interactively.

To start GHCi, simply run ghci in the terminal. One can then load and test Haskell code snippets directly. For example:

```
Prelude> :load Example.hs
[1 of 1] Compiling Main ( Example.hs, interpreted )
Ok, modules loaded: Main.
*Main> main
Hello, Haskell!
```

Within GHCi, several commands help manage the workflow:

- :load <filename> - Load a Haskell source file.
- :reload - Reload the current program, useful after making changes.
- :type <expression> - Display the type of the given expression.
- :info <identifier> - Show information about the specified identifier.

Error Handling and Debugging:

During compilation, GHC provides detailed error messages to aid in debugging. Common errors include syntax errors, type errors, and missing module imports. An example error message might look like this:

```
Example.hs:3:8: error:
    • Couldn't match expected type 'Int' with actual type 'String'
    • In the expression: "Hello"
      In an equation for 'main': main = "Hello"
```

This message indicates a type mismatch in Example.hs at line 3, character 8, helping you pinpoint and resolve the issue.

Through understanding the compilation stages, utilizing the various GHC commands, and making effective use of GHCi, Haskell programmers can optimize and streamline their development process, ensuring robust and performant applications.

1.7 Haskell's GHCi: Interactive Haskell

GHCi, short for Glasgow Haskell Compiler interactive, serves as an indispensable tool for Haskell programmers. It offers a Read-Eval-Print Loop (REPL) that enables users to interactively work with Haskell code, whether for experimentation, testing, or learning purposes.

To start GHCi, simply type ghci in your terminal:

```
$ ghci
GHCi, version 8.10.4: https://www.haskell.org/ghc/ :? for help
Loaded GHCi configuration from /home/user/.ghci
Prelude>
```

Once launched, GHCi presents a prompt (Prelude>), indicating readiness for input. The Prelude module, Haskell's standard library, is loaded by default. To close GHCi, use the command :quit or the shortcut :q.

Example:

```
Prelude> :quit
Leaving GHCi.
```

An essential feature of GHCi is the ability to load Haskell source files. Suppose you have a Haskell file named example.hs:

```
$ cat example.hs
module Example where

add :: Int -> Int -> Int
add x y = x + y
```

To load example.hs into GHCi, use the :load command followed by the filename:

```
Prelude> :load example.hs
[1 of 1] Compiling Example ( example.hs, interpreted )
Ok, one module loaded.
*Example>
```

The prompt changes from Prelude> to *Example>, signifying that the Example module is now in scope. The * indicates interactive mode, which allows for redefinitions and debugging.

Functions within the loaded module can now be used:

```
*Example> add 3 5
8
```

GHCi also supports inline code execution, making it ideal for rapid prototyping. Here's how you can define and evaluate functions directly:

```
Prelude> let square x = x * x
Prelude> square 4
16
```

The let keyword is required for defining functions and variables within GHCi.

GHCi's command suite enhances its functionality, including commands like:

- :type - Display the type of an expression.
- :info - Provide information about a name (e.g., functions, types).
- :reload - Reload the current module.
- :set - Modify GHCi settings.

Examples:

```
*Example> :type add
add :: Int -> Int -> Int

*Example> :info add
add :: Int -> Int -> Int  -- Defined at example.hs:4:1

*Example> :reload
Ok, one module loaded.

*Example> :set +t
*Example> add 2 3
5
it :: Int
```

Enhanced interaction can be achieved via GHCi's scripting capabilities. You can write a series of GHCi commands in a script file and run them using the :script command:

```
$ echo ":type add" > commands.ghci
$ echo "add 1 2" >> commands.ghci
*Example> :script commands.ghci
add :: Int -> Int -> Int
3
```

For persistent configurations, use the .ghci file, located in your home directory. Here you can preset commands to run every time GHCi starts. For example:

```
$ cat ~/.ghci
:set +t
:load example.hs
```

Upon starting GHCi, these settings are automatically applied:

```
$ ghci
GHCi, version 8.10.4: https://www.haskell.org/ghc/ :? for help
Loaded GHCi configuration from /home/user/.ghci
[1 of 1] Compiling Example ( example.hs, interpreted )
Ok, one module loaded.
*Example>
```

GHCi can also perform interactive debugging. By enabling breakpoints within your Haskell code and using GHCi's debugging commands (:break, :continue, :step, etc.), you can step through code execution to diagnose issues. Enable debugging with the -fbreak-on-error or -fbreak-on-exception flags:

```
$ ghci -fbreak-on-error -fbreak-on-exception example.hs
*Example> :break add
Breakpoint 0 activated at example.hs:4:1-4
*Example> add 1 2
Stopped at example.hs:4:1-4
_result :: Int = _
```

GHCi's flexibility and powerful toolset provide a robust environment for both novice and experienced Haskell developers to explore, prototype, and fine-tune their code with ease.

1.8 Basic Haskell Syntax Overview

Haskell syntax, designed for both clarity and conciseness, emphasizes readability and maintainability. This section will explore fundamental elements of Haskell syntax, including comments, basic types, functions, list comprehensions, and pattern matching.

Comments in Haskell are indicated by two hyphens (–) for single-line comments or a multi-line block enclosed in {- -}:

```
-- This is a single-line comment

{- This is a
   multi-line comment -}
```

Haskell is dynamically typed, but types can be explicitly declared for clarity and type-checking purposes. The basic types in Haskell include Int, Float, Bool, and Char. Type declarations follow a specific format:

```
x :: Int
x = 10

piValue :: Float
piValue = 3.14

isActive :: Bool
isActive = True

initial :: Char
initial = 'A'
```

Functions are central to Haskell programming. A function's type declaration specifies the type of its parameters and return value:

```
add :: Int -> Int -> Int
add x y = x + y
```

Haskell supports **list comprehensions**, which allow for constructing lists from existing lists.

```
-- List of squares from 1 to 10
squares = [x^2 | x <- [1..10]]

-- List of even numbers from 1 to 20
evens = [x | x <- [1..20], even x]
```

Next, **pattern matching** provides a way to deconstruct data structures. Patterns are matched against the form of the input data and executed accordingly:

```
factorial :: Int -> Int
factorial 0 = 1
factorial n = n * factorial (n - 1)

isZero :: Int -> Bool
isZero 0 = True
isZero _ = False
```

Tuples allow for storing fixed sized collections of elements possibly of different types. Unlike lists, which are homogeneous, tuples can hold a variety of types:

```
-- Tuple containing an Int and a Char
tupleExample :: (Int, Char)
tupleExample = (1, 'a')

-- Function that swaps the elements of a tuple
swap :: (a, b) -> (b, a)
swap (x, y) = (y, x)
```

Guards are a way to test whether conditions hold. They provide a way to specify different values or functions based on boolean expressions:

```
absoluteValue :: Int -> Int
absoluteValue n
    | n < 0 = -n
    | otherwise = n
```

Let expressions bind variables to values or functions. These can be used to simplify complex expressions:

```
cylinder :: Float -> Float -> Float
cylinder r h =
    let sideArea = 2 * pi * r * h
        topArea = pi * r^2
    in sideArea + 2 * topArea
```

Finally, **where clauses** offer a way to bind values that are used in a function:

```
maximum' :: (Ord a) => [a] -> a
maximum' [] = error "empty list"
maximum' [x] = x
maximum' (x:xs)
    | x > maxTail = x
    | otherwise = maxTail
    where maxTail = maximum' xs
```

This concise and systematic approach to Haskell syntax provides a foundation that facilitates both learning and practical application. As we progress, understanding these basic elements will be essential for mastering more intricate concepts.

1.9 Key Features of Haskell

Haskell is a purely functional programming language known for several key features that distinguish it from other languages. Understanding these features is crucial for leveraging Haskell's full potential and writing efficient, maintainable code.

1. Pure Functions

Haskell ensures that functions are pure, meaning they do not have side effects. A pure function's output relies solely on its input arguments, and it does not affect the program's state or interact with external states such as global variables. This characteristic makes reasoning about and testing Haskell programs straightforward.

```
-- A pure function example
add :: Int -> Int -> Int
add x y = x + y
```

The function add takes two integers and returns their sum. It only depends on the input values and does not alter any external state.

2. Lazy Evaluation

Haskell uses lazy evaluation, meaning expressions are not evaluated until their results are needed. This approach allows for the creation of infinite data structures and can lead to performance improvements by avoiding unnecessary calculations.

```
-- Infinite list of natural numbers
naturals :: [Int]
naturals = [0..]
```

In the above code, the list naturals represents an infinite list of natural numbers starting from 0. Haskell will only compute values from this list as they are required.

3. Type Inference

Haskell has a robust type inference system that reduces the need for explicit type annotations. The compiler deduces the types of expressions automatically, making code shorter and less error-prone while keeping strong type safety.

```
-- Haskell infers that x is of type Int
x = 10
```

Here, Haskell infers that x is an Int based on the assigned value 10.

4. Strong Static Typing

Haskell is a statically typed language with a strong type system. This feature ensures type errors are caught at compile-time, reducing runtime errors and improving code reliability.

```
-- Misleading type assignment will raise a compile-time error
badAdd :: Int -> Int -> String
badAdd x y = x + y
```

The function badAdd will cause a type error because it claims to return a String but attempts to perform an integer addition instead.

5. First-Class Functions

In Haskell, functions are first-class citizens, meaning they can be passed as arguments, returned from other functions, and assigned to variables.

```
-- Higher-order function that takes a function as an argument
applyTwice :: (a -> a) -> a -> a
applyTwice f x = f (f x)
```

The function applyTwice takes a function f and a value x, applying f to x twice.

6. Immutability

All variables in Haskell are immutable, meaning once a value is assigned to a variable, it cannot be changed. This immutability eliminates side effects, making programs easier to reason about.

```
-- Attempting to modify an immutable variable is incorrect
x = 5
x = x + 1 -- This is not allowed in Haskell
```

7. Pattern Matching

Haskell's pattern matching allows for checking a value against a pattern and deconstructing data structures easily. It is both a practical and expressive way to write conditional code.

```
-- Pattern matching on lists
sumList :: [Int] -> Int
sumList [] = 0
sumList (x:xs) = x + sumList xs
```

The function sumList uses pattern matching to recursively sum the elements of a list.

8. Algebraic Data Types (ADTs)

Haskell's ADTs enable the definition of composite types through a combination of existing types. They are essential for modeling complex data structures.

```
-- Define an algebraic data type for a binary tree
data Tree a = Empty | Node a (Tree a) (Tree a)

-- Function to compute the size of a binary tree
treeSize :: Tree a -> Int
treeSize Empty = 0
treeSize (Node _ left right) = 1 + treeSize left + treeSize right
```

The Tree type can represent a tree structure with nodes containing values of any type.

9. List Comprehensions

List comprehensions provide a concise way to build lists. This syntactic construct allows for expressing complex list operations in a readable manner.

```
-- Generate a list of even numbers up to 10
evens = [x | x <- [1..10], even x]
```

In the example, the comprehension constructs a list of even numbers from 1 to 10.

10. Monads and Do Notation

Monads in Haskell abstract and handle computational contexts, such as I/O, state, and exceptions. Do notation simplifies monadic code, making it clearer and more readable.

```
-- Using do notation for monadic operations
main :: IO ()
main = do
  putStrLn "Enter your name:"
```

```
name <- getLine
putStrLn ("Hello, " ++ name ++ "!")
```

The main function uses do notation to sequence I/O operations for reading and printing a user's name.

Haskell's features collectively contribute to its expressiveness and reliability as a functional programming language. These characteristics make it a powerful tool for developers, supporting both academic research and practical applications in industry. Understanding these features allows for writing more effective and efficient Haskell programs.

1.10 Resources for Learning Haskell

Understanding and mastering Haskell necessitates access to quality resources that provide a breadth and depth of knowledge. Here, we present a curated compilation of resources beneficial for learners at various levels, from beginners to those seeking expert proficiency.

- **Books**
  - *Learn You a Haskell for Great Good!* by Miran Lipovača. This book is highly recommended for beginners due to its accessible and humorous style. The author introduces Haskell concepts gradually, ensuring readers grasp the fundamentals before progressing to more complex topics.
  - *Real World Haskell* by Bryan O'Sullivan, Don Stewart, and John Goerzen. This book targets intermediate learners and focuses on practical application of Haskell in real-world scenarios. It includes numerous examples and exercises to reinforce learning.
  - *Haskell Programming from First Principles* by Christopher Allen and Julie Moronuki. This comprehensive guide is suitable for all levels, covering foundational concepts in detail and progressing to advanced topics. Known for its clarity and structured approach, it includes exercises to aid comprehension and mastery.
- **Online Courses**
  - *Introduction to Functional Programming* by Erik Meijer on Coursera. This course offers a solid foundation in functional programming using Haskell, ideal for beginners.

  - *Functional Programming in Haskell* on Pluralsight. This course is designed for intermediate learners, exploring Haskell's advanced features and applications.
  - *Haskell and Functional Programming on LinkedIn Learning*. This course dives into Haskell's functional programming paradigms, aimed at learners seeking to deepen their understanding.

- **Interactive Platforms**
  - *HackerRank*. Provides a range of Haskell challenges to practice problem-solving and coding skills in a competitive environment.
  - *Exercism*. Offers Haskell exercises with mentorship and feedback from experienced Haskell developers.
  - *Learn Haskell and Purely Functional Data Structures* on Codecademy. Interactive lessons designed to teach both the Haskell language and the principles of functional data structure design.

- **Documentation and Tutorials**
  - *The Haskell Wiki*. An extensive compilation of Haskell resources, tutorials, and documentation maintained by the Haskell community.
  - *Hoogle*. A Haskell API search engine that helps you find the right functions and libraries by type or name.
  - *Hackage*. The Haskell community's package database, containing libraries and tools that can significantly enhance Haskell programming.

- **Community and Support**
  - *Haskell-Café Mailing List*. A welcoming platform for discussions, queries, and knowledge sharing among Haskell programmers.
  - *Stack Overflow*. Numerous questions and detailed answers related to Haskell programming, useful for troubleshooting and advanced problem-solving.
  - *Reddit's Haskell Subreddit*. A community where learners and professionals discuss topics, share resources, and provide support about Haskell.

- *Haskell on Discord and Slack.* Real-time chat platforms for direct interaction with Haskell enthusiasts, offering quick support and collaborative learning.

For those looking to deepen their Haskell knowledge and expertise, combining multiple resources such as books, online courses, interactive platforms, and community support will provide a comprehensive learning experience. Engaging with diverse materials ensures a well-rounded understanding and practical proficiency in the Haskell programming language.

Chapter 2

Basic Syntax and Operations

This chapter covers the fundamental building blocks of Haskell programming, including writing a simple "Hello World" program, defining variables and constants, exploring basic data types and operations, and understanding arithmetic and logical operations. It also delves into conditional expressions, pattern matching, tuple and list manipulations, string operations, and the conventions for comments and documentation in Haskell.

2.1 Hello World in Haskell

To start with Haskell programming, the canonical "Hello World" example serves as an introduction to basic I/O operations. In Haskell, this involves understanding the main function and the putStrLn function for output.

The minimal "Hello World" program in Haskell is represented as follows:

```
main :: IO ()
main = putStrLn "Hello, World!"
```

The program has two parts: the type signature and the function implementation. The type signature main :: IO () indicates that the main function performs an input/output action that returns no meaningful value (unit type, ()).

The implementation of main uses putStrLn, a function that takes a string and prints it to the standard output, followed by a newline character.

When executed, the output is:

```
Hello, World!
```

To execute this program, save the code in a file named HelloWorld.hs. Open a terminal and navigate to the directory containing this file. Run the GHC (Glasgow Haskell Compiler) to compile and execute the program:

```
$ ghc -o HelloWorld HelloWorld.hs
$ ./HelloWorld
Hello, World!
```

First, the command ghc -o HelloWorld HelloWorld.hs compiles the source file into an executable named HelloWorld. The second command, ./HelloWorld, runs the executable, producing the output.

Haskell's approach to I/O operations, including this simple "Hello World" program, reflects the language's handling of side effects using monads. The IO type is a monad that encapsulates any side effects, ensuring purity across the language. This separation of pure and impure code is a central concept in Haskell.

Exploring I/O Actions

Consider altering the program to include additional I/O actions. For instance, printing multiple lines of text:

```
main :: IO ()
main = do
    putStrLn "Hello, World!"
    putStrLn "Welcome to Haskell programming."
```

Here, the do notation sequences multiple I/O actions. Each action is executed in the order specified. The putStrLn function is called twice, once for each line printed, producing:

```
Hello, World!
Welcome to Haskell programming.
```

Combining I/O with Pure Functions

You can combine I/O actions with pure functions to produce more dynamic output. Consider reading the user's name and then greeting them:

```
main :: IO ()
```

```
main = do
    putStrLn "What is your name?"
    name <- getLine
    putStrLn ("Hello, " ++ name ++ "!")
```

The function getLine reads a line of input from the standard input. The <- operator binds the result to the variable name. Finally, putStrLn outputs a personalized greeting by concatenating "Hello, ", name, and "!" using the ++ operator.

When executed, the interaction appears as:

```
What is your name?
Alice
Hello, Alice!
```

Error Handling in I/O

Handling errors is crucial in I/O operations. Using catch from Control.Exception, you can manage exceptions. For example, consider a program that attempts to read a file:

```
import System.IO
import Control.Exception

main :: IO ()
main = do
    putStrLn "Enter the filename:"
    filename <- getLine
    content <- readFileSafe filename
    putStrLn content

readFileSafe :: FilePath -> IO String
readFileSafe path = catch (readFile path) handler
  where
    handler :: IOError -> IO String
    handler _ = return "Error: Unable to read file."
```

In this program, readFileSafe attempts to read the specified file. If reading fails, it catches the IOError and returns an error message. The function catch takes the I/O action and an exception handler as arguments.

By integrating these I/O actions and techniques, learners can build a solid foundation in Haskell's approach to managing side effects while maintaining code purity.

2.2 Variables and Constants

In Haskell, variables and constants play a critical role in the development of programs by enabling the storage and manipulation of values.

Unlike in imperative programming languages, variables in Haskell are immutable, meaning once a value is assigned to a variable, it cannot be altered. This immutability is a key characteristic of functional programming and helps to avoid side effects. Constants, similarly, are fixed values that do not change throughout the execution of the program.

Variables

In Haskell, variables are essentially symbolic names bound to expressions. Let's examine how variables are defined and used. Here's a simple example:

```
x = 5
y = x + 10
```

In this example, x is bound to the value 5, and y is bound to the expression x + 10. Thus, y evaluates to 15. Importantly, once defined, the values of x and y remain constant throughout the program.

Constants

Constants in Haskell can be defined similarly to variables but usually represent fixed values that are not intended to be changed. Naming conventions often use uppercase letters to differentiate constants from variables, although this is not enforced by the language syntax itself. Here's an example:

```
PI = 3.14159
radius = 10
circumference = 2 * PI * radius
```

In the above example, PI is a constant representing the value of π, radius is a variable set to 10, and circumference is the computed value of the circle's circumference using the formula $2\pi r$.

Type Annotations

Haskell allows you to explicitly specify the types of variables and constants using type annotations, which can aid readability and provide additional safety by ensuring type correctness. For example:

```
x :: Int
x = 5

y :: Int
y = x + 10

PI :: Double
PI = 3.14159

radius :: Double
radius = 10
```

```
circumference :: Double
circumference = 2 * PI * radius
```

In this code snippet, x and y are explicitly declared to be of type Int, while PI, radius, and circumference are declared to be of type Double.

Laziness

An important aspect of Haskell is its lazy evaluation model, which means expressions are not evaluated until their values are actually needed. This implies that when you define a variable, Haskell does not immediately compute its value. Instead, it waits until the value is required in the computation. Consider the following example:

```
a = 3
b = 4
sum = a + b
main = print sum
```

In this example, the values for a and b are not computed immediately upon definition. They are only evaluated when sum is evaluated in the main function. This lazy evaluation allows Haskell to handle potentially infinite data structures and perform optimizations that can improve the overall performance of a program.

Scope and Shadowing

In Haskell, the scope of a variable or constant is determined by where it is defined. Variables can be defined globally or locally within a function. Shadowing occurs when a local variable has the same name as a variable in an outer scope, thus temporarily "hiding" the outer variable. Here is an example demonstrating variable scope and shadowing:

```
x = 10
computeSum x = x + y
  where y = 5
```

In the function computeSum, the parameter x shadows the global x. When computeSum is called, the local x is used, and the global x remains unaffected. Therefore, computeSum 20 evaluates to 25.

Understanding these principles of defining and manipulating variables and constants is fundamental to effective Haskell programming. These concepts maintain the integrity of values throughout computations and contribute to the robust and predictable behavior of Haskell programs.

2.3 Basic Data Types and Operations

Haskell, as a statically typed language, requires every expression to have a type known at compile time. There are various basic data types in Haskell which serve as the foundational building blocks for constructing more complex data structures and operations. Understanding these types is critical for effective Haskell programming.

The most commonly utilized basic data types in Haskell include Int, Integer, Float, Double, Char, and Bool. Each of these data types serves specific purposes and has unique properties.

Integer Types

The Int type represents fixed-precision integers. Typically, the range of Int is architecture dependent, often being at least -2^{31} to $2^{31} - 1$ on a 32-bit system.

The Integer type, in contrast, represents arbitrarily large integers. This flexibility comes with an increased computational cost but ensures that there are no overflow constraints.

```
exampleInt :: Int
exampleInt = 42

exampleInteger :: Integer
exampleInteger = 123456789012345678901234567890
```

Floating-Point Types

The Float type is a single-precision floating-point number, which roughly corresponds to a 32-bit floating point number in other languages. The Double type is a double-precision floating-point number, corresponding to a 64-bit floating point number.

```
exampleFloat :: Float
exampleFloat = 3.14

exampleDouble :: Double
exampleDouble = 2.718281828459045
```

Character and String Types

The Char type represents a single Unicode character enclosed in single quotes, while strings are lists of characters denoted by the type [Char] and enclosed in double quotes.

```
exampleChar :: Char
exampleChar = 'a'

exampleString :: [Char]
```

```
exampleString = "Hello, Haskell!"
```

Boolean Type

The Bool type is used to represent boolean values which can either be True or False. These boolean values are fundamental in enabling conditional operations and logical constructs.

```
exampleBoolTrue :: Bool
exampleBoolTrue = True

exampleBoolFalse :: Bool
exampleBoolFalse = False
```

Basic Operations

Each data type supports a variety of operations. Here, we explore the operations pertinent to each discussed data type.

Integer Operations

For integer types (Int and Integer), operations include standard arithmetic operations like addition, subtraction, multiplication, and division. Modulus and exponentiation are also commonly utilized operations.

```
addIntegers :: Int -> Int -> Int
addIntegers x y = x + y

subtractIntegers :: Int -> Int -> Int
subtractIntegers x y = x - y

multiplyIntegers :: Int -> Int -> Int
multiplyIntegers x y = x * y

divideIntegers :: Int -> Int -> Int
divideIntegers x y = div x y

modulusIntegers :: Int -> Int -> Int
modulusIntegers x y = mod x y
```

Floating-Point Operations

Floating-point types (Float and Double) support arithmetic operations that are akin to those supported by integer types, with each ensuring precision according to its specification.

```
addFloats :: Float -> Float -> Float
addFloats x y = x + y

subtractFloats :: Float -> Float -> Float
subtractFloats x y = x - y

multiplyFloats :: Float -> Float -> Float
multiplyFloats x y = x * y

divideFloats :: Float -> Float -> Float
```

```
divideFloats x y = x / y
```

It is important to note that unlike integers, dividing two floating-point numbers does not require a separate integer division function.

Character Operations

Character operations mainly involve comparisons, such as checking for equality or ordering. Characters can also be manipulated with functions like ord and chr, which convert between characters and their corresponding Unicode values.

```
compareChars :: Char -> Char -> Bool
compareChars x y = x == y

toUnicode :: Char -> Int
toUnicode c = ord c

fromUnicode :: Int -> Char
fromUnicode u = chr u
```

Boolean Operations

Boolean operations include logical conjunction (\&\&), logical disjunction (||), and logical negation (not).

```
andOperation :: Bool -> Bool -> Bool
andOperation x y = x && y

orOperation :: Bool -> Bool -> Bool
orOperation x y = x || y

notOperation :: Bool -> Bool
notOperation x = not x
```

Mastering these basic data types and operations is crucial as they form the foundation upon which more intricate Haskell programming concepts are built. Understanding how each data type behaves and how to manipulate them accurately is an indispensable skill for any Haskell programmer.

2.4 Arithmetic Operations

Arithmetic operations form a fundamental base for any programming language, enabling the developer to perform essential mathematical calculations. In Haskell, we will examine various arithmetic operations including addition, subtraction, multiplication, division, and modulus. The standard arithmetic operators in Haskell are intuitive and resemble those found in most programming languages. Below is a quick reference for these operations:

- Addition: $+$
- Subtraction: -
- Multiplication: $*$
- Division: $/$
- Modulus: mod

Haskell treats these operations on different numeric types such as Int, $\mathrm{Integer}$, Float, and Double. Let's explore these arithmetic operations through examples.

Addition, Subtraction, and Multiplication

The following Haskell code demonstrates the use of addition, subtraction, and multiplication with integers:

```
-- Addition
let a = 10
let b = 20
let sum = a + b
-- sum is 30

-- Subtraction
let difference = a - b
-- difference is -10

-- Multiplication
let product = a * b
-- product is 200
```

The variables a and b are defined as integers, and we use the $+$, -, and $*$ operators to perform the arithmetic operations. Haskell infers the types of these variables based on the assigned values and operations.

Division and Modulus

Division operation in Haskell can operate on both integer and floating-point numbers. The division operator (/) performs floating-point division, and the div function performs integer division.

The following Haskell code demonstrates the use of both integer and floating-point division:

```
-- Floating-point Division
let c = 10.0
let d = 3.0
```

```
let divisionResult = c / d
-- divisionResult is approximately 3.3333333333333335

-- Integer Division
let e = 10
let f = 3
let intDivisionResult = e `div` f
-- intDivisionResult is 3
```

Notice the backticks in the div function for integer division, which enables us to write it infix style, making it more readable.

For the modulus operation, Haskell provides the mod function, which returns the remainder of dividing two integers:

```
-- Modulus Operation
let modulusResult = e `mod` f
-- modulusResult is 1
```

The mod function is also used in an infix manner with backticks, similar to the div function.

Operator Precedence and Associativity

Understanding operator precedence and associativity is essential for correctly interpreting and debugging Haskell expressions. Operators with higher precedence bind more tightly than operators with lower precedence. For instance, multiplication and division have a higher precedence than addition and subtraction.

Consider the following expression:

```
let complexExpression = 10 + 5 * 2
-- complexExpression is 20, not 30
```

In this example, the multiplication operation has higher precedence than addition, so $5 * 2$ is evaluated first, resulting in $10 + 10$ which gives us 20.

To override the default precedence, we can use parentheses:

```
let overriddenExpression = (10 + 5) * 2
-- overriddenExpression is 30
```

In this case, the expression in parentheses is evaluated first, followed by the multiplication.

Special Cases and Type Casting

When performing arithmetic operations on mixed types, explicit type casting is necessary to avoid type mismatch errors. Haskell provides functions such as fromIntegral to convert an Int to a more general numeric type like Float or Double.

```
let intVal = 5 :: Int
let floatVal = 2.5 :: Float
let mixedTypeResult = fromIntegral intVal + floatVal
-- mixedTypeResult is 7.5
```

Using fromIntegral, we convert intVal from Int to Float to ensure compatibility with floatVal for the addition operation.

These examples cover the primary arithmetic operations in Haskell. Understanding their correct usage and behavior is fundamental for performing calculations and developing algorithms efficiently.

2.5 Boolean Logic

Boolean logic forms the bedrock of decision making in programming languages, including Haskell. It is crucial to understand the Boolean data type and the operations that can be performed with Boolean values to effectively utilize conditional expressions, perform pattern matching, and control program flow.

In Haskell, the Boolean data type is denoted as Bool. It has two values: True and False. These values are defined in the Prelude, the standard library that is imported by default.

Boolean operations in Haskell include the basic logical operations: AND, OR, and NOT. These operations use the following symbols:

- AND: &&
- OR: ||
- NOT: not

The AND operator (&&) returns True if both operands are True; otherwise, it returns False. The OR operator (||) returns True if at least one operand is True; it returns False only if both operands are False. The NOT operator (not) simply inverts the value of its operand: not True becomes False, and not False becomes True.

Here are some examples to illustrate the usage of these Boolean operators in Haskell:

```
-- Boolean AND operation
True && False -- evaluates to False
```

```
True && True -- evaluates to True

-- Boolean OR operation
True || False -- evaluates to True
False || False -- evaluates to False

-- Boolean NOT operation
not True -- evaluates to False
not False -- evaluates to True
```

Comparison operations also yield Boolean values. These operations compare values and return either True or False. The primary comparison operators in Haskell are:

- Equal to: ==
- Not equal to: /=
- Less than: <
- Greater than: >
- Less than or equal to: <=
- Greater than or equal to: >=

Consider the following examples that demonstrate the comparison operators:

```
-- Equality and inequality
5 == 5 -- evaluates to True
5 /= 3 -- evaluates to True

-- Comparison operations
3 < 5 -- evaluates to True
7 > 2 -- evaluates to True
5 <= 5 -- evaluates to True
9 >= 10 -- evaluates to False
```

Boolean expressions can also be combined using logical operators to form more complex conditions. Consider the following example that combines multiple Boolean and comparison operations:

```
-- Combining boolean and comparison operations
(5 > 3) && (3 < 4) -- evaluates to True
(5 == 5) || (6 /= 6) -- evaluates to True
not (2 < 1) -- evaluates to True
```

Furthermore, Boolean logic becomes particularly powerful when used with conditional expressions, which will be explored in detail in the next section. As a quick preview, let's consider an if expression that utilizes Boolean logic:

```
-- Using Boolean logic in an if expression
if (5 > 3) && (3 < 4) then "Condition is True" else "Condition is False"
-- evaluates to "Condition is True"
```

This illustrative if expression checks if both $5 > 3$ and $3 < 4$ evaluate to True. Since both conditions are true, the entire expression evaluates to the string "Condition is True".

Boolean logic in Haskell is essential for controlling program flow and enabling decision-making processes. It seamlessly integrates with other program constructs, making it a versatile and critical component of the language. Familiarity with Boolean operations and how to apply them will significantly enhance your Haskell programming capabilities.

2.6 Conditional Expressions

Conditional expressions in Haskell enable the execution of code based on whether certain conditions hold true or false. This functionality aligns with decision-making structures found in many programming languages, including if-else statements and guard clauses. In Haskell, conditional expressions are fundamental constructs that assist in controlling the flow of the program through expressions rather than statements.

Haskell predominantly uses if-then-else constructs and guards for expressing conditional logic.

The if-then-else Construct

The if-then-else construct in Haskell is an expression that evaluates a condition and returns a result based on whether the condition is true or false. The general syntax is as follows:

```
if <condition>
then <expression1>
else <expression2>
```

Here, <condition> is a boolean expression that evaluates to either True or False. If the condition is true, <expression1> is evaluated and returned. Otherwise, <expression2> is evaluated and returned.

Consider the example:

```
absVal :: Int -> Int
absVal x = if x >= 0
           then x
           else -x
```

In this function definition, absVal computes the absolute value of an integer x. The condition x >= 0 is evaluated; if it is true, x is returned. If the condition is false, -x is returned.

Guards

Guards offer an alternative and often more readable way to execute conditional logic in Haskell. They can be particularly beneficial when dealing with multiple conditions. The structure for guards is integrated within function definitions and case expressions.

The general syntax using guards is as follows:

```
functionName params
  | <condition1> = <expression1>
  | <condition2> = <expression2>
  | otherwise = <expressionDefault>
```

The | symbol initiates a guard. Each <condition> is evaluated in order. The first <condition> that evaluates to True causes the corresponding <expression> to be executed. The otherwise keyword acts as a catch-all guard, equivalent to a default case. It always evaluates to True if no previous conditions are met.

For example:

```
maxOfTwo :: Int -> Int -> Int
maxOfTwo a b
  | a >= b = a
  | otherwise = b
```

Here, maxOfTwo determines the greater of two integers. The first guard a >= b checks if a is greater than or equal to b. If true, a is returned; otherwise, the second guard otherwise returns b.

Nested if-else Expressions

It is feasible to nest if-else expressions within each other to handle multiple conditions. However, deeply nested if-else constructs can become difficult to read. Guards often provide a clearer alternative, but for completeness, consider the following example of nested if-else statements:

```
maxOfThree :: Int -> Int -> Int -> Int
maxOfThree a b c = if a >= b
                   then if a >= c
                        then a
                        else c
                   else if b >= c
                        then b
                        else c
```

This function maxOfThree returns the maximum of three integers a, b, and c. The innermost if-else expressions are evaluated by first comparing a and b, and then conditionally comparing the results with c.

Case Expressions

Haskell also offers case expressions for pattern matching, which can replace certain conditional constructs with potentially clearer code. The syntax of a case expression is as follows:

```
case expression of
  pattern1 -> result1
  pattern2 -> result2
  patternN -> resultN
```

Each pattern is compared against the value of expression. The first matching pattern's corresponding result expression is evaluated and returned.

Consider the example:

```
describeNumber :: Int -> String
describeNumber x = case x of
  0 -> "Zero"
  1 -> "One"
  _ -> "Many"
```

In the describeNumber function, the case expression matches the input integer against specified patterns. If x is 0, the function returns "Zero"; if x is 1, it returns "One"; otherwise, it returns "Many".

Understanding conditional expressions is crucial for distinguishing when and how to use Haskell's various constructs effectively, based on the specific requirements and readability of the code. Each of these methods offers unique strengths that can cater to differing scenarios in functional programming.

2.7 Pattern Matching

Pattern matching is a fundamental feature of Haskell that allows for the decomposition of data structures by specifying patterns to which data should conform. It is a powerful tool that simplifies complex conditional checks and deconstructs data structures in a concise and readable manner. This section explores the mechanisms of pattern matching, particularly in the context of function definitions, case expressions, and list operations.

In Haskell, patterns can be used in various contexts, including:

- Function definitions
- case expressions
- List comprehensions
- let and where clauses

A pattern matches a value if it has a compatible structure and the values of the pattern variables are consistent with the components of the value being matched. Here is an example of pattern matching in function definitions:

```
factorial :: Integer -> Integer
factorial 0 = 1
factorial n = n * factorial (n - 1)
```

In this example, the function factorial is defined with two patterns. The base case pattern 0 matches the input when it is zero, and the recursive case n matches any other integer. The factorial function calculates the factorial of a number using these patterns.

A function can have multiple patterns:

```
isZero :: Integer -> Bool
isZero 0 = True
isZero _ = False
```

In this definition, the underscore _ is a wildcard pattern that matches any value. The function isZero returns True if the input is zero and False otherwise.

Pattern matching can be extended to tuples and lists. For instance, consider the following function to add pairs of integer tuples:

```
addTuples :: (Integer, Integer) -> (Integer, Integer) -> (Integer, Integer)
addTuples (x1, y1) (x2, y2) = (x1 + x2, y1 + y2)
```

In the addTuples function, the pattern (x1, y1) matches the first pair, while (x2, y2) matches the second pair. The function returns a tuple consisting of the summed components.

For lists, pattern matching often involves specifying the head and tail of the list. For example:

```
sumList :: [Integer] -> Integer
sumList [] = 0
sumList (x:xs) = x + sumList xs
```

Here, sumList is defined using two patterns. The empty list [] matches the base case, returning 0. The pattern (x:xs) matches a non-empty list, where x is the first element (head) and xs is the rest of the list (tail). The function recursively calculates the sum of the list elements.

Pattern matching is also commonly used in case expressions to handle multiple cases within a function. Here is how the same sumList function can be written using a case expression:

```
sumList' :: [Integer] -> Integer
sumList' list = case list of
    [] -> 0
    (x:xs) -> x + sumList' xs
```

In this example, the case expression matches the value of list against the patterns [] and (x:xs), producing the same result as the function sumList defined earlier.

One important aspect of pattern matching is the ability to use it for deep pattern matching, wherein nested data structures are matched. Consider a function to extract the second element from a list of tuples:

```
secondElements :: [(a, b)] -> [b]
secondElements [] = []
secondElements ((_, y):xs) = y : secondElements xs
```

In secondElements, the pattern ((_, y):xs) matches a non-empty list of tuples. The underscore _ discards the first element of the tuple, while y captures the second element, and xs matches the rest of the list. The function constructs a list of the second elements.

Pattern matching is exhaustive, meaning that every possible input must be matched by some pattern. Failure to do so results in a runtime error known as a Non-exhaustive patterns error. Here is an example demonstrating safe pattern matching using a Maybe type:

```
safeHead :: [a] -> Maybe a
safeHead [] = Nothing
safeHead (x:_) = Just x
```

The safeHead function returns Nothing if the list is empty and Just x if the list is non-empty, where x is the first element of the list. This approach ensures that the function handles both cases explicitly, preventing runtime errors from unhandled patterns.

Overall, pattern matching not only allows for clear and concise code but also leverages the type system to ensure that all possible scenarios are accounted for explicitly. This technique is crucial in enabling Haskell programmers to write robust and understandable code.

2.8 Tuples and Lists

In Haskell, tuples and lists are fundamental data structures used to store and manipulate collections of values. Understanding these structures and their respective operations is crucial for effective Haskell programming.

Tuples are a fixed-size collection of heterogeneous elements, meaning they can contain elements of different types. For example, a tuple can contain an Int, a Char, and a String all at once. Tuples are defined using parentheses and commas.

```
-- A tuple containing an Int, Char, and String
myTuple :: (Int, Char, String)
myTuple = (1, 'a', "Hello")
```

To access the elements of a tuple, one typically employs pattern matching. The following example demonstrates how to extract values from a tuple.

```
-- Extracting elements from a tuple using pattern matching
extractTupleElements :: (Int, Char, String) -> (Int, Char, String)
extractTupleElements (x, y, z) = (x, y, z)

-- Usage
main :: IO ()
main = do
    let (a, b, c) = extractTupleElements myTuple
    print (a, b, c)
```

Lists, in contrast, are variable-length, homogeneous collections, meaning all elements in a list must be of the same type. Lists are defined using square brackets with elements separated by commas.

```
-- A list of Int
myList :: [Int]
myList = [1, 2, 3, 4, 5]
```

Haskell provides several built-in functions to perform operations on lists. For example, you can retrieve the head of the list, the tail of the list, or use pattern matching to destructure a list.

```
-- Getting the head and tail of the list
headOfList :: [Int] -> Int
headOfList lst = head lst

tailOfList :: [Int] -> [Int]
tailOfList lst = tail lst

-- Usage
main :: IO ()
main = do
```

```
    print (headOfList myList) -- Output: 1
    print (tailOfList myList) -- Output: [2, 3, 4, 5]
```

Lists can also be concatenated using the ++ operator, and elements can be added to the beginning of a list using the : (cons) operator.

```
-- Concatenating two lists
concatenateLists :: [Int] -> [Int] -> [Int]
concatenateLists lst1 lst2 = lst1 ++ lst2

-- Adding an element to the beginning of a list
prependElement :: Int -> [Int] -> [Int]
prependElement x lst = x : lst

-- Usage
main :: IO ()
main = do
    let list1 = [1, 2, 3]
    let list2 = [4, 5, 6]
    print (concatenateLists list1 list2) -- Output: [1, 2, 3, 4, 5, 6]
    print (prependElement 0 list1) -- Output: [0, 1, 2, 3]
```

List comprehensions provide a powerful way to create and process lists. They are similar to set comprehensions in mathematics and can be used to concisely generate new lists by transforming and filtering existing lists.

```
-- List comprehension to generate a list of squared numbers
squaredNumbers :: [Int] -> [Int]
squaredNumbers lst = [x * x | x <- lst]

-- List comprehension with a filter to generate even numbers
evenNumbers :: [Int] -> [Int]
evenNumbers lst = [x | x <- lst, even x]

-- Usage
main :: IO ()
main = do
    print (squaredNumbers [1, 2, 3, 4, 5]) -- Output: [1, 4, 9, 16, 25]
    print (evenNumbers [1, 2, 3, 4, 5]) -- Output: [2, 4]
```

Lists also support various higher-order functions, such as map, filter, and foldl, which can be used to apply functions to elements of the list, filter elements based on a predicate, and fold the list into a single value, respectively.

```
-- Using map to apply a function to each element of the list
incrementElements :: [Int] -> [Int]
incrementElements lst = map (+1) lst

-- Using filter to select elements that satisfy a predicate
selectEvenNumbers :: [Int] -> [Int]
selectEvenNumbers lst = filter even lst

-- Using foldl to sum the elements of a list
sumList :: [Int] -> Int
```

```
sumList lst = foldl (+) 0 lst

-- Usage
main :: IO ()
main = do
    print (incrementElements [1, 2, 3]) -- Output: [2, 3, 4]
    print (selectEvenNumbers [1, 2, 3, 4, 5]) -- Output: [2, 4]
    print (sumList [1, 2, 3, 4, 5]) -- Output: 15
```

Pattern matching is widely used with lists for various operations, including defining recursive functions. Here is an example of a recursive function to calculate the length of a list.

```
-- Recursive function to calculate the length of a list
lengthOfList :: [a] -> Int
lengthOfList [] = 0
lengthOfList (_:xs) = 1 + lengthOfList xs

-- Usage
main :: IO ()
main = do
    print (lengthOfList [1, 2, 3, 4, 5]) -- Output: 5
```

Understanding and effectively utilizing tuples and lists is foundational for mastering Haskell. Through practical implementation examples and operations, one can harness the full power of Haskell's data structures.

2.9 String Operations

In Haskell, strings are sequences of characters and are represented by the String type, which is synonymous with the type [Char]. String operations are fundamental to many Haskell applications, offering various built-in functions for manipulation, concatenation, and transformation. Understanding string operations allows us to handle textual data efficiently and perform common tasks such as concatenation, slicing, and pattern matching.

To illustrate string operations, consider the following example Haskell code snippets. Each example demonstrates a specific string function or operation.

Creating and Concatenating Strings

Creating a string in Haskell is straightforward:

```
hello :: String
hello = "Hello"
```

Concatenation of strings can be achieved using the ++ operator:

```
greet :: String
greet = hello ++ " World!"
```

Evaluating this concatenation in GHCi, Haskell's interactive environment, yields:

```
*Main> greet
"Hello World!"
```

Basic String Functions

Several built-in functions allow for common string operations. The length function returns the number of characters in a string:

```
stringLength :: Int
stringLength = length greet
```

The reverse function reverses the characters in a string:

```
reversedGreet :: String
reversedGreet = reverse greet
```

To transform a string, the map function applies a given function to each character. For example, to convert a string to uppercase, you can use:

```
import Data.Char (toUpper)

uppercaseGreet :: String
uppercaseGreet = map toUpper greet
```

Slicing Strings

Extracting substrings or slicing can be accomplished with take, drop, and splitAt. For instance, to take the first five characters of a string:

```
firstFive :: String
firstFive = take 5 greet
```

To drop the first six characters:

```
dropSix :: String
dropSix = drop 6 greet
```

To split a string at a specific index, returning a tuple of the two substrings:

```
splitGreet :: (String, String)
splitGreet = splitAt 5 greet
```

Evaluating splitGreet returns:

```
*Main> splitGreet
("Hello"," World!")
```

String Comparison

String comparison in Haskell uses standard relational operators: ==, /=, <, <=, >, and >=. Comparisons are lexicographic:

```
compareHelloWorld :: Bool
compareHelloWorld = "Hello" < "World"
```

Testing the comparison in GHCi:

```
*Main> compareHelloWorld
True
```

Pattern Matching with Strings

Pattern matching with strings is a powerful feature. You can match specific patterns and decompose strings:

```
matchGreeting :: String -> String
matchGreeting "Hello" = "Hello there!"
matchGreeting "Goodbye" = "See you later!"
matchGreeting _ = "Unknown greeting"
```

Testing matchGreeting:

```
*Main> matchGreeting "Hello"
"Hello there!"
*Main> matchGreeting "Goodbye"
"See you later!"
*Main> matchGreeting "Hi"
"Unknown greeting"
```

Advanced String Operations: Using Text Library

For more advanced and efficient string operations, the Data.Text library provides the Text type, which is more performant for large-scale string manipulations. Importing this library and converting between String and Text:

```
import qualified Data.Text as T

textExample :: T.Text
textExample = T.pack "Hello Text"

unpackExample :: String
unpackExample = T.unpack textExample
```

The Text library offers a rich set of functions analogous to those for String, such as T.concat, T.map, T.take, and T.drop.

The examples and functions presented establish a comprehensive understanding of string operations in Haskell. Mastery of these operations enables effective data manipulation and lays the groundwork for more advanced functional programming techniques.

2.10 Comments and Documentation

In Haskell, comments and proper documentation are critical for code readability and maintenance. Clear comments can greatly assist not only in understanding code written by yourself, but also by others who might need to work with or extend your code. Haskell provides two types of comments: single-line comments and multi-line comments. Additionally, there is a robust system for creating documentation through comments, which can be extracted to create formal documentation of the code.

Single-line comments begin with two hyphens – and extend to the end of the line. They are used for brief remarks or annotations in the code.

```
-- This is a single-line comment in Haskell
x = 42 -- Assignment of the value 42 to x
```

Multi-line comments begin with {- and end with -}. These comments can span multiple lines and be nested if necessary.

```
{-
  This is a multi-line comment.
  It spans multiple lines and can include descriptions,
  explanations, or other commentary.
-}
y = 7

{-
  Nested comments are also supported:
  {-
    Nested comment.
  -}
-}
```

For comprehensive documentation purposes, Haskell employs a system known as Haddock, which is the standard tool for automatically generating documentation from annotated Haskell source code. Haddock comments begin with – | (for documentation preceding a function or value) or –^ (for inline documentation related to data constructors or record fields).

Below is an example illustrating how Haddock comments can be used to create documentation:

```
-- | The 'square' function calculates the square of a number.
-- It takes one input of numeric type and returns the result
-- as the same numeric type.
square :: Num a => a -> a
square x = x * x

-- | The 'factorial' function calculates the factorial of a non-negative
```

```
-- integer.
--
-- ==== __Examples__
--
-- >>> factorial 5
-- 120
-- >>> factorial 0
-- 1
--
-- The function returns 1 when the input is 0 because the factorial of 0
-- is defined as 1.
factorial :: (Eq a, Num a) => a -> a
factorial 0 = 1
factorial n = n * factorial (n - 1)
```

In the example above, the -- | notation provides a description of the function square and factorial, including their purpose and usage. Additionally, the ==== __Examples__ section under factorial provides specific examples of how the function behaves with different inputs, which are particularly useful in documentation.

For documenting data types and type classes, Haddock comments can be equally detailed and informative. Here is an example of annotating a data type with Haddock comments:

```
-- | 'Point' represents a point in a 2D space.
data Point = Point
  { -- | The x-coordinate of the point
    xCoord :: Double
  , -- | The y-coordinate of the point
    yCoord :: Double
  } deriving (Show, Eq)
```

This detailed documentation through comments ensures that anyone reading the code will understand the purpose and structure of the Point data type, as well as the meaning of its fields.

It is also informative to include module-level documentation and comments to provide high-level overviews and context for the entire module. This can be done at the beginning of the Haskell source file:

```
{-|
Module : Geometry
Description : A module for geometric calculations
Copyright : (c) 2023, Your Name
License : MIT
Maintainer : your.email@example.com
Stability : experimental
Portability : portable

The 'Geometry' module provides various functions for calculations
involving geometric shapes, including areas and perimeters.
-}
module Geometry (areaOfCircle, areaOfRectangle) where
```

```
-- | Calculate the area of a circle given its radius.
-- Uses the formula  * r^2.
areaOfCircle :: Floating a => a -> a
areaOfCircle radius = pi * radius * radius

-- | Calculate the area of a rectangle given its width and height.
areaOfRectangle :: Num a => a -> a -> a
areaOfRectangle width height = width * height
```

Using these commenting techniques proficiently in Haskell ensures that code remains manageable, understandable, and well-documented. Properly documented code with both inline comments and formal Haddock annotations can significantly enhance collaborative efforts and streamline the development and maintenance processes.

Chapter 3

Functions in Haskell

This chapter explores the core concepts of functions in Haskell, including how to define and apply functions, use lambda expressions, and compose functions. It also covers advanced topics such as currying, recursion, using guards in function definitions, local bindings with 'let' and 'where' clauses, operator functions, and case expressions.

3.1 Defining Functions

In Haskell, defining a function is a fundamental task that involves specifying a function's name, its parameters, and the expression that computes the result of the function. Functions in Haskell are first-class citizens, meaning they can be passed as arguments to other functions, returned as results from other functions, and assigned to variables. This section will cover how to define functions in Haskell, including aspects such as naming conventions, type declarations, and pattern matching.

Basic Function Definition

A basic function definition in Haskell usually consists of the following components:

- The function name.
- A list of parameters.
- An equals sign (=).

- An expression that evaluates to the result of the function.

Consider the following example, which defines a simple function that adds two integers:

```
add :: Int -> Int -> Int
add x y = x + y
```

In this example, add is the name of the function. It takes two parameters, x and y, and returns their sum. The type declaration for the function is specified before the function definition using the double colon (::). The type declaration indicates that add is a function that takes two arguments of type Int and returns an Int.

Type Declarations

Type declarations are not mandatory but are considered a good practice because they make the code more readable and help catch errors during compilation. A type declaration specifies the types of the inputs and the output of the function. Here's how we can declare a type for a function that checks if a given number is even:

```
isEven :: Int -> Bool
isEven n = n `mod` 2 == 0
```

In this case, isEven takes an integer (Int) and returns a boolean (Bool) indicating whether the number is even.

Pattern Matching

Pattern matching is a powerful feature in Haskell that allows you to define functions more succinctly and clearly by directly specifying patterns to which the input data should conform. Pattern matching can be used with lists, tuples, and custom data types. Here is an example that demonstrates pattern matching with a list:

```
head' :: [a] -> a
head' [] = error "empty list"
head' (x:_) = x
```

In this function, head' takes a list and returns its first element. The pattern [] matches an empty list, and the function raises an error if the list is empty. The pattern (x:_) matches any list with at least one element, binding x to the head of the list and ignoring the tail.

Guards

Guards provide an elegant way to select between alternative patterns based on boolean expressions. Consider the following example of a function that categorizes an integer as positive, negative, or zero:

```
sign :: Int -> String
sign n
  | n > 0 = "positive"
  | n < 0 = "negative"
  | otherwise = "zero"
```

Here, sign uses guards to check the value of n and returns an appropriate string. Each guard is introduced by the pipe character (|) and is followed by a boolean expression and a corresponding result.

Multi-Clause Function Definitions

In Haskell, it is possible to define multiple clauses for a single function, each catering to different input cases. This is useful for functions that need different behaviors based on varying inputs. For instance, consider a function that returns the size category of a list:

```
listSize :: [a] -> String
listSize [] = "empty"
listSize [\_] = "singleton"
listSize [\_,\_] = "pair"
listSize \_ = "larger list"
```

In this example, listSize has different clauses for matching lists of varying lengths: an empty list, a list with one element, a list with two elements, and all other cases.

Local Definitions with let and where

Sometimes, it is necessary to create local bindings within a function. Haskell provides two constructs, let and where, for such purposes.

let expressions allow you to create local variables within an expression:

```
cylinder :: Float -> Float -> Float
cylinder r h =
  let sideArea = 2 * pi * r * h
      topArea = pi * r^2
  in sideArea + 2 * topArea
```

In this function, sideArea and topArea are local bindings visible only within the let expression.

where clauses serve a similar purpose but provide more readable code by placing the local bindings after the function body:

```
cylinder' :: Float -> Float -> Float
cylinder' r h = sideArea + 2 * topArea
  where
    sideArea = 2 * pi * r * h
    topArea = pi * r^2
```

By using where, the local variables sideArea and topArea are defined at the end, making the main computation easier to read.

Anonymous Functions

Haskell also allows the definition of anonymous functions using lambda expressions. These functions do not have names and are useful for short, throwaway functions. The following example demonstrates the use of a lambda expression to define an increment function:

```
increment = \x -> x + 1
```

In this case, increment is a function that takes one parameter, x, and returns x incremented by 1. The lambda expression is defined using the backslash (\) followed by the parameter and the arrow (->) separating the parameter from the return expression.

Understanding the intricacies of function definitions in Haskell, including type declarations, pattern matching, and local bindings, is critical for writing clear and efficient Haskell code. This foundation will facilitate exploration into more advanced topics covered in subsequent sections.

3.2 Function Application

Function application in Haskell is fundamental to how expressions are evaluated. In Haskell, function application is simply writing the function name followed by its arguments separated by spaces. For a function f and arguments x and y, the function application is represented as f x y. This syntax contrasts with many other programming languages where parentheses are used to enclose function arguments.

The function application syntax is left-associative. This means that an expression like f x y is interpreted as (f x) y. To help elucidate this, consider the following example function definitions and applications.

```
add :: Int -> Int -> Int
add x y = x + y

inc :: Int -> Int
inc = add 1
```

In the example above, add is a function that takes two Int arguments and returns their sum. The function inc is defined by partially applying add with the first argument set to 1. Here's how these functions can be applied:

```
result1 = add 3 4 -- result1 will be 7
result2 = inc 5 -- result2 will be 6
```

To evaluate add 3 4, Haskell first applies add to 3, resulting in a new function of type Int -> Int, which is then applied to 4, yielding the result 7. Similarly, inc 5 results in 6.

Haskell allows for more complex expressions involving multiple function applications and parentheses can be used to change the order of application.

```
mult :: Int -> Int -> Int
mult x y = x * y

result3 = mult (add 2 3) 4 -- result3 will be 20
result4 = add (mult 2 3) (mult 4 5) -- result4 will be 26
```

In mult (add 2 3) 4, the expression add 2 3 is evaluated first to 5, which is then multiplied by 4 to give 20. Similarly, in add (mult 2 3) (mult 4 5), mult 2 3 evaluates to 6 and mult 4 5 evaluates to 20, which are then added together to give 26.

Understanding function application in Haskell also requires knowing about how Haskell handles partially applied functions. When a function is applied to some, but not all, of its arguments, it returns a new function that takes the remaining arguments. This is related to the concept of currying where a function of multiple arguments can be transformed into a sequence of functions each with a single argument.

```
addThreeNumbers :: Int -> Int -> Int -> Int
addThreeNumbers x y z = x + y + z

partialAdd = addThreeNumbers 5 -- "partialAdd" is a function of type Int -> Int ->
    Int
result5 = partialAdd 3 4 -- result5 will be 12
```

In this case, partialAdd is a new function created by applying addThreeNumbers to the first argument. partialAdd itself is a function that takes two Int arguments and returns their sum with 5.

Another important concept related to function application is the use of the $ operator, which is used to reduce the need for parentheses in Haskell expressions. The $ operator is defined as:

```
(\$) :: (a -> b) -> a -> b
f \$ x = f x
```

The $ operator is right-associative and has the lowest precedence, making it convenient for writing cleaner code without deeply nested parentheses.

```
result6 = add 2 (mult 3 4) -- result6 will be 14
result7 = add 2 \$ mult 3 4 -- Using "$" operator, result7 will be 14
result8 = add 2 \$ mult 3 \$ add 4 5 -- result8 will be 32
```

Using $ helps in reading expressions from left to right without the clutter of multiple parentheses.

Advanced Haskell programming often involves higher-order functions, where functions take other functions as arguments. Function application becomes even more critical in these contexts. For instance:

```
applyTwice :: (a -> a) -> a -> a
applyTwice f x = f (f x)

result9 = applyTwice inc 5 -- result9 will be 7
```

Here, applyTwice is a higher-order function that takes a function f and a value x, applying the function to the value two times. The evaluation of applyTwice inc 5 first applies inc to 5 to get 6, and then applies inc again to 6, resulting in 7.

This section demonstrates the versatility and power of function application in Haskell. By understanding how functions are applied and evaluated, programmers can develop more succinct, readable, and efficient Haskell code.

3.3 Lambda Expressions

Lambda expressions in Haskell provide a way to define anonymous functions. Unlike named functions, which are defined using a function name, lambda expressions allow for ad-hoc function creation without needing to attach a name. A lambda expression is written using the syntax \args -> expression, where args represent the parameters of the function and expression represents the body of the function that operates on these parameters.

To create a basic lambda expression that adds two numbers together, you would write:

```
\addTwo = \x y -> x + y
```

In this example, \x y -> x + y is the lambda expression. It takes two arguments, x and y, and returns their sum. This expression can be applied like a regular function:

```
result = (\x y -> x + y) 5 3
```

8

Lambda expressions are particularly useful in situations where short, throw-away functions are required. For instance, they can be effectively used in higher-order functions like map, which applies a function to each element of a list:

```
doubleList = map (\x -> x * 2) [1,2,3,4]
```

[2,4,6,8]

Here, (\x -> x * 2) doubles each element in the list. Lambda expressions can be used wherever a function is expected, allowing for concise and readable code.

Lambda expressions can also be nested, facilitating the creation of more complex functions on the fly. For instance, consider the function to generate a list of functions that add specific numbers to their argument:

```
adders = map (\n -> \x -> x + n) [1,2,3]
```

In this example, (\n -> \x -> x + n) produces functions like (\x -> x + 1), (\x -> x + 2), and (\x -> x + 3).

Lambda expressions can be brilliantly combined with list comprehensions. A simple example that demonstrates filtering even numbers and then doubling them using list comprehension combined with a lambda expression:

```
processedList = [ (\x -> x * 2) x | x <- [1..10], even x ]
```

[4,8,12,16,20]

This code fragment shows the use of a lambda expression for doubling the filtered even numbers in the list from 1 to 10.

In cases where the lambda expression only operates using a single parameter, Haskell provides a way to omit parentheses for clarity. For example:

```
incrementList = map \x -> x + 1 [1, 2, 3, 4, 5]
```

It is essential, however, to consider readability. While lambda expressions can dramatically reduce verbosity, overuse or overly complex lambda expressions may make the code difficult to understand.

When combined with the let or where bindings, lambda expressions can be used to manipulate elements within a more extensive context:

```
sumEvenNumbers xs = let evenNumbers = filter even xs
                        add = \x y -> x + y
                    in foldr add 0 evenNumbers
```

10

Function bindings like foldr and filter masked by lambda expressions present a potent combination for succinctly expressing more complex operations on data structures.

Lambda expressions also shine in the context of partial function applications, enhancing their utility. Consider the situation with binary operations:

```
addThree = (\x y z -> x + y + z) 3
addToSeven = addThree 2
result = addToSeven 1
```

6

In this example, the lambda expression (\x y z -> x + y + z) is partially applied to 3 and 2, forming a chain of applications where each stage partially consumes the arguments.

Lambda expressions in Haskell articulate the possibilities of functional programming paradigms, offering elegant, concise mechanisms to write highly modular and easily understandable code.

3.4 Function Composition

Function composition is a powerful technique in Haskell, enabling the creation of new functions by combining existing ones. In Haskell, function composition is denoted by the (.) operator, which has the type signature:

```
(.) :: (b -> c) -> (a -> b) -> a -> c
```

This indicates that the (.) operator takes two functions as arguments: the first function (b -> c) and the second function (a -> b), and produces a new function (a -> c). Function composition is associative; that is, if you have three functions f, g, and h, then $(f \cdot g) \cdot h$ is equivalent to $f \cdot (g \cdot h)$.

Consider the following example, where we define two simple functions and compose them using (.):

```
increment :: Int -> Int
increment x = x + 1

square :: Int -> Int
square x = x * x

incrementThenSquare :: Int -> Int
incrementThenSquare = square . increment
```

Here, the incrementThenSquare function is defined by composing square and increment. When evaluating incrementThenSquare 3, the computation proceeds as follows:

```
incrementThenSquare 3
  = (square . increment) 3
  = square (increment 3)
  = square 4
  = 16
```

Function composition enhances code readability and reduces the need for explicit intermediate variables. Consider a more practical example using a list of numbers. Suppose we have a list of integers, and we want to filter out the odd numbers, increment the remaining even numbers, and then square the result. We can accomplish this as follows:

```
filterEven :: [Int] -> [Int]
filterEven xs = filter even xs

incrementList :: [Int] -> [Int]
incrementList xs = map increment xs

squareList :: [Int] -> [Int]
squareList xs = map square xs

processList :: [Int] -> [Int]
processList = squareList . incrementList . filterEven
```

In this example, the function processList is a composition of squareList, incrementList, and filterEven. Applying processList to the list [1, 2, 3, 4, 5] would produce:

```
processList [1, 2, 3, 4, 5]
  = (squareList . incrementList . filterEven) [1, 2, 3, 4, 5]
  = squareList (incrementList (filterEven [1, 2, 3, 4, 5]))
  = squareList (incrementList [2, 4])
  = squareList [3, 5]
  = [9, 25]
```

Haskell's standard library provides numerous combinators that work seamlessly with function composition. For example, map, filter, and foldr can be easily composed to create complex data transformations concisely.

Understanding function composition also encourages a more declarative programming style. When tackling a problem, instead of focusing on the sequence of steps required to solve it, you can focus on high-level transformations facilitated by composing simple functions. This approach often leads to more modular and maintainable code.

Function composition is not confined to unary functions. It can be extended to functions with multiple arguments through the use of curry and uncurry functions. The curry function converts a function that takes a tuple into a curried function, while the uncurry function reverses this transformation:

```
curry :: ((a, b) -> c) -> a -> b -> c
curry f x y = f (x, y)

uncurry :: (a -> b -> c) -> (a, b) -> c
uncurry f (x, y) = f x y
```

These transformations are particularly useful when dealing with functions in higher-order contexts. For instance, one may want to partially apply a curried function before composing it with other functions.

Here is an example using curry and uncurry:

```
sumPair :: (Int, Int) -> Int
sumPair (x, y) = x + y

sumCurried :: Int -> Int -> Int
sumCurried = curry sumPair

processListWithSum :: [Int] -> (Int, Int)
processListWithSum = (sumCurried 3) . head &&& last
```

In processListWithSum, the function composition involves sumCurried 3, head, and last, demonstrating the flexibility and expressiveness of function composition in Haskell.

3.5 Currying

Currying is a fundamental concept in Haskell, allowing functions to be transformed into a series of functions each with a single argument. In essence, currying converts a function that takes multiple arguments into a sequence of functions that each take a single argument. This is significant in Haskell due to its inherent support for higher-order functions and the flexibility it provides in function application.

In Haskell, all functions are curried by default. This means that a function that appears to take multiple arguments is actually a chain of functions, each consuming one argument and returning another function. Consider the following function definition:

```
add :: Int -> Int -> Int
add x y = x + y
```

Here, add appears to be a function of two arguments, x and y. In reality, it is a curried function that can be thought of in the following way:

```
add :: Int -> (Int -> Int)
add x = \y -> x + y
```

This transformation reveals how add is actually a function that takes an integer x and returns another function that takes an integer y and produces their sum.

To understand currying more concretely, observe how partial application works in Haskell. When you provide fewer arguments than a function expects, Haskell returns a new function waiting for the remaining arguments. For example:

```
addFive :: Int -> Int
addFive = add 5
```

Here, addFive is a partially applied function of add with the first argument fixed to 5. The resultant function addFive then takes just one integer argument and adds it to 5.

Currying also makes functions in Haskell highly composable, aiding in the construction of more complex functions from simpler ones. For instance, consider the function:

```
multiply :: Int -> Int -> Int
multiply x y = x * y
```

We can create a function that doubles a number through partial application:

```
double :: Int -> Int
double = multiply 2
```

Using the function double, one can then create another function to quadruple a number by composing it with itself:

```
quadruple :: Int -> Int
quadruple = double . double
```

Here, the composition operator (.) chains the two applications of double, effectively multiplying the input by four.

A key advantage of currying is its seamless integration with higher-order functions, which are prevalent in functional programming. For instance, one may use map, a higher-order function that applies a given function to each element of a list:

```
map double [1, 2, 3, 4]
```

The above expression results in [2, 4, 6, 8] by applying double to each element of the list.

Understanding the mechanism of currying prepares us to leverage anonymous functions, where functions without names are passed around and applied. This happens frequently when using inline computation without defining a named function:

```
map (\x -> x * 2) [1, 2, 3, 4]
```

Here, (\x -> x * 2) is a lambda expression representing an anonymous curried function that doubles its argument.

Currying also facilitates partial function application within custom higher-order functions. Consider a custom implementation of the zipWith function:

```
zipWith :: (a -> b -> c) -> [a] -> [b] -> [c]
zipWith _ [] _ = []
zipWith _ _ [] = []
zipWith f (x:xs) (y:ys) = f x y : zipWith f xs ys
```

With zipWith, we can combine elements of two lists with any binary function. For example, to zip two lists with addition:

```
zipWith add [1, 2, 3] [4, 5, 6]
```

The result is [5, 7, 9], where add is the curried function applied pairwise to elements of the two lists.

The concept of currying extends not only to user-defined functions but also to various combinators and operators in Haskell, offering enhanced modularity and reuse in function definitions and applications. Such abilities empower developers to construct versatile and concise code structures, fostering an environment where functions are primary constructs streamlined for higher-order operations and reusability.

3.6 Recursion in Functions

Recursion is a fundamental concept in Haskell, allowing functions to call themselves in their definition. This approach is particularly powerful for solving problems that can be broken down into smaller, identical subproblems. In Haskell, recursion is preferred over traditional iterative constructs like loops found in imperative programming languages. The elegance and expressiveness of recursive solutions are often more aligned with the declarative nature of Haskell.

To define a recursive function in Haskell, one must ensure the function has a base case that allows the recursion to terminate, preventing infinite loops. The base case provides an answer directly, without further recursion. Subsequent cases typically involve calling the function itself with modified arguments that progress towards the base case.

factorial is a classic example of a recursive function. Here, the factorial of a non-negative integer n is the product of all positive integers less than or equal to n. The mathematical definition is:

$$\text{factorial}(n) = \begin{cases} 1 & \text{if } n = 0 \\ n \times \text{factorial}(n-1) & \text{if } n > 0 \end{cases}$$

In Haskell, this can be directly translated into the following recursive function:

```
factorial :: Integer -> Integer
factorial 0 = 1
factorial n = n * factorial (n - 1)
```

This function definition uses pattern matching, where factorial 0 = 1 defines the base case and factorial n = n * factorial (n - 1) handles the recursive case. Each call to factorial with a positive integer reduces the problem size by one, eventually hitting the base case.

Consider the recursive calculation of the sum of an integer list. The sum of an empty list is 0, and for a non-empty list, it is the head of the list added to the sum of the tail:

```
sumList :: [Integer] -> Integer
sumList [] = 0
sumList (x:xs) = x + sumList xs
```

Here, sumList [] = 0 is the base case, and sumList (x:xs) = x + sumList xs handles the recursive case by splitting the list into the head x and the tail xs, summing x with the result of recursively summing xs.

Another useful example is the Fibonacci sequence, where each number is the sum of the two preceding ones. The recursive definition is straightforwardly translated into Haskell as follows:

```
fibonacci :: Integer -> Integer
fibonacci 0 = 0
fibonacci 1 = 1
fibonacci n = fibonacci (n - 1) + fibonacci (n - 2)
```

This function defines base cases for fibonacci 0 and fibonacci 1, and the recursive case sums the results of the previous two Fibonacci numbers.

While recursion is an elegant technique, it is essential to be cautious of performance concerns. Recursive functions like fibonacci can be extremely inefficient when recalculating the same values multiple times. Employing memoization or transforming the recursion into an iterative form via accumulators can enhance efficiency. Consider the following optimized version of the Fibonacci function using an accumulator and tail recursion:

```
fibonacci :: Integer -> Integer
fibonacci n = fibAux n 0 1
  where
    fibAux 0 a _ = a
    fibAux n a b = fibAux (n - 1) b (a + b)
```

In this improved version, fibAux uses an auxiliary function with two additional parameters to keep track of the intermediate results, ensuring tail-call optimization and efficient computation without redundant calculations.

Recursion is not only limited to numerical operations or lists. It can elegantly handle more complex data structures like trees. Consider a binary tree defined as:

```
data Tree a = Empty | Node a (Tree a) (Tree a)
```

A function to calculate the height of the binary tree can be written recursively:

```
treeHeight :: Tree a -> Integer
treeHeight Empty = 0
treeHeight (Node _ left right) = 1 + max (treeHeight left) (treeHeight right)
```

This function establishes the base case treeHeight Empty = 0, and recursively computes the height of the left and right subtrees, adding 1 to account for the root node at each level.

The versatility and natural fit of recursion in Haskell allow for concise, expressive, and often intuitive solutions to a wide range of problems. Properly handling base cases and ensuring progress towards those base cases are critical for correct recursive function definitions.

3.7 Guards in Function Definitions

Guards in Haskell function definitions enhance the expressiveness and readability of conditional logic. They allow you to specify a series of boolean expressions that are evaluated in order to determine which function body to execute. Guards can be utilized to elegantly handle cases which might otherwise require complex and nested if-then-else statements. This section delves into the syntax and application of guards, providing comprehensive examples to elucidate their use.

Syntax of Guards The basic syntax of guards in Haskell is as follows:

```
functionName args
  | condition1 = result1
  | condition2 = result2
  | conditionN = resultN
  | otherwise = defaultResult
```

Each guard is introduced with a vertical bar (|), followed by a boolean expression. If the expression evaluates to True, the corresponding result is returned. The otherwise keyword is a synonym for True and serves as a catch-all to ensure that one of the function bodies is always executed.

Example: Absolute Value Function Consider an example of defining an absolute value function using guards:

```
absolute :: (Num a, Ord a) => a -> a
absolute x
  | x < 0 = -x
  | otherwise = x
```

In this function, if x is less than zero, it returns the negative of x (thus making it positive). If x is zero or positive, it simply returns x.

Guards with Pattern Matching Guards can be combined with pattern matching to handle complex conditions concisely:

```
bmiTell :: (RealFloat a) => a -> String
bmiTell bmi
  | bmi <= 18.5 = "Underweight"
  | bmi <= 25.0 = "Normal weight"
  | bmi <= 30.0 = "Overweight"
  | otherwise = "Obese"
```

In this example, the function bmiTell evaluates the bmi and returns a string describing the category of the BMI value. The guards here ensure that the bmi value falls into one of the specified ranges, providing a clear and readable way to classify the BMI.

Nested Guards Guards can be nested within other guards to further refine the conditions:

```
max' :: (Ord a) => a -> a -> a
max' a b
  | a > b = a
  | otherwise = b

maxThree :: (Ord a) => a -> a -> a -> a
maxThree a b c
  | max' a b == a && max' a c == a = a
  | max' b c == b = b
  | otherwise = c
```

In maxThree, the function determines the maximum of three values by using nested guards. It utilizes an auxiliary function max' to compare pairs of values inside the guard conditions.

Performance Considerations with Guards When working with guards, the order of evaluation is significant for performance. Haskell evaluates guards in order from top to bottom. Once a condition is met, subsequent guards are not evaluated. Therefore, it's beneficial to place the most likely cases or the least computationally expensive checks first. This can lead to more efficient code execution.

Example: Calculating Fibonacci Numbers The definition of the Fibonacci sequence can benefit from guards to simplify the logic:

```
fibonacci :: (Integral a) => a -> a
fibonacci n
  | n == 0 = 0
  | n == 1 = 1
  | otherwise = fibonacci (n - 1) + fibonacci (n - 2)
```

Here, the function fibonacci uses guards to handle the special cases of n == 0 and n == 1 directly. For other cases, it recursively calls itself for (n - 1) and (n - 2).

Guards offer a powerful and transparent way to encode conditional logic in Haskell functions, enhancing readability and maintainability. Properly leveraging them can make your functions more understandable and your code more concise. This section has provided insight into defining and using guards effectively, aiming to bolster your Haskell programming skills.

3.8 Local Bindings with 'let' and 'where'

Local bindings in Haskell allow for the definition of local variables within a function or an expression. These bindings help in breaking down complex expressions into simpler, more readable components and establish local scopes for variables. In Haskell, this can be achieved using let expressions or the where clause.

The let Expression

The let expression is used to bind variables within an expression. It follows the syntax:

```
let <bindings> in <expression>
```

Here, <bindings> represents one or more variable bindings, and <expression> is the resultant expression that utilizes these bindings. The scope of the variables is limited to the <expression> part.

Example usage of let in Haskell:

```
calculateArea :: Double -> Double -> Double
calculateArea length width =
    let area = length * width
    in area
```

In the above example, the variable area is locally bound within the let expression and is used in the succeeding in part to compute the final result.

Multiple bindings can be included in a single let expression:

```
quadraticRoots :: (Double, Double, Double) -> (Double, Double)
quadraticRoots (a, b, c) =
    let discriminant = b^2 - 4*a*c
        root1 = (-b + sqrt(discriminant)) / (2*a)
        root2 = (-b - sqrt(discriminant)) / (2*a)
```

```
    in (root1, root2)
```

Here, discriminant, root1, and root2 are locally bound, allowing the calculation of quadratic roots in a clean and comprehensible manner.

The where Clause

The where clause is another method for local bindings in Haskell. It is conceptually similar to the let expression but is used to bind variables at the end of a function definition. These bindings are then accessible in the function's body.

The syntax for the where clause is as follows:

```
<function definition>
    where <bindings>
```

Example usage of where in Haskell:

```
calculatePerimeter :: Double -> Double -> Double
calculatePerimeter length width = perimeter
    where perimeter = 2 * (length + width)
```

In this example, the variable perimeter is defined in the where clause and subsequently used in the function body to compute the final result.

Similar to let expressions, multiple bindings can be included within a where clause:

```
quadraticRoots :: (Double, Double, Double) -> (Double, Double)
quadraticRoots (a, b, c) = (root1, root2)
    where discriminant = b^2 - 4*a*c
          root1 = (-b + sqrt(discriminant)) / (2*a)
          root2 = (-b - sqrt(discriminant)) / (2*a)
```

Both the let expression and where clause provide methods to simplify function definitions and enhance code readability by allowing the encapsulation of intermediate computations within a function. While let expressions are useful within single expressions, the where clause integrates seamlessly into function definitions. Choosing between them often depends on the specific context and style preferences in Haskell programming.

3.9 Operator Functions

In Haskell, operators are essentially functions that you can use in infix form. This feature allows for elegant and readable expressions in the program. Operators in Haskell are not strictly limited to the predefined ones like +, -, and *; you can define your own operators as well.

To illustrate the function and flexibility of operators, let's start with basic arithmetic operators. The definitions of these operators are predefined in Haskell, making them accessible for immediate use in expressions without additional declarations.

```
additionResult = 5 + 3
subtractionResult = 10 - 4
multiplicationResult = 7 * 2
```

The expression $5 + 3$ uses the + operator function in an infix manner, which is intuitive and results in additionResult equating to 8. Similarly, subtractionResult evaluates to 6, and multiplicationResult evaluates to 14.

Furthermore, you can define your own custom operators. In Haskell, an operator is defined by enclosing it with parentheses. Let's consider a custom operator, ***, which multiplies two numbers and then adds a constant value to the result.

```
(***) :: Int -> Int -> Int
a *** b = (a * b) + 2

customOpResult = 3 *** 4 -- Result: 14
```

In this example, the custom operator *** is defined using the standard function notation, and it specifies that a *** b equals $(a * b) + 2$. Hence, customOpResult would evaluate to 14.

Operators can also be used in a prefix form by enclosing them within parentheses. This is particularly useful in higher-order functions where operators can be passed as arguments.

```
result = (+) 5 3 -- Result: 8
```

The expression (+) 5 3 demonstrates the usage of the + operator as a function, resulting in result being 8.

Haskell allows the use of sections, a convenient feature for partially applying infix operators. A section is created by partially applying one argument to an operator and enclosing it within parentheses.

```
addFive = (5 +) -- Equivalent to \lambda x -> 5 + x
resultFive = addFive 7 -- Result: 12
```

In this case, addFive is a partially applied function that adds 5 to its argument. The resultFive will therefore be 12.

Operators can also be used for making code more readable, especially when dealing with custom data structures. Consider the following example where a point in a 2D space is defined:

```
data Point = Point Int Int

(.+.) :: Point -> Point -> Point
(Point x1 y1) .+. (Point x2 y2) = Point (x1 + x2) (y1 + y2)

origin = Point 0 0
pointA = Point 2 3
pointB = Point 4 6
resultPoint = pointA .+. pointB -- Result: Point 6 9
```

Here, the Point type is defined to represent a point in 2D space with integer coordinates. A custom operator .+. is defined to add two points together. When pointA and pointB are added using this custom operator, resultPoint will be Point 6 9.

Complex expressions often benefit from the introduction of new operators. Managing precedence and associativity of operators becomes critical to ensure correct evaluation. The default precedence of operators ranges from 0 (the lowest) to 9 (the highest). Associativity defines how operators of the same precedence group when multiple instances appear in an expression.

The precedence and associativity can be specified explicitly using the infix, infixl, or infixr declarations. These declarations precede the function definition.

```
infixl 6 .+.
```

The declaration infixl 6 .+. specifies that the operator .+. is left-associative with a precedence of 6. Understanding and controlling these properties is essential when defining multiple custom operators that may interact.

Operators thus provide a powerful means of creating expressive and concise code in Haskell. The careful definition and usage of operators can enhance code readability and functionality, enabling the writing of more idiomatic Haskell programs.

3.10 Case Expressions

Case expressions in Haskell provide a mechanism for branching based on the evaluation of an expression. This is essential for pattern matching, which is a fundamental feature of functional programming in Haskell. Case expressions facilitate the construction of functions that behave differently depending on the form of their inputs, enhancing code clarity and maintainability.

In Haskell, the case expression is used to choose among multiple patterns based on the value of an expression. The general syntax of a case expression is as follows:

```
case expression of
  pattern1 -> result1
  pattern2 -> result2
  ...
  patternN -> resultN
```

Each pattern is matched against the value resulting from the evaluation of the expression. If a match is found, the corresponding result is returned. The case expression is evaluated sequentially; hence, the order of patterns is significant.

Consider the following example where we define a function that classifies integers into three categories: negative, zero, and positive:

```
classifyInteger :: Int -> String
classifyInteger x = case x of
  n | n < 0 -> "Negative"
  0 -> "Zero"
  p | p > 0 -> "Positive"
```

Here, classifyInteger takes an integer and returns a string describing whether the integer is "Negative", "Zero", or "Positive". The patterns use guards (|) to express conditions directly within the case expression.

Another important usage of case expressions is to handle complex data structures. Consider an algebraic data type representing a binary tree:

```
data Tree a = Empty
            | Node a (Tree a) (Tree a)
```

We will define a function to calculate the depth of this tree. Using case expressions ensures that all possible forms of the Tree data type are handled explicitly:

```
treeDepth :: Tree a -> Int
treeDepth tree = case tree of
  Empty -> 0
  Node _ left right -> 1 + max (treeDepth left) (treeDepth right)
```

In this function, treeDepth returns the depth of a tree by recursively evaluating the left and right subtrees, selecting the deeper subtree, and adding one to account for the root node.

Pattern matching using case expressions is exhaustive. It ensures that all possible patterns are considered, preventing runtime errors due to unmatched patterns. If a pattern is missing, Haskell raises a compilation warning, thus encouraging robust and error-free code. For incomplete matches, a wildcard pattern (_) can be used as a catch-all case:

```
describeList :: [a] -> String
describeList xs = case xs of
  [] -> "The list is empty."
  [x] -> "The list has one element."
  (_:_:_) -> "The list has multiple elements."
```

In the describeList function, the wildcard pattern (_ : _ : _) matches any list with at least two elements, while the empty list and single-element list are matched explicitly.

Moreover, case expressions can be nested for more complex pattern matching scenarios. Consider a function that operates specifically on nested Maybe types:

```
maybeDepth :: Maybe (Maybe a) -> Int
maybeDepth x = case x of
  Nothing -> 0
  Just Nothing -> 1
  Just (Just _) -> 2
```

In maybeDepth, each level of the nested Maybe is matched explicitly, allowing the function to return the depth based on the level of nestedness.

Another important application involves pattern matching against tuples, allowing deconstruction of pairs, triples, etc., within case expressions:

```
sumPairElements :: (Int, Int) -> Int
sumPairElements pair = case pair of
  (x, y) -> x + y
```

In this example, sumPairElements takes a pair of integers and returns their sum by deconstructing the tuple into its components.

Case expressions in Haskell incorporate simplicity and power, promoting expressive and comprehensible function definitions. Proper utilization of this construct ensures effective pattern matching, enabling more reliable and maintainably structured programs.

Chapter 4

Lists and Recursion

This chapter examines the use of lists in Haskell, covering basic list operations, list comprehensions, and pattern matching with lists. It introduces recursive functions on lists and explores common recursive patterns. Additionally, it discusses higher-order functions, list filtering and mapping, fold and reduction operations, and the concept of infinite lists and laziness.

4.1 Introduction to Lists

In Haskell, lists are a fundamental data structure that plays a vital role in the language's functionality and elegance. Lists in Haskell are homogeneous, meaning each list contains elements of the same type. They are defined by square brackets, with elements separated by commas. The type of a list of elements of type a is denoted as $[a]$.

To illustrate, consider a list of integers:

```
[1, 2, 3, 4, 5]
```

This list has the type $[\mathrm{Int}]$ because all its elements are integers. One can create lists of other types, such as a list of characters:

```
['a', 'b', 'c']
```

This list's type is $[\mathrm{Char}]$, which is often synonymous with the String type in Haskell, as strings are just lists of characters.

Lists can be constructed using the cons operator (:), which adds an element to the front of a list. The expression x : xs constructs a new list with x as the head (first element) and xs as the tail (rest of the list). For instance,

```
1 : [2, 3, 4]
```

produces the list [1, 2, 3, 4].

An empty list is denoted by [] and can be used to signal the end of a list. For example, the list [1, 2, 3] can be explicitly constructed using the cons operator as follows:

```
1 : (2 : (3 : []))
```

Lists support various basic operations. Some of the most common ones include:

- head: retrieves the first element of a list.
- tail: provides the list minus its first element.
- length: gives the number of elements in a list.
- null: checks if a list is empty.
- reverse: reverses the elements of a list.

Here are examples demonstrating these functions:

```
head [1, 2, 3] -- 1
tail [1, 2, 3] -- [2, 3]
length [1, 2, 3] -- 3
null [] -- True
reverse [1, 2, 3] -- [3, 2, 1]
```

Haskell shows the elegance of its list notation through list comprehensions, allowing concise and readable construction of lists. A list comprehension has the form:

```
[ expression | qualifier1, qualifier2, ... ]
```

For example, the list of squares of numbers from 1 to 5 can be generated as follows:

```
[ x^2 | x <- [1..5] ]
```

which yields:

[1, 4, 9, 16, 25]

Qualifiers include if-then conditions and can filter elements. For instance, generating the list of even squares from 1 to 10 is done by:

```
[ x^2 | x <- [1..10], even x ]
```

producing:

[4, 16, 36, 64, 100]

Lists and pattern matching go hand-in-hand in Haskell. Pattern matching on lists allows the extraction and manipulation of elements directly. A common pattern is matching the head and tail of a list:

```
myFunction (x:xs) = ...
```

Patterns for empty lists and wildcards are also useful:

```
myFunction [] = ...
myFunction (_:xs) = ...
```

Here is an example function that sums all elements of an integer list using pattern matching:

```
sumList :: [Int] -> Int
sumList [] = 0
sumList (x:xs) = x + sumList xs
```

Executing sumList [1, 2, 3, 4] results in:

10

This section has laid the groundwork for understanding lists, their construction, fundamental operations, and an introduction to list comprehensions and pattern matching.

4.2 Basic List Operations

In Haskell, lists are fundamental structures used to store sequences of elements. Understanding basic list operations is crucial for effective programming. This section presents various operations including construction, concatenation, indexing, and slicing of lists, all of which are integral to manipulation and usage in functional programming.

A list in Haskell is constructed using square brackets, with elements separated by commas. For example, [1,2,3,4] represents a list of integers, while ['a','b','c'] represents a list of characters.

```
-- Constructing lists
intList = [1, 2, 3, 4]
charList = ['a', 'b', 'c']
```

The (++) operator is used to concatenate two lists. This operator appends the elements of the second list to the first list, forming a new list.

```
-- Concatenating lists
list1 = [1, 2, 3]
list2 = [4, 5, 6]
concatenatedList = list1 ++ list2 -- Result: [1, 2, 3, 4, 5, 6]
```

To access elements within a list, Haskell provides the !! operator, which indexes a list starting from 0. For instance, list !! 2 retrieves the third element from list.

```
-- Indexing lists
element = concatenatedList !! 2 -- Result: 3
```

Lists can be pre-pended with elements using the : operator, known as the cons operator. This operator adds an element at the beginning of a list.

```
-- Pre-pending elements to lists
newList = 0 : intList -- Result: [0, 1, 2, 3, 4]
charListPrepended = 'z' : charList -- Result: ['z', 'a', 'b', 'c']
```

Slicing lists to extract sublists can be achieved using the take and drop functions. The take function extracts the first n elements from a list, while drop removes the first n elements.

```
-- Slicing lists with take and drop
firstThree = take 3 concatenatedList -- Result: [1, 2, 3]
remaining = drop 3 concatenatedList -- Result: [4, 5, 6]
```

Checking for membership within a list is done using the elem function, which returns True if the element is found in the list and False otherwise.

```
-- Checking membership in lists
isThreeInList = 3 `elem` concatenatedList -- Result: True
isTenInList = 10 `elem` concatenatedList -- Result: False
```

The length function returns the number of elements in a list. This is useful for operations that need the list's size.

```
-- Getting the length of a list
listLength = length concatenatedList -- Result: 6
```

The head and tail functions are used to dissect lists. head returns the first element of a list, while tail returns the rest of the list excluding the first element.

```
-- Getting the head and tail of a list
firstElement = head concatenatedList -- Result: 1
restOfList = tail concatenatedList -- Result: [2, 3, 4, 5, 6]
```

The last and init functions are akin to head and tail; however, last returns the last element of a list and init returns the list minus the last element.

```
-- Getting the last and init of a list
lastElement = last concatenatedList -- Result: 6
exceptLast = init concatenatedList -- Result: [1, 2, 3, 4, 5]
```

It is important to note that applying head, tail, last, or init to an empty list will result in a runtime error. Appropriately handling empty lists is critical for robust Haskell programming.

For reverse operations, the reverse function provides a straightforward means to invert the order of elements in a list.

```
-- Reversing a list
reversedList = reverse concatenatedList -- Result: [6, 5, 4, 3, 2, 1]
```

Combining all these operations lays the foundation for developing more complex functions and algorithms using lists. Understanding these rudimentary operations enables efficient exploration and manipulation of data within a Haskell program.

4.3 List Comprehensions

Haskell provides a powerful and expressive way to construct and manipulate lists through the use of *list comprehensions*. List comprehensions offer a concise mechanism similar to set notation found in mathematics. They allow for the creation of lists by specifying their elements through a series of operations forming a sequence of transformations.

The basic syntax of a list comprehension in Haskell is as follows:

```
[ expression | qualifier1, qualifier2, ..., qualifierN ]
```

In this format, expression is an output function defining how elements of the resultant list are constructed, and each qualifier represents a limiting condition or a generator that supplies input list elements to the expression. The list comprehension can transform and filter these elements.

Consider an example where the task is to create a list of squares for numbers 1 to 5:

```
squares = [x * x | x <- [1..5]]
```

Here, x <- [1..5] is a generator that provides each integer from 1 to 5, and x * x computes the square of each of those numbers. The resulting list, assigned to squares, is:

```
[1, 4, 9, 16, 25]
```

List comprehensions can include multiple generators and perform cartesian products of the input lists. For instance, to generate pairs of elements from two lists:

```
pairs = [(x, y) | x <- [1, 2, 3], y <- ['a', 'b']]
```

This comprehension iterates through each combination of x from [1, 2, 3] and y from ['a', 'b'], producing:

```
[(1, 'a'), (1, 'b'), (2, 'a'), (2, 'b'), (3, 'a'), (3, 'b')]
```

Filters (also known as guards) can be included to restrict the values produced by the generators. By placing a Boolean expression in the list comprehension, only elements that satisfy the condition will be included. Examples include generating even numbers or pairs where the first element is less than the second:

```
evens = [x | x <- [1..10], even x]
```

Resulting in:

```
[2, 4, 6, 8, 10]
```

And to generate pairs where the first element is less than the second element:

```
pairsLt = [(x, y) | x <- [1..3], y <- [1..3], x < y]
```

This comprehension provides:

```
[(1, 2), (1, 3), (2, 3)]
```

Combining multiple generators and filters can yield complex list outputs. For instance, constructing a list of Pythagorean triples (triples of integers (a, b, c) such that $a^2 + b^2 = c^2$) for a given range can be achieved as follows:

```
pythagoreanTriples = [(a, b, c) | c <- [1..10], b <- [1..c], a <- [1..b], a^2 + b^2 == c^2]
```

This produces:

```
[(3, 4, 5), (6, 8, 10)]
```

List comprehensions can also be nested, allowing one comprehension to be enclosed within another. This technique can be used to flatten lists of lists. For example, flattening a list of lists into a single list can be performed as follows:

```
nestedList = [[1, 2, 3], [4, 5], [6]]
flattenedList = [x | sublist <- nestedList, x <- sublist]
```

Yielding:

```
[1, 2, 3, 4, 5, 6]
```

List comprehensions can enhance code readability and maintainability, especially when dealing with concise data transformations. By integrating list comprehensions into Haskell programs, developers can succinctly perform complex list manipulations while retaining clarity in their code.

4.4 Pattern Matching with Lists

Pattern matching is a fundamental feature in Haskell that is often utilized to simplify and elegantly express functions operating on list data structures. As previously discussed, lists in Haskell are an integral part of the language, and understanding how to pattern match on lists is crucial for performing various operations.

When you use pattern matching, you can directly deconstruct a list into its constituent elements, which allows for concise and readable code. Several patterns can be used to match lists: the empty list, a list with a head and tail, and lists with specific elements.

Matching an Empty List

In Haskell, the simplest pattern match is against the empty list, represented by []. This is particularly useful in functions where the base case needs to handle an empty list.

```
isEmpty :: [a] -> Bool
isEmpty [] = True
```

```
isEmpty _ = False
```

In the isEmpty function above, if the input list matches the empty list pattern ([]), it returns True. If it matches any other list (represented by _), it returns False.

Matching Non-Empty Lists

A non-empty list in Haskell can be matched using the (x:xs) pattern, where x is the first element (head) of the list, and xs represents the rest of the list (tail).

```
sumList :: [Int] -> Int
sumList [] = 0
sumList (x:xs) = x + sumList xs
```

Here, sumList recursively sums the elements of a list. When the list is empty, it returns 0. When it matches the pattern (x:xs), it adds x (head) to the sum of the rest of the list xs (tail).

Pattern Matching with Specific Elements

You can match lists with specific elements, including nested patterns, to directly access and work with certain parts of the list:

```
startWithOne :: [Int] -> Bool
startWithOne (1:_) = True
startWithOne _ = False
```

In the startWithOne function, the pattern (1:_) checks if the list starts with the integer 1. If it does, the function returns True. If the list does not start with 1, it matches the wildcard pattern _ and returns False.

Matching Nested Lists

Pattern matching can also be applied to lists within lists, allowing for complex data structures to be handled intuitively:

```
secondElement :: [[a]] -> Maybe a
secondElement ([]:_) = Nothing
secondElement ((x:[]):_) = Nothing
secondElement ((_:y:_):_) = Just y
secondElement _ = Nothing
```

In this example, the secondElement function is designed to extract the second element from the first sublist of a list of lists. It handles several patterns: - If the first sublist is empty ([]:_), it returns Nothing. - If the first sublist has only one element ((x:[]):_), it returns Nothing. - If the first sublist has at least two elements ((_:y:_):_), it returns Just y, extracting the second element. - For any other pattern, it returns Nothing.

Advantages of Pattern Matching

Pattern matching provides several key advantages in Haskell: - **Clarity:** It partitions functions into clearly defined cases, making the intentions of code immediate and obvious. - **Safety:** By covering all possible patterns, it ensures all cases are handled, which reduces bugs and enhances reliability. - **Conciseness:** It reduces the need for explicit checks and manipulations, allowing for more concise and readable code.

Consider a function that determines the length of a list:

```
listLength :: [a] -> Int
listLength [] = 0
listLength (_:xs) = 1 + listLength xs
```

The listLength function defines two patterns: one for an empty list and one for a non-empty list. In the non-empty list case, it discards the head with _ and recursively counts the elements in the tail xs, adding 1 for each element.

Pattern Matching as a Recurring Theme

Pattern matching is not limited to simple lists but is a recurring theme across Haskell, applicable to tuples, custom data types, and more. When working with lists, particularly in recursive functions, pattern matching allows us to break down problems into manageable parts, adhering to Haskell's declarative programming style.

```
maxElement :: (Ord a) => [a] -> a
maxElement [x] = x
maxElement (x:xs) = max x (maxElement xs)
```

In the maxElement function finding the maximum element of a list, pattern matching enables handling singleton lists [x] directly, and recursively comparing the head x with the maximum of the tail xs in the pattern (x:xs). This flexibility and expressiveness enable developers to implement efficient and elegant solutions.

4.5 Recursive Functions on Lists

In Haskell, recursion is a powerful method for performing operations on lists. It allows us to define functions in which a function calls itself as a subroutine, thereby providing a mechanism to iterate over the elements of a list implicitly. This section delves into the construction and utilization of recursive functions to manipulate and traverse lists, elucidating the conceptual and syntactical aspects crucial to proficient Haskell programming.

A recursive function on a list typically follows a similar structure: it handles the base case (usually the empty list) and the recursive case (usually the list with at least one element, deconstructed into its head and tail). The base case ensures termination, while the recursive case processes the head and recurs on the tail.

Consider the canonical example of the length function, which calculates the number of elements in a list:

```
length :: [a] -> Int
length [] = 0
length (_:xs) = 1 + length xs
```

In this definition, length is a polymorphic function operating over a list of any type. The base case length [] = 0 specifies that the length of an empty list is zero. The second equation, length (_:xs) = 1 + length xs, handles the recursive case. It decomposes the list into its head (which is ignored with the wildcard _) and its tail xs, recursively calculating the length of the tail and adding one (accounting for the head).

The sum function, which aggregates the elements of a list, provides another straightforward example:

```
sum :: Num a => [a] -> a
sum [] = 0
sum (x:xs) = x + sum xs
```

Here, sum operates on a list of numeric elements. The base case sum [] = 0 ensures that the sum of an empty list is zero. The recursive case sum (x:xs) = x + sum xs decomposes the list into its head x and tail xs, recursively summing the elements of the tail and adding the head.

Consider a more complex function, reverse, which reverses the order of elements in a list:

```
reverse :: [a] -> [a]
reverse [] = []
reverse (x:xs) = reverse xs ++ [x]
```

In this function, the base case reverse [] = [] states that reversing an empty list results in an empty list. The recursive case reverse (x:xs) = reverse xs ++ [x] posits that reversing a non-empty list (x:xs) involves reversing the tail xs and appending the head x to the end of the reversed tail. The ++ operator denotes list concatenation.

As another example, consider the function filter, which removes elements from a list that do not satisfy a predicate:

```
filter :: (a -> Bool) -> [a] -> [a]
filter _ [] = []
filter pred (x:xs)
    | pred x = x : filter pred xs
    | otherwise = filter pred xs
```

The filter function takes a predicate pred and a list, returning a list of elements for which pred evaluates to True. The base case filter _ [] = [] means filtering an empty list always yields an empty list. The recursive case inspects the head x: if pred x is True, x is included in the result, followed by filtering the tail xs. If pred x is False, x is excluded, and the filter is applied to xs.

Lastly, let us consider the map function, which applies a given function to each element of a list:

```
map :: (a -> b) -> [a] -> [b]
map _ [] = []
map f (x:xs) = f x : map f xs
```

The map function transforms a list by applying a function f to each element. The base case map _ [] = [] specifies that mapping over an empty list returns an empty list. The recursive case map f (x:xs) = f x : map f xs applies f to the head x and recurs on the tail xs, constructing a new list with the transformed elements.

Below, we define an algorithm using the algorithm2e package to illustrate the process of a generic recursive list operation:

This pseudocode formalizes the recursive processing of any list, abstracting away the specifics into a generic Process function. The base case returns an empty list when the input is empty. The recursive case processes the head and recurs on the tail, constructing a new list by

Algorithm 1: Generic Recursive List Operation

```
Input: List L of elements of type a
Output: Processed list L' of elements of type b
Function RecursiveOperation(L):
    if L is empty then
        return Empty List
    else
        head ← head(L);
        tail ← tail(L);
        processedHead ← Process(head);
        processedTail ← RecursiveOperation(tail);
        return processedHead : processedTail
    end
```

prepending the processed head to the result of the recursive call on the tail.

Understanding such recursive paradigms equips Haskell programmers to tackle complex list manipulations effectively. Each recursive function processing lists embodies a core concept: breaking down the problem into smaller subproblems, solving the base case directly, and combining the results of recursive calls to achieve the final solution.

4.6 Common Recursive Patterns

In Haskell, recursion is a fundamental technique for operating on lists. By leveraging recursive patterns, one can solve complex problems by breaking them down into simpler subproblems. This section elaborates on several common recursive patterns often used in Haskell programming to process lists.

Sum of Elements: The sum of elements in a list is a classic example of a recursive function. The base case is an empty list, which has a sum of zero. The recursive case is a list with a head x and a tail xs, where the sum is the head x added to the sum of the tail xs.

```
sumList :: [Int] -> Int
sumList [] = 0
sumList (x:xs) = x + sumList xs
```

In this definition, sumList matches the empty list as the base case, returning 0. For the non-empty list, it calculates the sum by adding the head element x to the result of the recursive call on the tail xs.

Product of Elements: Similarly, the product of elements in a list can be implemented recursively. The base case for an empty list is defined as 1 because multiplying by 1 does not change the product. The recursive case multiplies the head x with the product of the tail xs.

```
productList :: [Int] -> Int
productList [] = 1
productList (x:xs) = x * productList xs
```

Length of a List: The length of a list is another frequently used recursive pattern. The base case for the length of an empty list is 0. For a nonempty list, it is 1 plus the length of the tail.

```
lengthList :: [a] -> Int
lengthList [] = 0
lengthList (_:xs) = 1 + lengthList xs
```

In this function, lengthList, underscores _ are used to ignore the head value, as it is not needed to compute the length.

Map: The map function applies a given function to each element of a list, returning a list of results. The base case is an empty list, resulting in an empty list. The recursive case applies the function to the head and cons the result onto the mapped tail.

```
mapList :: (a -> b) -> [a] -> [b]
mapList _ [] = []
mapList f (x:xs) = f x : mapList f xs
```

Here, mapList takes a function f and a list of type a, and it applies f to each element in the list, yielding a list of type b.

Filter: The filter function selects elements from a list that satisfy a predicate. The base case is an empty list, which results in an empty list. For a nonempty list, the head element is included in the result if it satisfies the predicate, and the function recurses on the tail.

```
filterList :: (a -> Bool) -> [a] -> [a]
filterList _ [] = []
filterList p (x:xs)
  | p x = x : filterList p xs
  | otherwise = filterList p xs
```

In filterList, the predicate p determines whether each element should be included in the resulting list.

Append: Appending two lists together is another common recursive pattern. The base case is appending an empty list to another list, yielding the second list. The recursive case appends the head of the first list to the result of appending the tail of the first list to the second list.

```
appendList :: [a] -> [a] -> [a]
appendList [] ys = ys
appendList (x:xs) ys = x : appendList xs ys
```

Reverse a List: Reversing a list in a recursive manner involves moving the head of the list to the end. The base case is an empty list, which is already reversed. The recursive case involves calling the reverse function on the tail and appending the head to the result.

```
reverseList :: [a] -> [a]
reverseList [] = []
reverseList (x:xs) = reverseList xs ++ [x]
```

Notice that reverseList xs ++ [x] appends the head element x to the end of the reversed tail.

Take: The take function selects the first n elements from a list. If n is zero or the list is empty, the result is an empty list. Otherwise, the head of the list is taken, and take (n 1) is called on the tail.

```
takeList :: Int -> [a] -> [a]
takeList _ [] = []
takeList 0 _ = []
takeList n (x:xs) = x : takeList (n-1) xs
```

Drop: The drop function removes the first n elements from a list. If n is zero or the list is empty, the entire list is returned. For n greater than zero, the head is dropped and drop (n 1) is called on the tail.

```
dropList :: Int -> [a] -> [a]
dropList _ [] = []
dropList 0 xs = xs
dropList n (_:xs) = dropList (n-1) xs
```

Zip: The zip function combines two lists into a list of pairs. The recursion stops when either list is empty. In each recursive step, the heads of both lists are paired, and zip is called on the tails.

```
zipList :: [a] -> [b] -> [(a, b)]
zipList [] _ = []
zipList _ [] = []
zipList (x:xs) (y:ys) = (x, y) : zipList xs ys
```

These examples illustrate fundamental recursive patterns on lists in Haskell. Understanding and applying these patterns allows for solving a variety of problems efficiently and elegantly using recursion.

4.7 Higher-Order Functions with Lists

In Haskell, higher-order functions are those that take other functions as arguments or return them as results. They are essential for writing concise and expressive code, particularly when dealing with lists. This section will delve into common higher-order functions for lists, exploring their definitions, usages, and implications in functional programming.

A higher-order function can simplify operations that would otherwise require verbose explicit recursion. Prominent higher-order functions for lists include map, filter, and fold.

Map

The map function applies a given function to every element of a list, resulting in a new list where each element is the result of the applied function.

```
map :: (a -> b) -> [a] -> [b]
map _ [] = []
map f (x:xs) = f x : map f xs
```

For instance, using map to increment each element in a list:

```
increment :: [Int] -> [Int]
increment xs = map (+1) xs

-- Execution
increment [1, 2, 3]

-- Output
[2, 3, 4]
```

Filter

The filter function takes a predicate and a list, returning a new list containing only the elements that satisfy the predicate.

```
filter :: (a -> Bool) -> [a] -> [a]
filter _ [] = []
filter p (x:xs)
  | p x = x : filter p xs
  | otherwise = filter p xs
```

An example of using filter to extract even numbers from a list:

```
evenNumbers :: [Int] -> [Int]
evenNumbers xs = filter even xs

-- Execution
evenNumbers [1, 2, 3, 4, 5, 6]

-- Output
```

```
[2, 4, 6]
```

Folds

The foldl and foldr functions (folds) reduce a list to a single value by iteratively applying a combining function to the elements of the list and an accumulator.

```
foldl :: (b -> a -> b) -> b -> [a] -> b
foldl _ acc [] = acc
foldl f acc (x:xs) = foldl f (f acc x) xs

foldr :: (a -> b -> b) -> b -> [a] -> b
foldr _ acc [] = acc
foldr f acc (x:xs) = f x (foldr f acc xs)
```

Consider calculating the sum of a list using foldl:

```
sumList :: [Int] -> Int
sumList xs = foldl (+) 0 xs

-- Execution
sumList [1, 2, 3, 4]

-- Output
10
```

Or finding the product of a list using foldr:

```
productList :: [Int] -> Int
productList xs = foldr (*) 1 xs

-- Execution
productList [1, 2, 3, 4]

-- Output
24
```

Function Composition and Pipelines

Higher-order functions can be combined to create complex data transformations. Consider a pipeline where a list is incremented and then filtered to retain only even numbers:

```
processList :: [Int] -> [Int]
processList xs = filter even (map (+1) xs)

-- Execution
processList [1, 2, 3, 4]

-- Output
[2, 4]
```

Equivalently, using function composition (.):

```
processList :: [Int] -> [Int]
```

```
processList = filter even . map (+1)
```

Laziness and Infinite Lists

The laziness of Haskell allows higher-order functions to operate on potentially infinite lists without immediate evaluation. For example, generating an infinite list of numbers and mapping a function over them:

```
numbersFrom :: Int -> [Int]
numbersFrom n = n : numbersFrom (n + 1)

incrementedNumbers :: [Int]
incrementedNumbers = map (+1) (numbersFrom 1)

-- Accessing the first few elements
take 5 incrementedNumbers

-- Output
[2, 3, 4, 5, 6]
```

Higher-order functions encapsulate powerful patterns for list manipulation, enhancing both expressiveness and efficiency in Haskell programming. Through them, abstraction is elevated, and the readability of complex data processing is significantly improved. Understanding and mastering these functions is vital for developing advanced Haskell applications.

4.8 Filtering and Mapping Lists

Filtering and mapping are two fundamental operations that can be performed on lists in Haskell to transform and retrieve data. Filtering involves selecting elements from a list that satisfy a given predicate, while mapping involves applying a function to each element of a list to produce a new list.

Filtering Lists

In Haskell, the filter function is used to filter elements of a list based on a predicate. A predicate is a function that returns a Bool value, indicating whether an element should be included in the resulting list. The type signature of filter is:

```
filter :: (a -> Bool) -> [a] -> [a]
```

The filter function takes a predicate and a list as arguments and returns a list of elements that satisfy the predicate.

Consider the following example, where we filter out even numbers from a list:

```
isEven :: Int -> Bool
isEven x = x `mod` 2 == 0

evenNumbers = filter isEven [1, 2, 3, 4, 5, 6]
```

Here, evenNumbers would be [2, 4, 6].

Mapping Lists

To apply a function to each element of a list, Haskell provides the map function. The type signature of map is:

```
map :: (a -> b) -> [a] -> [b]
```

The map function takes a function and a list as arguments and returns a new list obtained by applying the function to each element of the input list.

Consider the example where we add 3 to each element of a list:

```
addThree :: Int -> Int
addThree x = x + 3

incrementedList = map addThree [1, 2, 3, 4, 5]
```

Here, incrementedList would be [4, 5, 6, 7, 8].

Combining Filtering and Mapping

It is often necessary to both filter and map over a list. These operations can be chained together to create more complex transformations. For example, to first filter even numbers from a list and then double the remaining numbers, we can compose filter and map:

```
double :: Int -> Int
double x = x * 2

evenDoubledNumbers = map double (filter isEven [1, 2, 3, 4, 5, 6])
```

In this case, evenDoubledNumbers would be [4, 8, 12].

Lambda Expressions

Using lambda expressions, we can create anonymous functions on the fly without the need to define them separately. This is particularly useful for short, simple functions used within map or filter. Here is the earlier example using a lambda for doubling:

```
evenDoubledNumbers = map (\x -> x * 2) (filter (\x -> x `mod` 2 == 0) [1, 2, 3, 4, 5,
    6])
```

This achieves the same result, [4, 8, 12], without the need to separately define isEven and double.

Higher-Order Functions with Lists

The map and filter functions are important examples of higher-order functions—functions that take other functions as arguments. The strength of higher-order functions lies in their ability to abstract out common patterns of computation, making code more reusable and easier to reason about.

Consider a task where you need to transform a list of numbers by doubling even numbers and incrementing odd numbers and then filter to keep numbers greater than 10. This can be accomplished as follows:

```
transformAndFilter :: [Int] -> [Int]
transformAndFilter xs = filter (> 10) (map transform xs)
  where
    transform x = if x `mod` 2 == 0 then x * 2 else x + 1

result = transformAndFilter [1, 2, 3, 4, 5, 6]
```

The variable result is [11, 12, 13] as it first transforms the list to [2, 4, 4, 8, 6, 12] and then filters elements greater than 10.

Efficiency Considerations

While chaining map and filter operations is a powerful technique, it is important to consider efficiency. Each function application creates a new list, which can lead to performance overhead in both time and space. In cases where performance is critical, these operations can be combined into a single list traversal to improve efficiency. For instance:

```
efficientTransformAndFilter :: [Int] -> [Int]
efficientTransformAndFilter [] = []
efficientTransformAndFilter (x:xs)
  | transformed > 10 = transformed : efficientTransformAndFilter xs
  | otherwise = efficientTransformAndFilter xs
  where
    transformed = if x `mod` 2 == 0 then x * 2 else x + 1

resultEfficient = efficientTransformAndFilter [1, 2, 3, 4, 5, 6]
```

By combining mapping and filtering in one recursive function, resultEfficient will also be [11, 12, 13], but accomplished in a single traversal.

Filtering and mapping are essential list operations in Haskell that demonstrate the power of functional programming. Utilizing these operations effectively allows for clear and expressive data transformations, facilitating sophisticated data processing tasks while maintaining concise and readable code. Proper understanding and application of these functions enable optimized performance and harness the full potential of higher-order functions in Haskell.

4.9 Folds and Reductions

In Haskell, folds are an essential functional programming technique that provide a versatile method to traverse and manipulate lists. They generalize a pattern of recursion for processing an entire list and accumulating a result. Understanding folds requires comprehending two primary functions: foldl and foldr. These functions systematically reduce a list to a single value by applying a binary operation.

foldl stands for "fold left," and it processes the list from left to right. Its type signature is foldl :: (b -> a -> b) -> b -> [a] -> b. The parameters are the binary function, the initial accumulator, and the list to be folded.

```
foldl (\acc x -> acc + x) 0 [1, 2, 3, 4]
-- Results in 10
```

In this example, the binary function adds the elements of the list [1, 2, 3, 4] to the accumulator, starting with an initial value of 0. The process can be visualized as follows:

```
foldl (+) 0 [1, 2, 3, 4]
= foldl (+) (0 + 1) [2, 3, 4]
= foldl (+) (1 + 2) [3, 4]
= foldl (+) (3 + 3) [4]
= foldl (+) (6 + 4) []
= 10
```

foldr stands for "fold right," and it processes the list from right to left. Its type signature is foldr :: (a -> b -> b) -> b -> [a] -> b. The parameters are similar to those of foldl but in reverse order.

```
foldr (\x acc -> x + acc) 0 [1, 2, 3, 4]
-- Results in 10
```

Here, the binary function adds elements starting from the rightmost element of the list:

```
foldr (+) 0 [1, 2, 3, 4]
= 1 + (foldr (+) 0 [2, 3, 4])
= 1 + (2 + (foldr (+) 0 [3, 4]))
= 1 + (2 + (3 + (foldr (+) 0 [4])))
= 1 + (2 + (3 + (4 + foldr (+) 0 [])))
= 1 + (2 + (3 + (4 + 0)))
= 10
```

The difference between foldl and foldr is not only in the direction of processing but also in how they handle infinite lists. foldr can operate on infinite lists under certain conditions, while foldl typically cannot, because foldl requires complete traversal of the list to begin the reduction.

When deciding between foldl and foldr, if the binary function is associative, either can be employed. However, foldr should be preferred if the reduction can benefit from lazy evaluation. Consider the following example of a list concatenation:

```
foldr (:) [] [1, 2, 3, 4]
-- Results in [1, 2, 3, 4]
```

foldr constructs the list by inserting each element from the right, preserving the original order effectively. Using foldl, the complexity of such an operation would be inefficient due to the necessity of reversing intermediate results:

```
foldl (\acc x -> acc ++ [x]) [] [1, 2, 3, 4]
-- Results in [1, 2, 3, 4]
```

Given Haskell's strength in functional programming paradigms, let's discuss foldl' from the Data.List module, which offers a strict version of foldl. The primary difference is that foldl' evaluates the accumulator eagerly, which can provide performance benefits by preventing the build-up of thunks (deferred operations):

```
import Data.List (foldl')

foldl' (\acc x -> acc + x) 0 [1, 2, 3, 4]
-- Results in 10
```

Haskell's versatility in handling folds extends to several specialized folding functions in the Data.Foldable module, such as foldMap and foldlM. foldMap combines mapping and folding by allowing elements to be transformed before folding, leveraging monoids:

```
import Data.Foldable (foldMap)
import Data.Monoid (Sum(..))

foldMap Sum [1, 2, 3, 4]
-- Results in Sum {getSum = 10}
```

foldlM, on the other hand, is a monadic fold that allows incorporating monadic effects during the reduction process, useful for accumulation requiring effectful computations.

```
import Control.Monad (foldM)

foldM (\acc x -> return (acc + x)) 0 [1, 2, 3, 4]
-- Results in Just 10
```

In scenarios where side effects or computations intertwined with the folding process are necessary, foldM simplifies implementation by embedding monadic actions within the fold operation.

Overall, mastering folds provides efficient means to decompose various complex operations into coherent, reusable patterns in Haskell. By internalizing these concepts, the power to manipulate and traverse data structures functionally becomes substantially clear, streamlining many common programming tasks into more elegant, declarative forms.

4.10 Infinite Lists and Laziness

Haskell's robust handling of infinite lists is one of its distinctive features, enabling programmers to define and work with lists that do not have a terminal element. This capability hinges on Haskell's key concept of laziness, or more formally, non-strict evaluation. Before delving into the practical applications and implications of infinite lists, it is essential to understand how laziness operates in Haskell.

In Haskell, expressions are not evaluated when they are bound to variables; rather, they are evaluated only when their results are needed. This strategy is known as "call-by-need". As a result, infinite structures can be defined and manipulated seamlessly, because elements of these structures are computed on-demand.

Consider the simplest infinite list – the list of all natural numbers:

```
naturals :: [Integer]
naturals = [0..]
```

In this code snippet, naturals is defined as an infinite list starting from 0, incremented by 1 indefinitely. Here the range notation [0..] is used, where Haskell's list comprehension syntax allows for such elegant definitions.

When working with infinite lists, it is crucial to access only a finite portion of the list at a time. Below, we extract the first ten elements of naturals:

```
take 10 naturals
```

The take function in Haskell retrieves a specified number of elements from a list, allowing functional interaction with infinite lists without causing non-terminating computations.

```
[0,1,2,3,4,5,6,7,8,9]
```

Combining infinite lists with list comprehensions enables sophisticated definitions. For example, generating an infinite list of multiples of 3 can be achieved as follows:

```
multiplesOfThree :: [Integer]
multiplesOfThree = [x | x <- [0..], x `mod` 3 == 0]
```

Here, we use list comprehension to filter the infinite list of natural numbers, retaining only those elements that are divisible by 3.

Another practical example involves the Fibonacci sequence, an essential numeric series in mathematics and computer science. Utilizing laziness, the infinite sequence of Fibonacci numbers can be defined concisely:

```
fibs :: [Integer]
fibs = 0 : 1 : zipWith (+) fibs (tail fibs)
```

In this definition, the Fibonacci sequence starts with 0 and 1. The zipWith function is employed to pairwise add corresponding elements of fibs and tail fibs (the list of Fibonacci numbers with the first element removed). This construct ensures that only needed elements are computed lazily.

To illustrate the practical usage, the following command extracts the first 15 Fibonacci numbers:

```
take 15 fibs
```

```
[0,1,1,2,3,5,8,13,21,34,55,89,144,233,377]
```

Beyond sequences, other infinite structures such as streams of random numbers can also be handled. The System.Random module can be referenced to illustrate this via an infinite list of random values:

```
import System.Random

randomsList :: (RandomGen g, Random a) => g -> [a]
randomsList gen = randoms gen

-- Initialize with a new standard generator
gen <- newStdGen
randomsList' = randomsList gen :: [Int]
```

Here, the randoms function generates an infinite list of random values starting with a given generator. Note that a finite segment of this list should be used in practical applications to avoid infinite loops.

Finally, infinite lists can often be combined using Haskell's higher-order functions. For example, producing an infinite list of tuples containing powers of 2 paired with their indices:

```
powersOfTwo :: [(Integer, Integer)]
powersOfTwo = zip [0..] (iterate (*2) 1)
```

In this instance, the iterate function successively applies the multiplication by 2 starting from 1, effectively generating all powers of 2. The iterator is paired with the infinite list of indices using zip, creating an infinite list of tuples.

Laziness in Haskell not only enables the definition and utility of infinite lists but also ensures resource efficiency by computing elements only when they are demanded. This paradigm, when mastered, opens versatile programming possibilities, interleaving elegance with functionality.

Chapter 5

Types and Type Classes

This chapter delves into Haskell's type system, explaining type inference, basic types, and type variables. It covers parameterized types, algebraic data types, and type synonyms. The chapter also provides an in-depth look at type classes, how to create type class instances, and an overview of commonly used type classes. Advanced features of type classes are also discussed.

5.1 Introduction to Types

In Haskell, types are a fundamental aspect of the language that plays a crucial role in ensuring code correctness and reliability. Types help to specify the kind of values that can be used in different parts of the program, thereby allowing the compiler to catch errors at compile-time. Understanding types is essential for mastering Haskell programming, as they provide critical information about how functions interact with data.

A type in Haskell is a classification that specifies which kind of data a variable or expression can hold. For instance, the type Int represents integer values, while Bool represents boolean values. Haskell's type system is extremely powerful and expressive, enabling the creation of complex types that can model a wide variety of data structures and behaviors.

```
-- Example of type declarations
x :: Int
```

```
x = 5

y :: Bool
y = True
```

In the example above, x is declared to be of type Int and is assigned the value 5, while y is of type Bool and is assigned the value True. The double colon :: is used to specify the type of a variable or expression.

Type Signatures

A type signature explicitly states the type of a function or expression. It specifies the types of inputs a function can accept and the type of output it will produce. Providing type signatures for functions is considered good practice because it serves as documentation and helps the compiler ensure that the implementation matches the developer's intentions.

```
-- Function with a type signature
add :: Int -> Int -> Int
add a b = a + b
```

In the add function above, the type signature Int -> Int -> Int denotes that add takes two Int values as arguments and returns an Int value. The arrow -> is used to separate the input and output types.

Type Inference

Haskell features a robust type inference engine that can automatically deduce the types of expressions without explicit type annotations. This feature allows the programmer to write less boilerplate code while maintaining the benefits of a statically-typed language.

```
-- Type inference in action
increment a = a + 1
```

For the increment function, Haskell's type inference system deduces that a must be of type Num (a numeric type) because it is used with the + operator. The inferred type of increment is:

```
increment :: Num a => a -> a
```

This means increment is a function that takes a value of any type that is an instance of the Num type class (discussed in a later section) and returns a value of the same type.

Polymorphic Types

In Haskell, functions can be polymorphic, meaning they can operate on arguments of various types. Polymorphic types use type variables, typically denoted by lowercase letters like a, b, etc.

```
-- Polymorphic function example
identity :: a -> a
identity x = x
```

The identity function has the type a -> a, indicating it takes a value of some type a and returns a value of the same type. The specific type a can be any type, making identity a polymorphic function.

Parametric and Adhoc Polymorphism

Haskell supports two kinds of polymorphism: parametric polymorphism and ad-hoc polymorphism. Parametric polymorphism allows functions to be written generically, so they can handle values uniformly without depending on their type.

```
-- Parametric polymorphism in action
swap :: (a, b) -> (b, a)
swap (x, y) = (y, x)
```

The swap function can interchange the elements of any tuple regardless of their types.

Ad-hoc polymorphism, on the other hand, is achieved through type classes. This allows functions to operate differently based on the type of their arguments. For instance, the + operator can add integers, floating-point numbers, and so on, depending on the type context.

```
-- Usage of type class constraints
describe :: Show a => a -> String
describe x = "The value is " ++ show x
```

The describe function uses a type class constraint (Show a =>) to ensure that show can be applied to x. The Show type class includes types that can be converted to a string representation.

Understanding the concepts introduced here is crucial for appreciating Haskell's type system. As we delve deeper into parameterized types, algebraic data types, and type classes, the real power and flexibility of Haskell types will become evident. This foundational knowledge sets the stage for exploring how types can be harnessed to write robust, maintainable, and expressive Haskell programs.

5.2 Type Inference

Haskell's type inference mechanism is one of its most powerful features, allowing programmers to write concise code without the need for explicit type annotations. The Haskell compiler, GHC (Glasgow Haskell Compiler), can deduce the types of expressions automatically by using the Hindley-Milner type inference algorithm, which forms the backbone of its type system.

Type inference operates by examining the structure of functions and expressions, deriving the most general type that satisfies all constraints imposed by the usage of these expressions. This process can be broken down into several key steps: gathering type constraints, unifying types, and generalizing type variables.

```
-- Example of type inference
exampleFunction x y = x + y
```

For the function exampleFunction, Haskell will infer the types of x and y by analyzing the + operator. The + operator is defined in the Prelude as:

```
(+) :: Num a => a -> a -> a
```

Here, the Num type class constraint ensures that + operates on any type a that is an instance of the Num type class. Therefore, the type of exampleFunction is inferred to be:

```
exampleFunction :: Num a => a -> a -> a
```

Haskell's type inference not only spares the programmer from writing type annotations but also ensures type safety by catching type errors at compile time. This capability is leveraged through unification, a process that finds a common type among several type expressions.

Consider the following example with polymorphic types:

```
pair :: a -> b -> (a, b)
pair x y = (x, y)
```

In this function, a and b are type variables, indicating that pair can take arguments of any type and return a tuple consisting of these arguments. The type of pair is inferred due to its construction, which matches the form (x, y), thereby making use of generalized type variables.

Constraints play a crucial role in type inference. When the compiler encounters an expression, it generates type constraints based on the structure and operators used. These constraints are subsequently solved to obtain the most general type. As seen in the exampleFunction, the use of the Num type class places specific constraints on the variables being inferred.

Another significant aspect is the process of generalization. After resolving type constraints, the compiler generalizes the type variables, converting them into polymorphic types if they are not constrained by specific type classes. Consider the type inference for a simple identity function:

```
identity :: a -> a
identity x = x
```

The expression x = x imposes no constraints on a, thereby allowing a to remain fully polymorphic.

Type inference with more complex structures, such as higher-order functions, proceeds similarly by recursively inferring types of subexpressions:

```
applyTwice :: (a -> a) -> a -> a
applyTwice f x = f (f x)
```

Here, the function applyTwice takes a function f as its first argument and infers that f must be applicable to its own result, thus forcing the type (a -> a) for f and a for x.

The power of Haskell's type inference enables work with algebraic data types without explicit type annotations:

```
data Maybe a = Nothing | Just a

safeHead :: [a] -> Maybe a
safeHead [] = Nothing
safeHead (x:_) = Just x
```

For the safeHead function, the type inference mechanism deduces that when applied to a list, the outcome matches the Maybe type, specifically Maybe a.

Understanding type inference is fundamental to harnessing the full potential of Haskell. It allows developers to write flexible, type-safe code while the compiler transparently manages type correctness behind the scenes.

5.3 Basic Types in Haskell

Haskell, as a statically typed language, features a robust type system to ensure that errors are minimized at compile time. One of the essential aspects of understanding Haskell is learning the basic types that the language provides. This section will cover the most fundamental and commonly used types.

1. Bool

The Bool type represents boolean values, which can either be True or False. It is a simple algebraic data type with two possible values.

```
True :: Bool
False :: Bool
```

Boolean values are primarily used in conditional expressions and predicates.

2. Char

The Char type is used to represent single characters. It is defined to store Unicode characters.

```
'a' :: Char
'\n' :: Char -- newline character
'\x03C0' :: Char -- Unicode for pi ()
```

Characters are typically enclosed in single quotation marks.

3. String

Although String is not a primitive type, it is essentially a list of characters. The type synonym for String is defined as:

```
type String = [Char]
```

Strings are sequences of characters and are enclosed in double quotation marks.

```
"Hello, World!" :: String
```

4. Int

The Int type is used to represent fixed-precision integers. The range of Int depends on the system but is generally sufficient for most arithmetic operations.

```
42 :: Int
-7 :: Int
``
```

5. Integer

Unlike Int, the Integer type represents arbitrary precision integers. This means that Integer can handle very large numbers that exceed the bounds of Int.

```
12345678901234567890 :: Integer
```

The trade-off for using Integer is performance, as they are less efficient than Int for smaller values.

6. Float

The Float type represents single-precision floating-point numbers. It is suitable for operations requiring moderate precision.

```
3.14 :: Float
-0.001 :: Float
```

7. Double

The Double type offers double-precision floating-point numbers, providing a greater degree of accuracy and range compared to Float.

```
2.718281828459045 :: Double
1.0e-4 :: Double
``
```

8. Rational

The Rational type is used to represent rational numbers, which are fractions of two integers. It leverages the Ratio type to manage the numerator and the denominator.

```
import Data.Ratio

(3 % 4) :: Rational
(10 % 3) :: Rational
```

Using Rational values ensures precision that floating-point representations might not offer.

9. Complex

For complex numbers, Haskell provides the Complex type from the Data.Complex module. Complex numbers are expressed with real and imaginary parts.

```
import Data.Complex
```

```
(3 :+ 4) :: Complex Double -- Represents 3 + 4i
(1.0 :+ 2.0) :: Complex Float -- Represents 1.0 + 2.0i
```

10. Type Inspection with :t

Haskell provides an interactive way to check the type of expressions using the GHCi command :t. For example:

```
Prelude> :t True
True :: Bool

Prelude> :t 'a'
'a' :: Char

Prelude> :t "Hello"
"Hello" :: String

Prelude> :t 42
42 :: Num p => p

Prelude> :t 3.14
3.14 :: Fractional p => p
```

Understanding these basic types and their usage is foundational for writing robust Haskell code. As you become more familiar with these types, you will also learn how Haskell's type system ensures type safety and assists in writing more reliable programs.

5.4 Type Variables

Type variables are a fundamental aspect of Haskell's type system, allowing for the creation of generic and reusable code components. By abstracting over specific types, type variables enable functions, data types, and type classes to be defined in a flexible manner that can operate over a range of different types.

A type variable is typically represented by a lowercase letter, often a, b, c, etc. Unlike concrete types such as Int or String, type variables can stand in for any type. This concept is crucial for defining polymorphic functions and data types.

Consider the function id, which returns its argument unchanged:

```
id :: a -> a
id x = x
```

In this example, the type signature a -> a indicates that the function id takes a value of some type a and returns a value of the same type a. The type variable a signifies that id can operate on any type, making it a polymorphic function.

Furthermore, type variables allow the definition of parameterized data types. For instance, the Maybe type is parameterized by a type variable:

```
data Maybe a = Nothing | Just a
```

Here, Maybe a is a type that can represent an optional value of type a. The type variable a in the definition allows Maybe to be used with any type, such as Maybe Int, Maybe String, etc.

The presence of type variables can be extended to more complex data types, such as binary trees:

```
data Tree a = Empty | Node a (Tree a) (Tree a)
```

In this definition, Tree a represents a binary tree that stores values of type a. The constructors Empty and Node respectively define an empty tree and a node containing a value of type a and two subtrees.

It is essential to note that type variables do not impose any restrictions on the types they can represent. However, constraints can be introduced using type classes to restrict the kinds of types that can be substituted for a type variable.

For example, consider a function that requires its arguments to be comparable using the Ord type class:

```
max :: Ord a => a -> a -> a
max x y
    | x >= y = x
    | otherwise = y
```

In this case, the type signature Ord a => a -> a -> a indicates that max can only be applied to types that are instances of the Ord type class, such as Int or String. The Ord a => part of the type signature is a type class constraint, specifying that the type variable a must belong to the Ord type class.

This feature allows for a fine-grained control over the types that can be used with a polymorphic function or data type. Another illustration is the Functor type class, which facilitates mapping a function over a structure without altering the structure itself:

```
class Functor f where
    fmap :: (a -> b) -> f a -> f b
```

The type variable f in the Functor type class definition stands for a type constructor that takes one type argument. The fmap function maps a function from type a to type b over a structure f that contains elements of type a, producing a new structure containing elements of type b.

To provide a concrete example, consider the Maybe type as a Functor:

```
instance Functor Maybe where
    fmap _ Nothing = Nothing
    fmap g (Just x) = Just (g x)
```

This instance declaration specifies how fmap operates on the Maybe type. If the input is Nothing, the result is Nothing. If the input is Just x, the function g is applied to x, and the result is wrapped in Just.

Type variables thus play a pivotal role in Haskell, fostering code generality and reusability. Their integration with type classes further enriches the language's expressive power, enabling the definition of robust and versatile abstractions.

5.5 Parameterized Types

Parameterized types, also known as generic types, enable the definition of data structures and functions that operate uniformly on a variety of types, enhancing the flexibility and reusability of code. In Haskell, we can define parameterized types using type variables, which allow us to create data structures without specifying their exact types.

Consider the simple example of a list type, which is parameterized by the type of elements it contains. In Haskell, the definition of a list can be represented as follows:

```
data List a = Empty | Cons a (List a)
```

Here, List is a parameterized type, and a is a type variable. The list can be either Empty or a Cons cell containing a value of type a followed by another list of the same type. This definition allows List to be used with any type of elements. For instance, we can have List Int, List Char, or even List (List Int).

To illustrate the versatility of parameterized types, we will define a simple binary tree data structure where nodes contain values of any type:

```
data Tree a = Leaf a | Node (Tree a) (Tree a)
```

In this definition, Tree a can either be a Leaf containing a value of type a, or a Node that connects two subtrees.

Next, we explore how to write functions that operate on parameterized data types. Let's implement a function to calculate the size of the tree (i.e., the number of nodes):

```
size :: Tree a -> Int
size (Leaf _) = 1
size (Node left right) = size left + size right
```

The size function recursively traverses the tree, counting each Leaf and Node it encounters. This function is completely generic and works for Tree a regardless of the specific type of a.

We can also define a function to transform each value in the tree using a provided function:

```
mapTree :: (a -> b) -> Tree a -> Tree b
mapTree f (Leaf x) = Leaf (f x)
mapTree f (Node left right) = Node (mapTree f left) (mapTree f right)
```

The mapTree function takes a function f that transforms values of type a to type b, and applies it across all elements of the Tree a, producing a Tree b.

Parameterized types also work seamlessly with other Haskell features like type classes. For example, consider implementing the Functor type class for the Tree type:

```
instance Functor Tree where
    fmap = mapTree
```

Here, we make Tree an instance of the Functor type class by providing an implementation for fmap, which is a synonym for our previously defined mapTree function.

Another important use case for parameterized types is defining more complex data structures like key-value pairs or dictionaries. Here's a simple example of a parameterized Pair type:

```
data Pair a b = Pair a b
```

The Pair type takes two type parameters, a and b, allowing combinations of different types. We might have pairs such as Pair Int String or Pair Bool Char. Functions operating on Pair can similarly be generic:

```
swap :: Pair a b -> Pair b a
swap (Pair x y) = Pair y x
```

The swap function exchanges the elements in a Pair, changing its type from Pair a b to Pair b a. This demonstrates the powerful abstraction capabilities afforded by parameterized types.

In practice, parameterized types are prevalent across many standard and custom Haskell libraries, contributing to the language's expressive type system. The examples provided here form a foundation for understanding the use and utility of parameterized types, paving the way for more advanced type constructions and abstractions in Haskell.

5.6 Algebraic Data Types

Algebraic Data Types (ADTs) are a fundamental concept in Haskell and functional programming in general. They allow the creation of composite types, which can be used to represent more complex data structures. ADTs are particularly powerful because they combine properties from other data types to form new types. In Haskell, ADTs include two primary constructs: sum types and product types.

Sum types, also known as tagged unions or variant records, allow a variable to hold a value that could be one of several different possibilities. Each possibility is tagged with a constructor. An example of a sum type is the Maybe type, which can either be Nothing or Just a, where a is some value.

```
data Maybe a = Nothing | Just a
```

In this definition, Maybe a is an ADT with two constructors: Nothing, which represents the absence of a value, and Just a, which represents the presence of a value of type a.

Product types, on the other hand, allow combining multiple values together, each potentially of different types, into a single composite value. A classic example of a product type is a tuple. Here's an example of a custom product type representing a 2D coordinate:

```
data Coordinate2D = Coordinate2D Int Int
```

This Coordinate2D type has a single constructor, also called Coordinate2D, which takes two Int arguments.

Combining both sum and product types allows defining more complex structures. Consider the following ADT for a binary tree containing integer values:

```
data BinaryTree = Empty
```

```
                | Node Int BinaryTree BinaryTree
```

In this definition, BinaryTree is a sum type with two constructors: Empty, representing an empty tree, and Node, representing a tree node containing an integer value and two subtrees (left and right).

Algebraic Data Types are more expressive when combined with recursive definitions. They enable the representation of recursive data structures such as lists and trees. Here's an example of the list type using an ADT:

```
data List a = Cons a (List a)
            | Nil
```

In this definition, List a can be either Nil, representing the empty list, or Cons a (List a), representing a non-empty list where a is the head element and (List a) is the tail of the list.

Pattern matching is a powerful feature of Haskell that works seamlessly with ADTs. It allows the deconstruction of values and the application of different actions based on their constructors. Here is an example of a function using pattern matching with the Maybe type:

```
isJust :: Maybe a -> Bool
isJust Nothing = False
isJust (Just _) = True
```

This function, isJust, checks if a Maybe value is Just or Nothing. Pattern matching makes the function definition straightforward and eliminates the need for explicit checks.

In another example, consider a function that calculates the depth of a binary tree:

```
depth :: BinaryTree -> Int
depth Empty = 0
depth (Node _ left right) = 1 + max (depth left) (depth right)
```

In this function, depth, pattern matching is used to handle different cases of BinaryTree. If the tree is Empty, its depth is 0. If it is a Node, the depth is calculated as 1 plus the maximum depth of its left and right subtrees.

Another benefit of ADTs is that they can express invariants of the data types directly in their definitions. By leveraging well-defined constructors, it is possible to ensure that only valid data is represented. For instance, consider an ADT for non-empty lists:

```
data NonEmptyList a = NonEmpty a [a]
```

This NonEmptyList type ensures that there is always at least one element in the list, which can be verified at compile-time.

Additionally, ADTs can be combined with type classes to create more generic and reusable code. Suppose we want to define an equality check for BinaryTree. We can derive it by making BinaryTree an instance of the Eq type class:

```
instance Eq BinaryTree where
    Empty == Empty = True
    (Node x left1 right1) == (Node y left2 right2) = (x == y) && (left1 == left2) &&
            (right1 == right2)
    _ == _ = False
```

This instance declaration uses pattern matching to check for equality between BinaryTree values.

In summary, Algebraic Data Types in Haskell provide a robust way to model complex data by combining simpler types in meaningful ways. They support abstraction, enforce invariants, and integrate seamlessly with type classes and pattern matching, making them indispensable tools for Haskell programmers.

5.7 Type Synonyms

Type synonyms in Haskell provide a way to create alternative names for existing types. This feature enhances code readability and maintainability by giving meaningful names to complex types. Unlike new data types, type synonyms do not create new distinct types, but rather aliases for existing ones, allowing for more expressive type signatures without additional runtime overhead.

A type synonym is declared using the type keyword. The basic syntax for defining a type synonym looks like this:

```
type String = [Char]
```

In the example above, String is defined as a synonym for the list of Char. This allows us to use String in place of [Char] throughout the code, enhancing clarity when dealing with functions that operate on textual data.

```
printString :: String -> IO ()
printString str = putStrLn str
```

Here, String is used in the type signature of the printString function, making it immediately clear that the function expects a string input.

Type synonyms can also be parameterized, similar to types in Haskell. This can be especially useful when dealing with complex type signatures that involve type constructors. For instance, consider a generic representation of a pair:

```
type Pair a b = (a, b)
```

In this case, Pair is a type synonym for a tuple that holds two types, a and b. This makes function signatures more concise and readable.

```
swap :: Pair a b -> Pair b a
swap (x, y) = (y, x)
```

The swap function's type signature uses the Pair type synonym, making it evident that the function swaps the elements of a tuple.

More complex examples involve type synonyms for deeply nested or higher-kinded types. For instance, let's consider a synonym for a type of a function returning a computation in the I/O Monad:

```
type IOFunc a = a -> IO a
```

This allows for easier-to-read type signatures:

```
applyTwice :: IOFunc a -> a -> IO a
applyTwice f x = f x >>= f
```

Here, IOFunc clarifies that applyTwice takes a function which performs an I/O action and applies it twice to the input.

Type synonyms play a crucial role in dealing with complex type errors and type signatures, especially when working with libraries and frameworks that involve sophisticated types. For example, in web frameworks that may have complicated types for representing request handlers, type synonyms can dramatically simplify type signatures.

```
type Handler m = Request -> m Response
```

In this case, Handler m abstracts the specific type of a request handler into a more understandable form.

Another noteworthy point is the interaction of type synonyms with type classes. While type synonyms can enhance readability, they do not affect type class instances. Consequently, when defining type class instances, one must use the actual underlying type. However, type synonyms can still make the instance declarations more readable:

```
type UserID = Int
type UserName = String

data User = User UserID UserName

instance Eq User where
  (User id1 _) == (User id2 _) = id1 == id2

instance Show User where
  show (User id name) = "User " ++ show id ++ ": " ++ name
```

In the example above, UserID and UserName are type synonyms for Int and String respectively. They make the User data type definition and the associated instance declarations more descriptive and easier to understand.

Additionally, it is important to note that type synonyms cannot be recursive. Attempting to define a recursive type synonym results in a compilation error. For instance:

```
type BadType = (Int, BadType)
```

This will result in an error, as Haskell does not support recursive type synonyms to prevent potential infinity loops and ensure type safety.

By leveraging type synonyms effectively, one can achieve a high level of code clarity and maintainability, allowing for more intuitive and understandable Haskell code, especially in large and complex codebases.

5.8 Type Classes

In Haskell, *type classes* play a critical role in capturing shared behavior among different types. They provide a means to define commonly shared functionality that can be implemented by various data types. A *type class* can be thought of as a collection of types that support a specific set of operations, encapsulating functionality in an abstract way. This section delves into the concept, definition, and usage of type classes in Haskell, aiming to establish a comprehensive understanding of this powerful feature.

Definition of Type Classes:

A type class in Haskell is defined using the class keyword, followed by the class name and the type variable that will represent the types implementing the type class. Here is a basic structure of a type class definition:

```
class Eq a where
    (==) :: a -> a -> Bool
    (/=) :: a -> a -> Bool
```

In this example, the Eq type class is defined with a single type variable a. This type class specifies two functions: (==) and (/=). Any type that wants to be an instance of the Eq type class will need to implement these two functions.

Creating Type Class Instances:

To make a type an instance of a type class, the instance keyword is used. Let's consider the data type Bool. We can create an instance of Eq for Bool as follows:

```
instance Eq Bool where
    True == True = True
    False == False = True
    _ == _ = False

    x /= y = not (x == y)
```

Here, we define how the equality functions (==) and (/=) work for Bool. This enables the comparison of Bool values using these functions.

Type Class Constraints:

Type class constraints are used to specify that a function or a type must be an instance of a particular type class. This is achieved using the => symbol. For example:

```
sort :: (Ord a) => [a] -> [a]
sort = ...
```

The function sort takes a list of elements of type a and returns a sorted list. The constraint (Ord a) specifies that the type a must be an instance of the Ord type class, which provides an ordering for elements.

Defining Custom Type Classes:

We can also define our own type classes. Suppose we want a type class Shape that defines an operation for computing the area of a shape:

```
class Shape a where
    area :: a -> Double
```

Next, we implement this type class for some specific shapes:

```
data Circle = Circle Double
data Rectangle = Rectangle Double Double
```

```
instance Shape Circle where
    area (Circle r) = pi * r^2

instance Shape Rectangle where
    area (Rectangle w h) = w * h
```

In this example, we have defined Shape and provided implementations for Circle and Rectangle, allowing us to calculate their areas.

Type Classes and Type Inference:

Haskell's type inference system works seamlessly with type classes. When you define a function that uses a type class operation, the compiler infers the necessary constraints. For instance:

```
isEqual :: (Eq a) => a -> a -> Bool
isEqual x y = x == y
```

Haskell automatically infers that isEqual requires its arguments to be instances of the Eq type class based on the use of the (==) function.

Multi-parameter Type Classes and Functional Dependencies:

Although basic type classes involve single type variables, it is possible to define multi-parameter type classes using multiple type variables. Here is an example:

```
class Convertible a b where
    convert :: a -> b
```

This type class Convertible specifies a conversion between types a and b. However, multi-parameter type classes can lead to ambiguities, which can often be resolved with functional dependencies. Functional dependencies, introduced via the | symbol, specify relationships between type variables:

```
class Convertible a b | a -> b where
    convert :: a -> b
```

The functional dependency | a -> b indicates that type a uniquely determines type b, ensuring that there is no ambiguity in type inference.

Type Classes and Polymorphism:

Type classes enable a form of polymorphism called *ad-hoc polymorphism*, allowing functions to operate on any type that conforms to a specific interface described by a type class. This contrasts with *parametric polymorphism* where functions are written generically to operate on any type.

For instance, consider a generic function to find the maximum element in a list:

```
maximum :: (Ord a) => [a] -> a
maximum = foldr1 max
```

Here, maximum can operate on any list of elements, provided the element type a is an instance of the Ord type class, which defines an ordering.

The concept of type classes and their implementations in Haskell emphasize that shared behavior can be abstracted and reused across disparate types, providing flexibility and extensibility in code design and implementation. As we delve deeper into type classes in subsequent sections, we will explore creating and working with instances, commonly used type classes, and some advanced features that further extend the utility of Haskell's type system.

5.9 Creating Type Class Instances

In Haskell, type classes allow us to define a set of functions that operate uniformly across various types. A type class defines a behavior, and types that can exhibit this behavior are known as instances of that type class. Creating type class instances is fundamental to harnessing Haskell's type system fully. This section delves into how to define instances for user-defined types and explores common patterns and best practices.

To create an instance of a type class, we use the instance keyword followed by the type class name and the type for which we are creating the instance. Here is the general syntax for defining an instance:

```
instance TypeClassName Type where
    -- Definitions of the type class functions
```

Let us consider a straightforward example with the Eq type class, which includes the equality operator (==) and the inequality operator (/=). We will create an instance of the Eq type class for a custom data type.

```
data Color = Red | Green | Blue

instance Eq Color where
    Red == Red = True
    Green == Green = True
    Blue == Blue = True
    _ == _ = False
```

The above code defines a simple Color data type with three constructors: Red, Green, and Blue. We then create an Eq instance for Color, providing the implementation of the == function. Notice that we use pattern matching to compare the Color values.

In a similar vein, we can define instances for other type classes such as Show, which is used for converting values to strings, and Ord, which is used for ordering values. Below is an instance of the Show type class for the Color data type:

```
instance Show Color where
    show Red = "Red"
    show Green = "Green"
    show Blue = "Blue"
```

Haskell's compiler can derive instances for some common type classes automatically. The Eq and Show type classes, for instance, support automatic derivation. Here is an example:

```
data Color = Red | Green | Blue deriving (Eq, Show)
```

This approach is convenient and reduces boilerplate code. However, for more complex behaviors that automatic derivation cannot handle, manual instance definitions are required.

Let us delve into a type class that requires more intricate definitions. The Ord type class is used for types that have a total ordering. When creating an Ord instance, we typically need to define compare or the relational operators (<, <=, >, >=).

Consider a custom data type representing a two-dimensional point:

```
data Point = Point Int Int

instance Eq Point where
    (Point x1 y1) == (Point x2 y2) = (x1 == x2) && (y1 == y2)

instance Ord Point where
    (Point x1 y1) <= (Point x2 y2) = (x1 < x2) || (x1 == x2 && y1 <= y2)
```

Here, we define a Point data type and create instances for both the Eq and Ord type classes. In the Eq instance, we define when two Point values are considered equal. In the Ord instance, we define the ordering by comparing the x-coordinates first, and if they are equal, we compare the y-coordinates.

When working with parameterized types, the process is similar. Consider the following example with a simple binary tree data structure:

```
data Tree a = Empty | Node a (Tree a) (Tree a)
```

```
instance Eq a => Eq (Tree a) where
    Empty == Empty = True
    Node x left1 right1 == Node y left2 right2 = (x == y) && (left1 == left2) && (
          right1 == right2)
    _ == _ = False

instance Show a => Show (Tree a) where
    show Empty = "Empty"
    show (Node x left right) = "Node " ++ show x ++ " (" ++ show left ++ ") (" ++
          show right ++ ")"
```

In this example, we define a generic binary tree data type Tree and create instances for both Eq and Show. The instances are defined for Tree holding any type a, provided that a itself is an instance of the respective type class (Eq or Show).

When working with type classes, one might need to create instances for multiple type classes simultaneously. Haskell supports multi-parameter type classes, allowing you to define more complex relationships between types. Here is an illustration using a multi-parameter class called GShow:

```
class GShow a b where
    gshow :: a -> b -> String

instance GShow Int Char where
    gshow i c = show i ++ " and " ++ [c]
```

In this example, GShow is a type class that takes two parameters. We define an instance of GShow for Int and Char, implementing the gshow function by concatenating the string representations of an Int and a Char.

Creating type class instances in Haskell is a powerful way to make your types behave uniformly within the language's type system. The process involves defining how your types meet the requirements set by the type class, allowing for reusable and extendable code. Understanding and utilizing type class instances effectively underscores much of what makes Haskell's type system both robust and expressive.

Next, we will explore commonly used type classes, building on the concepts introduced here and illustrating their practical applications in various contexts.

5.10 Commonly Used Type Classes

Haskell's type classes are a powerful feature that allows for ad-hoc polymorphism, enabling functions to operate on different types. This section discusses some of the most commonly used type classes in Haskell, covering their functionality, purposes, and usage with code examples.

Eq and Ord

The Eq type class is fundamental in Haskell as it provides an interface for equality testing. The Eq class defines two primary methods: (==) for equality and (/=) for inequality.

```
class Eq a where
    (==) :: a -> a -> Bool
    (/=) :: a -> a -> Bool
```

For instance, standard types like Int, Char, and Bool have Eq instances that allow comparisons.

```
-- Example usage of Eq
5 == 5 -- Evaluates to True
5 /= 3 -- Evaluates to True
'a' == 'b' -- Evaluates to False
```

The Ord type class is used for types that have an ordering. It extends the Eq class, inheriting its methods and adding functionality for comparison. It includes methods like compare, (<), (<=), (>), (>=):

```
class Eq a => Ord a where
    compare :: a -> a -> Ordering
    (<), (<=), (>=), (>) :: a -> a -> Bool
    min, max :: a -> a -> a
```

The Ordering type can be LT, EQ, or GT.

```
-- Example usage of Ord
compare 5 3 -- Evaluates to GT
5 > 3 -- Evaluates to True
'a' < 'b' -- Evaluates to True
```

Show and Read

The Show type class is for types whose values can be converted to strings. This conversion is done via the show function.

```
class Show a where
    show :: a -> String
```

Standard instances of Show include types like Int, Char, Bool, lists and tuples, making it easy to represent these values as strings.

```
-- Example usage of Show
show 123 -- Evaluates to "123"
show 'a' -- Evaluates to "'a'"
show True -- Evaluates to "True"
show [1,2,3] -- Evaluates to "[1,2,3]"
```

Conversely, the Read type class is for types that can be parsed from strings. It defines the read function, which parses a string representation of a value.

```
class Read a where
    read :: ReadS a

type ReadS a = String -> [(a, String)]
```

```
-- Example usage of Read
read "123" :: Int -- Evaluates to 123
read "[1,2,3]" :: [Int] -- Evaluates to [1,2,3]
read "True" :: Bool -- Evaluates to True
```

Note that read requires an explicit type annotation, as the compiler cannot infer the type.

Enum and Bounded

The Enum type class is used for types that have predecessors and successors. It includes methods like succ, pred, and list range creation.

```
class Enum a where
    succ, pred :: a -> a
    toEnum :: Int -> a
    fromEnum :: a -> Int
    enumFrom :: a -> [a]
    enumFromThen :: a -> a -> [a]
```

Examples include numeric types and Char.

```
-- Example usage of Enum
succ 'A' -- Evaluates to 'B'
pred 5 -- Evaluates to 4
['a'..'e'] -- Evaluates to "abcde"
```

The Bounded type class is for types that have an upper and lower bound. It includes methods minBound and maxBound.

```
class Bounded a where
    minBound, maxBound :: a
```

Integer types and Char, among others, have Bounded instances.

```
-- Example usage of Bounded
minBound :: Int -- Evaluates to -9223372036854775808 (on a 64-bit system)
```

```
maxBound :: Char -- Evaluates to '\1114111'
```

Functor

The Functor type class is for types that can be mapped over. It includes the method fmap which applies a function to every element in a structure.

```
class Functor f where
    fmap :: (a -> b) -> f a -> f b
```

Lists, Maybe, and Either are some instances of Functor.

```
-- Example usage of Functor
fmap (+1) [1,2,3] -- Evaluates to [2,3,4]
fmap (*2) (Just 3) -- Evaluates to Just 6
fmap (show . (*2)) (Left 3 :: Either Int Int) -- Evaluates to Left "6"
```

Monad

The Monad type class is for types that support binding operations, allowing sequential actions. It builds on the Applicative type class and introduces the (»=) (bind) operation.

```
class Applicative m => Monad m where
    (>>=) :: m a -> (a -> m b) -> m b
    (>>) :: m a -> m b -> m b
    return :: a -> m a
    return = pure
```

The (»=) operation chains monadic operations.

```
-- Example usage of Monad
Just 3 >>= \x -> Just (x + 1) -- Evaluates to Just 4
[1,2] >>= \x -> [x, -x] -- Evaluates to [1,-1,2,-2]
```

These type classes enhance Haskell's flexibility and power, making it possible to write generic and reusable code. They serve as the bedrock for many functional programming patterns and paradigms.

5.11 Advanced Type Class Features

Haskell's type classes provide a powerful mechanism for ad-hoc polymorphism, enabling functions to operate on multiple types that support common operations. Once the basic understanding of type classes is established, we can delve into advanced features that further enhance the expressiveness and usability of type classes in complex scenarios.

Multi-Parameter Type Classes

Multi-parameter type classes extend the capabilities of single-parameter type classes by allowing more than one type parameter. This makes it possible to define relationships between multiple types. The syntax for defining a multi-parameter type class is straightforward. Consider the following example that introduces a type class, Transform, which relates two types:

```
class Transform a b where
    transform :: a -> b
```

An instance of this type class could be defined to transform a list of any type to an integer, where the transformation might involve computing the length of the list:

```
instance Transform [a] Int where
    transform = length
```

To use the transform function, make a call like this:

```
result :: Int
result = transform [1, 2, 3, 4] -- result will be 4
```

Note that MultiParamTypeClasses extension needs to be enabled:

```
{-# LANGUAGE MultiParamTypeClasses #-}
```

Functional Dependencies

When utilizing multi-parameter type classes, it can be beneficial to indicate how certain type parameters depend on others. This is done using functional dependencies, helping the compiler determine the types more precisely. Functional dependencies are declared using the pipe symbol (|):

```
{-# LANGUAGE FunctionalDependencies #-}

class Transform a b | a -> b where
    transform :: a -> b
```

The functional dependency a -> b signifies that type b is uniquely determined by type a. This reduces ambiguity in type inference, allowing the compiler to infer types more efficiently.

Flexible Instances

Haskell's default rule for instance selection prefers earlier-defined instances, but there are instances where more flexibility is needed. The FlexibleInstances extension allows the creation of more general instances. Here is an example demonstrating this concept:

```
{-# LANGUAGE FlexibleInstances #-}

class Example a where
    exampleFunc :: a -> String

instance Example [Int] where
    exampleFunc _ = "List of Ints"

instance Example [a] where -- More general instance
    exampleFunc _ = "Generic List"
```

Now, exampleFunc when called with a list of Int will use the more specific instance; otherwise, it will fall back to the more general instance.

Overlapping Instances

There are cases where instances overlap, and the most specific instance should be chosen. The OverlappingInstances extension allows Haskell to choose the best matching instance in case of an overlap.

```
{-# LANGUAGE OverlappingInstances #-}

instance Example [Int] where
    exampleFunc _ = "List of Ints"

instance Example [a] where
    exampleFunc _ = "Generic List"
```

With OverlappingInstances enabled, a call to exampleFunc [1, 2, 3] will correctly identify and use the [Int] instance.

Type Families

Type families provide another advanced mechanism to associate types. Unlike functional dependencies, type families blend more naturally into Haskell's type system. They are declared using the type family keyword, which introduces a type-level function. There are two kinds of type families: open and closed.

Open Type Families

Open type families allow for extensible relationships between types. Here is an example of an open type family:

```
{-# LANGUAGE TypeFamilies #-}

type family ElementType a

type instance ElementType [a] = a
type instance ElementType (Maybe a) = a

extractElement :: (ElementType a) -> String
extractElement = show
```

Closed Type Families

Closed type families encapsulate all their logic within one definition, similar to a function with branches:

```
{-# LANGUAGE TypeFamilies #-}

type family Compare a b where
    Compare Int Int = Bool
    Compare a b = Ordering

compareValues :: Compare Int Int -> String
compareValues = show
```

In this example, Compare maps pairs of types to either Bool or Ordering depending on the input types. Closed type families provide type-level pattern matching, proving extremely useful in complex type manipulation.

Generalized Algebraic Data Types (GADTs)

GADTs extend the expressive power of Haskell's type system by allowing more precise typing of data constructors. To use GADTs, enable the GADTs extension:

```
{-# LANGUAGE GADTs #-}

data Expr a where
    IVal :: Int -> Expr Int
    BVal :: Bool -> Expr Bool
    Add :: Expr Int -> Expr Int -> Expr Int
    Eq :: Expr Int -> Expr Int -> Expr Bool

eval :: Expr a -> a
eval (IVal n) = n
eval (BVal b) = b
eval (Add x y) = eval x + eval y
eval (Eq x y) = eval x == eval y
```

GADTs allow the type of each constructor to specify precisely what type of Expr it constructs, making functions like eval very typesafe.

By employing these advanced features, we can achieve finer control over type classes, ensuring more robust and maintainable Haskell code. With multi-parameter type classes, functional dependencies, flexible and overlapping instances, type families, and GADTs, the Haskell programmer can succinctly capture complex type relationships and behaviors.

Chapter 6

Higher-Order Functions

This chapter focuses on higher-order functions in Haskell, explaining their definition and use, as well as function pointers. It discusses map, filter, and fold operations, anonymous functions and lambdas, and function composition. Partial application, the use of higher-order functions with lists, and operators as functions are also covered, along with control flow using higher-order functions and practical examples.

6.1 Introduction to Higher-Order Functions

In Haskell, higher-order functions are a fundamental concept that significantly enhances the language's expressiveness and flexibility. A higher-order function is one that can take one or more functions as arguments or return a function as its result. This capability allows for a concise and readable code that abstracts common patterns of computation.

To understand higher-order functions, it is essential first to be comfortable with the notion of functions as first-class citizens in Haskell. This means that functions can be passed as arguments to other functions, returned as results from other functions, and assigned to variables. Consider the definition of a function in Haskell that takes another function as an argument:

```
applyTwice :: (a -> a) -> a -> a
applyTwice f x = f (f x)
```

In this example, applyTwice is a higher-order function. The type signature indicates that applyTwice takes a function f (which itself takes an argument of type a and returns a result of the same type) and a variable x of type a. The function applyTwice applies the function f to the argument x twice.

To further illustrate, consider using applyTwice with a simple function like (+1):

```
result = applyTwice (+1) 5
```

The resulting computation can be described step-by-step as follows:

```
applyTwice (+1) 5
=> (+1) ((+1) 5)
=> (+1) 6
=> 7
```

Another common pattern with higher-order functions involves returning a function as a result. This is a powerful feature that enables function creation on-the-fly and supports advanced techniques like currying and partial application, which will be discussed in later sections. Below is an example that returns a new function:

```
addN :: Int -> (Int -> Int)
addN n = \x -> x + n
```

Here, addN is a higher-order function that takes an integer n and returns a new function. The returned function takes an integer x and adds n to it. This can be seen in the following usage:

```
addFive = addN 5
result = addFive 10 -- result is 15
```

Higher-order functions extend beyond simple examples. They are the building blocks of more abstract concepts like function composition and currying. Consider the function composition operator (.). The definition of the composition operator is given as:

```
(.) :: (b -> c) -> (a -> b) -> (a -> c)
(f . g) x = f (g x)
```

This operator takes two functions, f and g, and returns a new function that is the composition of f and g. That new function applies g to an input x and then applies f to the result of g x. This allows for chaining functions together in a concise manner.

Another frequent use of higher-order functions in Haskell is in list processing. Functions like map, filter, and fold encapsulate common list operations. The map function applies a given function to each element of a list:

```
map :: (a -> b) -> [a] -> [b]
map _ [] = []
map f (x:xs) = f x : map f xs
```

In this definition, map takes a function f and a list of type [a], and returns a list of type [b]. The application of map applies the function to each element of the list:

```
result = map (+1) [1, 2, 3, 4] -- result is [2, 3, 4, 5]
```

The above example demonstrates how map applies the function $(+1)$ to each element of the list $[1, 2, 3, 4]$, resulting in a new list $[2, 3, 4, 5]$.

Higher-order functions underpin the elegance and power of functional programming in Haskell. They enable abstraction over actions, not just values, and form the basis for many sophisticated functional programming techniques and libraries. As one delves deeper into the language, mastering higher-order functions will unlock more advanced and expressive coding paradigms.

6.2 Function Pointers

In Haskell, the concept of function pointers is expressed through the more abstract notion of treating functions as first-class citizens. This means that functions can be passed as arguments to other functions, returned as results from functions, and assigned to variables. In languages like C or C++, function pointers are used to achieve similar behavior, but in Haskell, function pointers are seamlessly integrated into the type system and syntactic structure of the language.

To begin with, let us examine the syntactic and semantic nuances of using functions as values. When a function is passed as an argument, it is crucial to understand the types involved. Consider the following example where we define a simple function add:

```
add :: Int -> Int -> Int
add x y = x + y
```

The type signature of add indicates that it takes two Int arguments and returns an Int. Now, suppose we want to create a function applyFunction that takes a function and two integers as arguments and returns the result of applying the function to the integers:

```
applyFunction :: (Int -> Int -> Int) -> Int -> Int -> Int
applyFunction f x y = f x y
```

Here, applyFunction has the type (Int -> Int -> Int) -> Int -> Int -> Int, which means it takes a function from Int to Int to Int, followed by two Int values, and returns an Int. We can use applyFunction to apply add as follows:

```
*Main> applyFunction add 3 4
7
```

This demonstrates that functions in Haskell can be passed around just like any other values.

Next, let us explore more complex scenarios involving higher-order functions. Consider a scenario where we want to create a function composeFunctions that takes two functions and returns their composition. The composition of two functions g and h is another function that applies h first and then g to the result of h:

```
composeFunctions :: (b -> c) -> (a -> b) -> (a -> c)
composeFunctions g h = \x -> g (h x)
```

In composeFunctions, the type signature (b -> c) -> (a -> b) -> (a -> c) indicates that it takes a function from b to c and a function from a to b, and returns a function from a to c. This is a direct implementation of function composition.

For instance, consider the functions negate and length, whose type signatures are as follows:

```
negate :: Int -> Int
negate x = -x

length :: [a] -> Int
length = foldr (\_ acc -> acc + 1) 0
```

We can use composeFunctions to compose negate and length:

```
*Main> let negLength = composeFunctions negate length
*Main> negLength [1, 2, 3, 4]
-4
```

In this example, negLength is a function that first computes the length of a list and then negates the result.

Another powerful technique is the use of function pointers to create higher-order functions that operate on other functions. For example, the map function takes a function and a list, and applies the function to each element of the list:

```
map :: (a -> b) -> [a] -> [b]
map _ [] = []
map f (x:xs) = f x : map f xs
```

The map function demonstrates the utility of function pointers by abstracting over the function to be applied to list elements. It can be used with any function of type a -> b. For instance:

```
*Main> map negate [1, 2, 3, 4]
[-1, -2, -3, -4]
*Main> map length ["hello", "world"]
[5, 5]
```

The function map can be utilized with various functions, showcasing the flexibility granted by treating functions as first-class citizens.

Function pointers, or higher-order functions, provide a foundation for creating abstract, reusable components in Haskell. They allow for elegant code that can be easily composed and reused. This section has highlighted how Haskell leverages the concept of function pointers to simplify complex operations and promote code reuse and abstraction.

6.3 Map, Filter, and Fold Operations

The map, filter, and fold operations are fundamental higher-order functions in Haskell that allow for functional-style processing of lists. They are essential tools in a Haskell programmer's toolkit and provide powerful methods for applying functions to lists, creating new lists based on conditions, and aggregating list values, respectively.

The map function applies a given function to each element of a list, producing a new list with the results. Here's a typical usage of the map function:

```
map :: (a -> b) -> [a] -> [b]

-- Example:
squaredList = map (\x -> x * x) [1, 2, 3, 4, 5]
```

The output of this operation will be:

```
[1, 4, 9, 16, 25]
```

In this example, the anonymous function (\x -> x * x) is applied to each element of the input list [1, 2, 3, 4, 5], resulting in a new list where each element is the square of the corresponding element in the original list.

The filter function constructs a new list containing only those elements of the original list that satisfy a given predicate function. Here's how filter can be defined and used:

```
filter :: (a -> Bool) -> [a] -> [a]

-- Example:
evenNumbers = filter (\x -> x `mod` 2 == 0) [1, 2, 3, 4, 5, 6]
```

The output of this example will be:

```
[2, 4, 6]
```

In this case, the anonymous function (\x -> x `mod` 2 == 0) serves as a predicate to check if an element is even. Only elements that satisfy this predicate (i.e., the even numbers) are included in the resulting list.

The foldr and foldl functions, collectively referred to as fold operations, are used to reduce a list to a single value by iteratively applying a binary function. foldr (fold right) processes the list from right to left, while foldl (fold left) processes it from left to right. Here are their type signatures:

```
foldr :: (a -> b -> b) -> b -> [a] -> b
foldl :: (b -> a -> b) -> b -> [a] -> b
```

foldr is often used when dealing with lists because of its ability to handle infinite lists and its generally lazy nature. A common usage of foldr is to implement a sum of the elements of a list:

```
sumList = foldr (\x acc -> x + acc) 0 [1, 2, 3, 4, 5]
```

The output of this fold operation will be:

```
15
```

In this example, the binary function (\x acc -> x + acc) is applied starting from the rightmost element of the list [1, 2, 3, 4, 5], with 0 as the initial accumulator.

Similarly, one can use foldl to achieve the same result by processing the list from the left:

```
sumList' = foldl (\acc x -> acc + x) 0 [1, 2, 3, 4, 5]
```

The result of foldl in this context will be:

```
15
```

Although the end result is the same for foldr and foldl, their usages differ based on specific requirements such as the direction of traversal and memory efficiency.

These higher-order functions are not only concise but also express powerful abstractions that eliminate explicit loops, making Haskell code more declarative and expressive. When combined, map, filter, and fold operations become even more potent, enabling intricate data transformations with minimal code.

Understanding how to effectively use these functions is crucial for any Haskell programmer aiming to leverage the full power of functional programming paradigms. Practical proficiency in these operations is foundational to writing elegant and efficient Haskell programs.

6.4 Anonymous Functions and Lambdas

Anonymous functions, often referred to as lambdas, allow for the creation of functions without the need to assign them explicitly to a name. This is particularly useful for short-lived operations or for passing functions as arguments in higher-order functions. Haskell's syntax for anonymous functions is concise and powerful, adhering to the functional programming paradigm where functions are treated as first-class citizens.

To declare an anonymous function in Haskell, we use the backslash (\) followed by the function's parameters, an arrow (→), and the function body. The general syntax is:

```
\x y -> x + y
```

This represents a function that takes two arguments, x and y, and returns their sum. Such a function can be immediately used in the context where it is defined. Consider the following example using the map function, which applies a given function to each element of a list:

```
map (\x -> x * 2) [1, 2, 3, 4]
```

In this case, the anonymous function `\x -> x * 2` is applied to each element of the list [1, 2, 3, 4] to produce the output:

```
[2, 4, 6, 8]
```

Lambdas are particularly powerful when combined with higher-order functions. They enable us to define short, one-off functions inline without cluttering the namespace with additional function names. Consider another example using the filter function, which selects elements from a list that satisfy a given condition:

```
filter (\x -> x > 2) [1, 2, 3, 4]
```

Here, the anonymous function \x -> x > 2 filters the list, yielding:

```
[3, 4]
```

Anonymous functions can also be used with the foldr function, which reduces a list to a single value by recursively applying a binary function. In conjunction with a lambda, foldr can be used as follows:

```
foldr (\x acc -> x + acc) 0 [1, 2, 3, 4]
```

This anonymous function takes two arguments, x and acc, and adds them together. Starting with an initial accumulator value of 0, foldr processes the list [1, 2, 3, 4] to produce:

```
10
```

It is essential to note that anonymous functions can have multiple parameters. For instance:

```
(\x y -> x * y) 3 4
```

This anonymous function multiplies its two parameters, x and y, and, when applied to the values 3 and 4, the output is:

```
12
```

Haskell's anonymous functions support capturing variables from their surrounding scope, a concept known as closures. Consider the following example:

```
let addN n = \x -> x + n in map (addN 2) [1, 2, 3, 4]
```

In this example, addN is a function that returns an anonymous function. The anonymous function adds the parameter n to its argument x. By applying addN 2 to the list [1, 2, 3, 4] with map, the result is:

```
[3, 4, 5, 6]
```

Anonymous functions and lambdas offer a succinct way to define small functions inline without cluttering the global namespace. They are indispensable in functional programming, allowing for concise and expressive code, especially when working with higher-order functions.

6.5 Function Composition

Function composition is a fundamental concept in functional programming that allows the combination of functions to build more complex operations. In Haskell, function composition is performed using the (.) operator, which takes two functions as arguments and returns a new function. The new function applies the second argument function first and then applies the first argument function to the result. Mathematically, if you have functions f and g, the composition $(f \circ g)(x)$ is equivalent to $f(g(x))$.

The (.) operator has the following type signature:

```
(.) :: (b -> c) -> (a -> b) -> a -> c
```

The type signature indicates that (.) takes a function from b to c and a function from a to b, and produces a new function from a to c.

Consider the following example where we have two simple functions:

```
addOne :: Int -> Int
addOne x = x + 1

timesTwo :: Int -> Int
timesTwo x = x * 2
```

We can define a new function addOneThenTimesTwo which is the composition of addOne and timesTwo:

```
addOneThenTimesTwo :: Int -> Int
addOneThenTimesTwo = timesTwo . addOne
```

Using the composed function, we can see the following behavior:

```
main :: IO ()
main = do
   print (addOneThenTimesTwo 3) -- Output: 8
```

8

Here, addOneThenTimesTwo 3 translates to timesTwo (addOne 3), yielding 8 as the result.

Function composition is particularly powerful when dealing with functions that transform data. For instance, suppose we need to perform a series of transformations on a list of integers:

```
incrementEach :: [Int] -> [Int]
incrementEach = map (\x -> x + 1)

squareEach :: [Int] -> [Int]
```

```
squareEach = map (\x -> x * x)

incrementAndSquare :: [Int] -> [Int]
incrementAndSquare = squareEach . incrementEach
```

In this example, incrementAndSquare will increment each value in the list and then square the result:

```
main :: IO ()
main = do
    print (incrementAndSquare [1, 2, 3, 4]) -- Output: [4, 9, 16, 25]
```

```
[4, 9, 16, 25]
```

Function composition in Haskell is not limited to functions that operate on the same type of data. Consider the following more diverse example:

```
showBool :: Bool -> String
showBool True = "True"
showBool False = "False"

isEven :: Int -> Bool
isEven x = x `mod` 2 == 0

describeEvenness :: Int -> String
describeEvenness = showBool . isEven
```

Here, describeEvenness takes an integer, determines if it is even using isEven, and then converts the result to a string using showBool. When we run the following:

```
main :: IO ()
main = do
    print (describeEvenness 4) -- Output: "True"
    print (describeEvenness 7) -- Output: "False"
```

```
"True"
"False"
```

The ability to compose functions seamlessly enables the creation of highly modular and reusable code. Small, specialized functions can be developed and then composed to achieve complex behaviors without the need for repetitive code.

Moreover, function composition is associative, a property that allows us to compose multiple functions in any grouping without changing the result. Specifically, for any functions f, g, and h, we have:

```
(f . (g . h)) == ((f . g) . h)
```

This means we can chain multiple compositions together naturally, as shown:

```
f :: Int -> Int
f x = x + 10

g :: Int -> Int
g x = x * 2

h :: Int -> Int
h x = x - 5

composedFunction :: Int -> Int
composedFunction = f . g . h

main :: IO ()
main = do
    print (composedFunction 5) -- Output: 10
```

10

Lastly, it is worth noting that function composition can also be utilized in defining control flow structures and integrating different functional paradigms. This flexibility contributes to Haskell's expressiveness and power, enabling sophisticated and concise function definitions.

6.6 Partial Application

In functional programming, partial application is a powerful concept where a function that takes multiple arguments is transformed into a function that takes fewer arguments. The resulting function can be seen as a "partial" application of the original function, with some of its arguments fixed. This not only improves code reusability but also increases the clarity and conciseness of the code.

Consider a function with three parameters. Its type can be represented as (a -> b -> c -> d). Through partial application, we can fix one or more of its parameters, transforming it into functions of types (b -> c -> d), (c -> d), or ultimately, into a function that returns the final value directly, d.

In Haskell, every function is inherently a curried function. This means that we can apply a function partially by simply providing fewer arguments than the function requires. Haskell automatically handles the reduction and returns a new function expecting the remaining arguments.

For example, consider the following function:

```
addThreeNumbers :: Int -> Int -> Int -> Int
addThreeNumbers x y z = x + y + z
```

We can partially apply addThreeNumbers by fixing its first argument:

```
addTwoNumbersToFive :: Int -> Int -> Int
addTwoNumbersToFive = addThreeNumbers 5
```

In this case, addTwoNumbersToFive is a new function that takes two Int parameters and adds them to the fixed value 5. We can invoke it as follows:

```
result = addTwoNumbersToFive 3 4
```

result = 12

To illustrate further, let's look at a more practical example involving lists. Suppose we have a function that multiplies every element in a list by a given factor:

```
multiplyList :: Int -> [Int] -> [Int]
multiplyList factor xs = map (* factor) xs
```

We can partially apply multiplyList to create a new function that multiplies every element by 10:

```
multiplyByTen :: [Int] -> [Int]
multiplyByTen = multiplyList 10
```

Thus, we can use multiplyByTen naturally:

```
tenTimesList = multiplyByTen [1, 2, 3, 4, 5]
```

tenTimesList = [10, 20, 30, 40, 50]

Partial application is also advantageous when working with higher-order functions. Consider the function filter, which requires a predicate function to filter elements in a list. By partially applying a predicate, we can create various specialized filter functions. For example:

```
isEven :: Int -> Bool
isEven n = n `mod` 2 == 0

filterEvens :: [Int] -> [Int]
filterEvens = filter isEven
```

In this scenario, filterEvens is derived from filter by partially applying the isEven function. It filters out even numbers from any given list:

```
evenList = filterEvens [1, 2, 3, 4, 5, 6]
```

evenList = [2, 4, 6]

Moreover, Haskell's infix operators can also be partially applied. For instance, the operator + can be partially applied to create a function that adds 10 to any given number:

```
addTen :: Int -> Int
addTen = (10 +)
```

When we utilize addTen:

```
addedValue = addTen 5
```

```
addedValue = 15
```

This pervasiveness of partial application in Haskell streamlines code, making it more modular and expressive. As functions become more specialized through partial application, they align closely with the desired operations, enhancing both readability and maintainability of the code.

6.7 Using Higher-Order Functions with Lists

Higher-order functions in Haskell find extensive utility when dealing with lists. This section will delve into key techniques and functions used to manipulate and interact with lists using higher-order functions. We will explore the built-in Haskell functions map, filter, and fold (both foldl and foldr), illustrating their applications through comprehensive examples.

map is a higher-order function that applies a specified function to each element of a list, producing a new list. The type signature of map is:

```
map :: (a -> b) -> [a] -> [b]
```

This indicates that map takes a function from type a to type b and a list of type a, returning a list of type b.

Consider an example where we want to square each element in a list of integers:

```
squareList :: [Int] -> [Int]
squareList xs = map (^2) xs
```

Evaluating squareList [1, 2, 3, 4] produces:

```
[1, 4, 9, 16]
```

Another powerful higher-order function is filter, which constructs a new list containing only those elements of the original list that satisfy a given predicate. Its type signature is:

```
filter :: (a -> Bool) -> [a] -> [a]
```

To illustrate, consider filtering out only the even numbers from a list of integers:

```
evenList :: [Int] -> [Int]
evenList xs = filter even xs
```

Evaluating evenList [1, 2, 3, 4, 5, 6] yields:

```
[2, 4, 6]
```

The fold function family (foldl and foldr) are fundamental for reducing a list to a single value by iteratively applying a binary function. The type signatures for these functions are:

```
foldl :: (b -> a -> b) -> b -> [a] -> b
foldr :: (a -> b -> b) -> b -> [a] -> b
```

foldl processes the list from the left, while foldr processes it from the right. To compute the sum of a list using foldl, consider:

```
sumList :: [Int] -> Int
sumList xs = foldl (+) 0 xs
```

For evaluating sumList [1, 2, 3, 4], the result is:

```
10
```

In contrast, to concatenate a list of strings using foldr, we have:

```
concatStrings :: [String] -> String
concatStrings xs = foldr (++) "" xs
```

Evaluating concatStrings ["Hello", " ", "World", "!"] results in:

```
"Hello World!"
```

zipWith is another higher-order function, which applies a function to corresponding elements of two lists, creating a new list. Its type signature is:

```
zipWith :: (a -> b -> c) -> [a] -> [b] -> [c]
```

To add corresponding elements of two lists, you can use:

```
addLists :: [Int] -> [Int] -> [Int]
addLists xs ys = zipWith (+) xs ys
```

Evaluating addLists [1, 2, 3] [4, 5, 6] produces:

```
[5, 7, 9]
```

Additionally, higher-order functions can be effectively combined. Consider the problem of finding the product of the squares of even numbers from a list:

```
productEvenSquares :: [Int] -> Int
productEvenSquares xs = foldl (*) 1 (map (^2) (filter even xs))
```

Evaluating productEvenSquares [1, 2, 3, 4] yields:

```
16
```

Leveraging higher-order functions with lists facilitates concise, expressive, and functional code, enhancing both readability and maintainability.

6.8 Operators as Functions

In Haskell, operators are a fundamental part of the language syntax and they behave like functions. This functionality allows operators to be manipulated in the same way as functions, enabling their use in higher-order functions, mapping, and function composition. Understanding this concept is critical for leveraging the full expressive power of Haskell.

Operators in Haskell, such as +, -, *, and /, are infix by default, meaning they are placed between their arguments. For example, the expression $2 + 3$ uses the + operator infix. In Haskell, any infix operator can also be used as a prefix function. To use an infix operator as a prefix function, you simply enclose it in parentheses. Here is an example:

```
Prelude> (+) 2 3
5
```

In this example, (+) is the prefix version of the + operator, and it takes two arguments, 2 and 3, yielding the result 5. Similarly, other operators can also be converted to their prefix forms. For example:

```
Prelude> (*) 4 5
20
Prelude> (-) 10 2
8
Prelude> (/) 20 4
5.0
```

This mechanism allows operators to be passed as arguments to higher-order functions. For instance, the map function can apply an operator to each element in a list. Consider the following example, where we add 5 to each element of a list using the + operator:

```
Prelude> map (+5) [1, 2, 3, 4, 5]
[6, 7, 8, 9, 10]
```

In this example, (+5) is a partially applied function created from the + operator. It takes one argument and adds 5 to it. The map function then applies this partially applied function to each element of the list [1, 2, 3, 4, 5].

Operators can also be used in a similar manner with the filter function. For example, suppose we want to filter out all elements in a list that are less than 10 using the less-than operator $<$:

```
Prelude> filter (<10) [5, 12, 8, 20, 1]
[5, 8, 1]
```

In this case, <10 is a partially applied function that takes one argument and checks if it is less than 10. The filter function then returns a list of elements satisfying this condition.

Operators can also be employed with the foldl and foldr functions. For instance, to compute the sum of a list of numbers using the + operator with foldl:

```
Prelude> foldl (+) 0 [1, 2, 3, 4, 5]
15
```

In this example, foldl takes the + operator, an initial accumulator value 0, and the list [1, 2, 3, 4, 5]. It then applies the + operator cumulatively from the left, resulting in the sum 15.

Additionally, operators can be used in function composition, allowing you to create new functions by combining existing operators or functions. The composition operator (.) is used to compose functions. For example:

```
Prelude> let negateSum = negate . sum
Prelude> negateSum [1, 2, 3, 4, 5]
-15
```

Here, the negateSum function is the composition of the negate function and the sum function. It takes a list of numbers, computes their sum, and then negates the result.

Furthermore, operators can be used as sections, which are special forms of partial application. An operator section involves fixing one operand of a binary operator and leaving the other operand free. For example:

```
Prelude> let addFive = (5+)
Prelude> addFive 10
15
```

In this case, (5+) is a section that adds 5 to its argument. Sections are particularly useful for creating simple functions without writing explicit lambda expressions.

Understanding the usage of operators as functions highlights the flexibility of Haskell and enhances your ability to write concise and expressive code. The ability to treat operators as first-class functions is one of the many features that makes Haskell a powerful language for functional programming.

6.9 Control Flow with Higher-Order Functions

Control flow in programming refers to the order in which individual statements, instructions, or function calls are executed or evaluated. In Haskell, where functions are first-class citizens, higher-order functions can be leveraged to manage control flow effectively and elegantly. This section explores how higher-order functions such as map, filter, and foldr can be used for control flow, and details the application of function composition and partial application in structuring flow of control.

Using higher-order functions to dictate control flow can lead to more expressive, concise, and readable code. Rather than relying on traditional loop constructs seen in imperative languages, Haskell programmers often use functional paradigms to achieve looping behavior and decision-making.

Iterating with map, filter, and foldr

The map function applies a given function to each element of a list, effectively iterating over the list. This approach can be seen as a functional replacement for a for loop in imperative languages. Consider the following example where we double each element in a list:

```
doubleList :: [Int] -> [Int]
doubleList = map (*2)
```

Here, map takes the function (*2) and applies it to each element of the input list, returning a new list of doubled values. The control flow is managed by the higher-order function map.

The filter function is used to select elements of a list that satisfy a predicate. It serves a similar purpose to if statements within loops for conditional filtering in imperative languages:

```
filterEven :: [Int] -> [Int]
filterEven = filter even
```

In this example, filter even retains only the even elements from the input list. The predicate even is a function that determines the condition for inclusion in the output list, thus directing the flow based on the condition.

The foldr function reduces a list to a single value by traversing the list and applying a binary function. It can be seen as a way to implement iteration with accumulation. For instance, summing the elements of a list can be elegantly expressed using foldr:

```
sumList :: [Int] -> Int
sumList = foldr (+) 0
```

In this code, foldr takes the binary function (+) and an initial value 0, then traverses the list, accumulating the sum.

Function Composition for Control Flow

Function composition, denoted by the (.) operator, allows the creation of new functions by composing existing ones. This capability can streamline control flow by eliminating the need for intermediate variables and making the code more readable.

Consider a scenario where we want to first increment each element of a list and then filter out the odd numbers. This can be accomplished by composing map and filter:

```
incrementAndFilterOdd :: [Int] -> [Int]
incrementAndFilterOdd = filter odd . map (+1)
```

Here, (map (+1)) increments each element, and (filter odd) filters out the increments that are odd. The composition filter odd . map (+1) dictates the control flow in a single, readable statement.

Partial Application for Constructing Control Flow

Partial application is another powerful tool in Haskell that can simplify control flow. By fixing some arguments of a function, new functions with reduced arity are created. This can be particularly useful when creating specialized functions for later use.

For example, if we frequently need to sum a list of integers but always starting with an initial sum of 10, we can create a partially applied version of foldr:

```
sumListStartingAt10 :: [Int] -> Int
sumListStartingAt10 = foldr (+) 10
```

This new function, sumListStartingAt10, automatically starts the fold operation with an initial sum of 10, encapsulating the specific control behavior within the partially applied function.

Leveraging Higher-Order Functions in Control Structures

The && and || operators can be combined with lambda expressions to provide conditional control based on multiple predicates:

```
allEvenAndGreaterThanFive :: [Int] -> Bool
allEvenAndGreaterThanFive = all (\x -> even x && x > 5)
```

In this code, all is a higher-order function that returns True only if all elements in the list satisfy the combined predicate, enabling a concise and clear control flow representation.

Similarly, lists or other data structures can be processed in a cumulative manner using combinations of higher-order functions, effectively directing the control of values and operations through the pipeline of functions.

Utilizing higher-order functions for control flow not only reduces the need for explicit recursion or iteration constructs but also aligns with the principles of functional programming, promoting code reuse, modularity, and readability.

6.10 Practical Examples of Higher-Order Functions

In Haskell, higher-order functions provide a powerful abstraction mechanism, allowing functions to be manipulated in a manner similar to other data types. This section provides practical examples that demonstrate the versatility and capability of higher-order functions in various scenarios.

map is a quintessential higher-order function in Haskell, used to apply a function to each element of a list. Consider the following example where we double each element in a list of integers:

```
doubleList :: [Int] -> [Int]
doubleList = map (*2)
```

To apply doubleList to a specific list and observe the result, we can execute:

```
main :: IO ()
main = print (doubleList [1, 2, 3, 4, 5])
```

The output will be:

```
[2, 4, 6, 8, 10]
```

Another common higher-order function is filter, which selects elements of a list that satisfy a given predicate. For instance, we can filter out even numbers from a list:

```
filterEvens :: [Int] -> [Int]
filterEvens = filter even
```

Executing this function would look like:

```
main :: IO ()
main = print (filterEvens [1, 2, 3, 4, 5, 6])
```

The output will be:

```
[2, 4, 6]
```

The foldr function is a powerful accumulator that allows us to recursively process a list. For example, we can sum the elements of a list:

```
sumList :: [Int] -> Int
sumList = foldr (+) 0
```

Invocation of sumList can be seen as follows:

```
main :: IO ()
main = print (sumList [1, 2, 3, 4, 5])
```

The output reflects the sum:

```
15
```

Anonymous functions, or lambdas, are particularly useful for succinctly expressing functionality, especially when used in conjunction with higher-order functions. For instance, the following uses a lambda to increment each number in a list:

```
incrementList :: [Int] -> [Int]
incrementList = map (\x -> x + 1)
```

To observe the effect:

```
main :: IO ()
main = print (incrementList [1, 2, 3, 4, 5])
```

The resulting output will be:

```
[2, 3, 4, 5, 6]
```

Next, we demonstrate function composition, enabling the creation of complex operations by combining simpler functions. The following example first doubles a number and then increments it:

```
doubleAndIncrement :: Int -> Int
doubleAndIncrement = (+1) . (*2)
```

Application of doubleAndIncrement is straightforward:

```
main :: IO ()
main = print (doubleAndIncrement 3)
```

Yielding the output:

```
7
```

Partial application empowers functions to be called with fewer arguments than they normally require, returning a new function. For example, we can create a function that adds three to a number:

```
addThree :: Int -> Int
addThree = (+3)
```

The immediate application and result can be demonstrated as follows:

```
main :: IO ()
main = print (addThree 5)
```

This produces:

```
8
```

Using higher-order functions with lists, let's implement a function that returns a list of squares of even numbers. Combining map and filter achieves this:

```
evenSquares :: [Int] -> [Int]
evenSquares = map (^2) . filter even
```

Calling evenSquares looks like:

```
main :: IO ()
main = print (evenSquares [1, 2, 3, 4, 5, 6])
```

Generating the output:

```
[4, 16, 36]
```

Lastly, operators as functions can be particularly concise. For instance, we can use the addition operator in a map operation to add one to each element:

```
addOneToList :: [Int] -> [Int]
addOneToList = map (+1)
```

An execution script to observe the results:

```
main :: IO ()
main = print (addOneToList [1, 2, 3, 4, 5])
```

The output resonates with our expectations:

```
[2, 3, 4, 5, 6]
```

These practical examples underscore the extensive possibilities afforded by higher-order functions in Haskell, showcasing their ability to simplify complex operations and enhance functional programming paradigms.

Chapter 7

Modules and Packages

This chapter introduces Haskell's module system, including how to create, use, export, and import modules, as well as qualified imports and standard library modules. It provides examples of custom modules and an introduction to Haskell packages, detailing the use of Cabal for package management, managing dependencies, and creating and publishing packages.

7.1 Introduction to Modules

Modules in Haskell play a crucial role in organizing code into manageable and reusable components. A module is essentially a collection of functions, types, and type classes grouped together under a single name. Modular programming aids in encapsulating code, making it easier to understand, maintain, and reuse. This section delves into the definition, purpose, and practical uses of modules in Haskell programming.

A Haskell module serves several core purposes: it defines a namespace, provides encapsulation, and promotes code reuse. The namespace ensures that names defined in one module do not clash with names in another. Encapsulation allows module authors to expose only the interface of a module while hiding the implementation details, thus adhering to the principle of information hiding.

To define a module, Haskell uses the module keyword followed by the module name and the where keyword. The code within a module follows this declaration.

Below is an example of defining a simple module named Geometry:

```
module Geometry where

area :: Float -> Float -> Float
area width height = width * height

perimeter :: Float -> Float -> Float
perimeter width height = 2 * (width + height)
```

In the example, the Geometry module exports two functions: area and perimeter. These functions can be used by any other module that imports the Geometry module.

The file name of the Haskell module should match the module name, with a .hs extension. In this case, the module Geometry should be saved in a file named Geometry.hs.

To use functions from another module, Haskell provides the import keyword. By importing a module, one gains access to the functions, types, and type classes exported by that module.

Here is an example of a module that imports the Geometry module:

```
module Main where

import Geometry

main :: IO ()
main = do
  let width = 5.0
      height = 10.0
  print ("Area: " ++ show (area width height))
  print ("Perimeter: " ++ show (perimeter width height))
```

In this Main module, the Geometry module is imported and its functions are used to compute and print the area and perimeter of a rectangle. The main function serves as the entry point of the Haskell program, leveraging the IO monad for output operations.

It's important to note that Haskell's import mechanism is quite flexible. By default, an import brings all exported names from the module into scope. However, one can also choose to import only specific functions or types using an import list, or qualify the import to avoid name clashes.

For instance, if only the area function from the Geometry module is required, the import statement can be modified as follows:

```
import Geometry (area)
```

Conversely, if the full module is imported but the names should be kept qualified, thus avoiding conflicts, a qualified import can be used:

```
import qualified Geometry as Geo

main :: IO ()
main = do
  let width = 5.0
      height = 10.0
  print ("Area: " ++ show (Geo.area width height))
  print ("Perimeter: " ++ show (Geo.perimeter width height))
```

In this adjusted example, the functions from the Geometry module must be prefixed with Geo., the alias specified by the as clause in the import statement. This practice makes clear the origin of the functions, aiding readability and maintenance of larger codebases with potential name overlaps.

Modules can also re-export entities from other modules. This feature facilitates the creation of higher-level interfaces. For example, one can create a module Geometry3D that re-exports functions from Geometry and adds new functionality:

```
module Geometry3D (module Geometry, volume) where

import Geometry

volume :: Float -> Float -> Float -> Float
volume width height depth = width * height * depth
```

Here the Geometry3D module brings in all exports from the Geometry module and introduces a new function volume. Users importing Geometry3D will have access to area, perimeter, and the new volume function.

Through modules, Haskell encourages a structured approach to code design, enhancing code clarity and facilitating large-scale software development.

7.2 Creating and Using Modules

In Haskell, the concept of modules serves to organize code into separate namespaces, thereby facilitating modular programming and code reuse. A module collects related functions, types, and typeclasses, encapsulating them into a single unit. This section will elucidate the process of creating and using modules in Haskell, including proper syntax, conventions, and practical examples.

Creating a Module

To create a Haskell module, first, create a new file with the .hs extension. The name of the file should correspond to the module name, capitalized. For instance, creating a module named MathUtils entails creating a file named MathUtils.hs.

At the beginning of the file, declare the module name and list the functions and types to be exported. The module keyword accomplishes this:

```
module MathUtils (add, subtract) where

add :: Int -> Int -> Int
add x y = x + y

subtract :: Int -> Int -> Int
subtract x y = x - y
```

Here, MathUtils is the module name. The (add, subtract) specification indicates that only the add and subtract functions are exported.

Using a Module

To utilize functions and types from a module, they must be imported into another Haskell file. Use the import keyword to achieve this. Suppose we have another file named Main.hs aiming to use MathUtils:

```
import MathUtils (add, subtract)

main :: IO ()
main = do
    let sumResult = add 5 3
    let subtractResult = subtract 5 3
    putStrLn ("5 + 3 = " ++ show sumResult)
    putStrLn ("5 - 3 = " ++ show subtractResult)
```

The import statement at the beginning of Main.hs imports the add and subtract functions from the module MathUtils. Consequently, these functions can be used within the main function.

Default Imports

By default, Haskell includes several commonly used modules that are automatically available, such as Prelude. This built-in module comprises basic functions, such as map, filter, and common operators. Explicit importing of Prelude is not necessary unless you opt to hide or replace it with custom implementations.

Managing Name Conflicts in Modules

In contexts where different modules define functions with identical names, resolving name conflicts becomes imperative. Consider the following scenario:

```
import MathUtils (add)
import AnotherModule (add)
```

Both MathUtils and AnotherModule provide a function named add. To handle such conflicts, Haskell supports qualified imports, allowing the use of module qualifiers:

```
import qualified MathUtils as MU
import qualified AnotherModule as AM

main :: IO ()
main = do
    let sumResultMU = MU.add 5 3
    let sumResultAM = AM.add 5 3
    putStrLn ("MathUtils add: 5 + 3 = " ++ show sumResultMU)
    putStrLn ("AnotherModule add: 5 + 3 = " ++ show sumResultAM)
```

Here, MU and AM serve as aliases for MathUtils and AnotherModule, respectively. Function calls are prefixed with these aliases, ensuring clarity and avoiding conflicts.

Hiding Functions

If you need to import a module excluding specific functions, the hiding clause is useful. For instance:

```
import MathUtils hiding (add)
```

This statement imports the entire MathUtils module except for the add function. This approach helps prevent unintended function usage while retaining access to other functionalities of the module.

Organizing Larger Projects

For larger projects, organizing code into multiple modules becomes essential. Hierarchical module names are employed for this purpose, using a dot separator to denote structure. Consider a project directory structure:

```
src/
    Main.hs
    Utils/
        MathUtils.hs
        StringUtils.hs
```

Modules within this structure would be named based on their paths:

```
// File: src/Utils/MathUtils.hs
module Utils.MathUtils (add, subtract) where

...

// File: Main.hs
import Utils.MathUtils (add)
```

```
main :: IO ()
main = ...
```

Hierarchical modules clarify code organization, simplifying maintenance and enhancing readability.

To create and utilize modules effectively, understanding the syntax and conventions is pivotal. By encapsulating related functions and types within modules, Haskell promotes modular programming and code reuse, essential for maintaining complex software systems. Systematic module management, proper use of imports, and handling potential conflicts through qualified imports and function hiding are crucial practices for efficient Haskell development.

7.3 Exporting and Importing Functions

When working with larger codebases in Haskell, modularity is essential for maintaining clean, reusable, and maintainable code. Exporting and importing functions between modules allows you to achieve this modularity effectively. This section covers the syntax and semantics of exporting and importing functions, which are foundational for any Haskell programmer aiming to build larger systems.

When a module is created, it can explicitly state which of its functions, types, and type classes are available to other modules. By default, nothing is exported; hence, to use functions from one module in another, you must explicitly specify what to expose.

```
module Geometry
    ( sphereVolume
    , sphereArea
    ) where

sphereVolume :: Float -> Float
sphereVolume radius = (4.0 / 3.0) * pi * (radius ^ 3)

sphereArea :: Float -> Float
sphereArea radius = 4 * pi * (radius ^ 2)

cubeVolume :: Float -> Float
cubeVolume side = side ^ 3

cubeArea :: Float -> Float
cubeArea side = 6 * (side ^ 2)
```

In the above example, the Geometry module exports only sphereVolume and sphereArea. Hence, any other module importing Geometry will not have access to cubeVolume and cubeArea unless explicitly stated. The Haskell module system enforces this encapsulation, which is key for data hiding and abstraction.

To use the exported functions in another module, an import declaration is required.

```
module Main where

import Geometry (sphereVolume, sphereArea)

main :: IO ()
main = do
    let radius = 5.0
    putStrLn ("The volume of the sphere: " ++ show (sphereVolume radius))
    putStrLn ("The area of the sphere: " ++ show (sphereArea radius))
```

Here, the Main module imports only the sphereVolume and sphereArea functions from the Geometry module. This makes the dependencies explicit and ensures that only the necessary functions are available in the current module's namespace.

In Haskell, it is also possible to import all exportable functions from a module without specifying each one individually by employing the module name.

```
module Main where

import Geometry

main :: IO ()
main = do
    let radius = 5.0
        side = 3.0
    putStrLn ("The volume of the sphere: " ++ show (sphereVolume radius))
    putStrLn ("The area of the sphere: " ++ show (sphereArea radius))
    putStrLn ("The volume of the cube: " ++ show (cubeVolume side))
    putStrLn ("The area of the cube: " ++ show (cubeArea side))
```

This approach is less specific and imports all the exported members of the module, potentially increasing namespace pollution, which can lead to name clashes.

Qualified imports help resolve naming conflicts by allowing the usage of functions with their module names as prefixes.

```
module Main where

import qualified Geometry as Geo

main :: IO ()
main = do
    let radius = 5.0
        side = 3.0
    putStrLn ("The volume of the sphere: " ++ show (Geo.sphereVolume radius))
```

```
    putStrLn ("The area of the sphere: " ++ show (Geo.sphereArea radius))
    putStrLn ("The volume of the cube: " ++ show (Geo.cubeVolume side))
    putStrLn ("The area of the cube: " ++ show (Geo.cubeArea side))
```

By using qualified imports, we prefix each function with Geo, reducing the chance of accidental name conflicts and improving code readability, especially in larger projects.

It is also possible to hide certain functions while importing a module, which allows you to avoid naming conflicts more selectively.

```
module Main where

import Geometry hiding (cubeVolume)

main :: IO ()
main = do
    let radius = 5.0
    putStrLn ("The volume of the sphere: " ++ show (sphereVolume radius))
    putStrLn ("The area of the sphere: " ++ show (sphereArea radius))
```

In this example, all the functions from the Geometry module are imported except cubeVolume. This can be especially useful when redefining functions in the current scope without totally excluding a module.

Lastly, Haskell supports importing modules themselves so that certain functions can be re-implemented or extended.

```
module GeometryExtended
    ( module Geometry
    , ellipsoidVolume
    ) where

import Geometry

ellipsoidVolume :: Float -> Float -> Float -> Float
ellipsoidVolume r1 r2 r3 = (4.0 / 3.0) * pi * r1 * r2 * r3
```

Here, the GeometryExtended module re-exports everything from Geometry and adds an additional function ellipsoidVolume. This approach builds upon existing modules, promoting code reuse and extension without modification.

By understanding and utilizing the principles covered here, you will improve your ability to structure Haskell programs efficiently, leverage modularity, and manage dependencies effectively. This will result in code that is more readable, maintainable, and scalable.

7.4 Qualified Imports

Qualified imports in Haskell provide a mechanism to avoid name clashes and improve code clarity when working with multiple modules that might export functions or types with the same names. When performing a qualified import, entities from the imported module must be prefixed with the module name (or an alias) followed by a dot.

Qualification allows developers to define a clear namespace for the usage of functions and types, thus making the code more readable and maintainable. This is particularly useful in large projects where functions like map, filter, or fold might be defined in multiple modules.

To use qualified imports, the import keyword is used with the qualified keyword. Additionally, an optional alias can be provided using the as keyword to shorten the prefix needed for qualified names. Here are the general forms:

```
import qualified ModuleName
import qualified ModuleName as Alias
```

Using Qualified Imports without Alias When a module is imported using qualified imports without an alias, all functions and types from the module must be prefixed with the full module name.

Consider the following example:

```
import qualified Data.List

main :: IO ()
main = do
    let nums = [1, 2, 3, 4, 5]
    print (Data.List.sort nums)
```

In this code snippet, Data.List.sort is used to sort the list nums. The Data.List.sort syntax explicitly indicates that the sort function being called is from the Data.List module. This explicit qualification helps avoid any confusion with other sort functions that might be present in different modules.

Using Qualified Imports with Alias To reduce the verbosity of the module name when using qualified imports, an alias can be assigned to the module using the as keyword.

Consider the following example with an alias:

```
import qualified Data.List as L

main :: IO ()
```

```
main = do
    let nums = [1, 2, 3, 4, 5]
    print (L.sort nums)
```

In this code snippet, Data.List is imported as L, allowing the use of L.sort instead of Data.List.sort. This aliasing reduces the verbosity while retaining the benefits of qualified imports, making the code more concise and easier to read.

Resolving Name Clashes with Qualified Imports Name clashes occur when two or more modules export entities with the same name. Qualified imports help resolve such clashes by differentiating the entities through their respective module names or aliases.

Consider the following scenario where two modules export a function named sort:

```
import qualified Data.List as L
import qualified Data.Vector as V

main :: IO ()
main = do
    let nums = [1, 2, 3, 4, 5]
    print (L.sort nums)
    let vec = V.fromList [1, 2, 3, 4, 5]
    print (V.sort vec)
```

Here, Data.List and Data.Vector are both imported with different aliases (L and V). This allows the code to use both sort functions unambiguously: L.sort for lists and V.sort for vectors.

Selective Imports with Qualification It's also possible to combine qualified imports with selective imports to bring only specific entities into scope. This further limits the namespace pollution and improves code clarity.

Consider the following example:

```
import Data.List (nub)
import qualified Data.Map as M

main :: IO ()
main = do
    let items = [1, 2, 2, 3, 4, 4, 5]
    print (nub items) -- from Data.List
    let mapItems = M.fromList [(1, 'a'), (2, 'b')]
    print (M.lookup 2 mapItems) -- from Data.Map
```

In this code snippet, nub from Data.List is imported normally, while Data.Map is imported qualified with the alias M. This selective and qualified import approach allows clean usage of nub and qualified usage of Data.Map functions without any clashes.

Understanding and effectively utilizing qualified imports is essential for managing larger Haskell projects where multiple modules interact. Properly qualified imports lead to more maintainable and less error-prone code, ensuring that entities are clearly disambiguated and easily referencable within their respective namespaces.

7.5 Standard Library Modules

Haskell's standard library is a comprehensive collection of modules that provide a wide range of functionality essential for various programming tasks. These modules cover fundamental data structures, mathematical operations, input/output handling, system interaction, and more. The standard library helps Haskell programmers avoid rewriting common functions and enables the use of well-tested and optimized code components.

One of the central modules in Haskell's standard library is Prelude. It is implicitly imported by default in every Haskell module, offering a vast array of functions and types necessary for basic programming. However, the standard library extends far beyond Prelude, organizing functions and types into specialized modules that can be imported as needed.

To utilize these modules, a programmer can import them using the import statement. Here, we will explore how to import and use some key standard library modules, highlighting their primary functions and usage examples.

```
import Data.List
import Data.Maybe
import Control.Monad
import System.IO
import Text.Printf
```

Data.List is a module that provides functions for manipulating lists. Functions such as sort, nub, intercalate, and group are defined here. For example, the sort function sorts a list in ascending order:

```
import Data.List (sort)

main :: IO ()
main = do
  let unsortedList = [3, 1, 4, 1, 5, 9, 2, 6, 5, 3, 5]
  let sortedList = sort unsortedList
  print sortedList
```

The output of the above code will be:

```
[1,1,2,3,3,4,5,5,5,6,9]
```

Data.Maybe contains functions for working with the Maybe type, including isJust, isNothing, fromJust, fromMaybe, and maybe. These functions help handle optional values gracefully. For instance, fromMaybe can be used to provide a default value if a Maybe is Nothing:

```
import Data.Maybe (fromMaybe)

main :: IO ()
main = do
  let value1 = Just 10
  let value2 = Nothing
  print $ fromMaybe 0 value1 -- Output: 10
  print $ fromMaybe 0 value2 -- Output: 0
```

Control.Monad offers a collection of functions and types for monadic operations, such as mapM, forM, liftM, and several other utility functions crucial for working with monads. These functions simplify chaining and transforming of monadic values:

```
import Control.Monad (mapM)

main :: IO ()
main = do
  names <- mapM (\x -> return ("User: " ++ x)) ["Alice", "Bob", "Charlie"]
  print names
```

The result will be:

```
["User: Alice","User: Bob","User: Charlie"]
```

System.IO deals with input and output operations, including file handling, reading from and writing to the console, and manipulating I/O modes. Functions such as openFile, hGetContents, hPutStr, and hClose are vital for file operations:

```
import System.IO

main :: IO ()
main = do
  handle <- openFile "example.txt" ReadMode
  contents <- hGetContents handle
  putStrLn contents
  hClose handle
```

If example.txt contains the line "Hello, Haskell!", the program's output will be:

```
Hello, Haskell!
```

Lastly, the Text.Printf module provides functions for formatted printing, similar to C's printf. This can be particularly useful for constructing strings with embedded values:

```
import Text.Printf (printf)

main :: IO ()
main = do
  let language = "Haskell"
  let year = 2023
  printf "Welcome to %s programming in the year %d\n" language year
```

This code will output:

```
Welcome to Haskell programming in the year 2023
```

These examples only scratch the surface of Haskell's standard library. Programmers are encouraged to explore the documentation of the standard modules to fully leverage their capabilities in building efficient and concise Haskell programs.

7.6 Custom Module Examples

A solid understanding of modules is fundamental to organizing complex Haskell applications. This section provides comprehensive examples of creating and using custom modules, illustrating how to structure and manage code effectively. We shall construct two modules: MathOperations and StringUtilities, and demonstrate their integration within a Haskell program.

```
module MathOperations (
    add,
    subtract,
    multiply,
    divide
) where

add :: Int -> Int -> Int
add x y = x + y

subtract :: Int -> Int -> Int
subtract x y = x - y

multiply :: Int -> Int -> Int
multiply x y = x * y

divide :: Int -> Int -> Maybe Int
divide _ 0 = Nothing
divide x y = Just (x `div` y)
```

The MathOperations module defines four arithmetic functions: add, subtract, multiply, and divide. The divide function returns a Maybe Int to handle division by zero gracefully, returning Nothing for such cases.

Next, consider the StringUtilities module:

```
module StringUtilities (
    toUpperCase,
    toLowerCase,
    reverseString
) where

import Data.Char (toUpper, toLower)

toUpperCase :: String -> String
toUpperCase = map toUpper

toLowerCase :: String -> String
toLowerCase = map toLower

reverseString :: String -> String
reverseString = reverse
```

The StringUtilities module provides string manipulation functions: toUpperCase, toLowerCase, and reverseString. It makes use of the Data.Char module for case conversion.

To use these modules in a Haskell program, we create a new Haskell file named Main.hs:

```
import MathOperations (add, divide)
import StringUtilities (toUpperCase, reverseString)

main :: IO ()
main = do
    let sumResult = add 5 7
        divisionResult = divide 20 4
        upperCased = toUpperCase "hello"
        reversed = reverseString "world"

    putStrLn $ "Sum: " ++ show sumResult
    putStrLn $ "Division Result: " ++ show divisionResult
    putStrLn $ "Upper Case: " ++ upperCased
    putStrLn $ "Reversed String: " ++ reversed
```

The Main module imports specific functions from MathOperations and StringUtilities, demonstrating selective imports which help in avoiding namespace collisions and unnecessary imports. The main function exemplifies invoking these functions and printing the results.

Running this Haskell program yields:

```
Sum: 12
Division Result: Just 5
Upper Case: HELLO
Reversed String: dlrow
```

These examples illustrate the encapsulation of functionality within modules, enabling code reuse and improving maintainability. The MathOperations module encapsulates arithmetic operations, while the

StringUtilities module provides common string manipulations. The Main module orchestrates the use of these functionalities, showcasing how custom modules integrate seamlessly within a Haskell program.

This clear separation of concerns is advantageous for collaborative projects, as it allows multiple developers to work on different modules independently. Additionally, it provides a blueprint for testing each module separately before integration, promoting a robust development workflow.

7.7 Introduction to Packages

In Haskell, a package refers to a collection of modules bundled together, which can be distributed and reused as a single unit. The primary purpose of using packages is to manage and encapsulate code, promote code reuse, and facilitate sharing within the Haskell community. Packages play a significant role in extending the functionalities available to Haskell programs beyond the standard libraries.

A Haskell package typically includes source code files, metadata about the package such as its name, version, and dependencies, and possibly other resources such as documentation. The information about the package is usually contained in a *.cabal file, named after the Cabal (Common Architecture for Building Applications and Libraries) system used for package management.

To create a Haskell package, follow these steps with an appropriate project directory structure:

```
my-haskell-package/
 src/
    ModuleA.hs
    ModuleB.hs
 test/
    Spec.hs
 my-haskell-package.cabal
 Setup.hs
```

The src directory contains the source code files for different modules in the package, whereas the test directory contains test files. The my-haskell-package.cabal file includes metadata about the package, and Setup.hs is typically a minimal file required to build the package.

A typical *.cabal file may look as follows:

```
name: my-haskell-package
version: 0.1.0.0
```

```
synopsis: A brief description of the package.
description: A longer description of your package.
category: Specific category of the package
license: BSD3
license-file: LICENSE
author: Your Name
maintainer: your.email@example.com
build-type: Simple
cabal-version: >=1.10

library
  exposed-modules: ModuleA, ModuleB
  hs-source-dirs: src
  build-depends: base >=4.7 \&\& <5
  default-language: Haskell2010

test-suite test-suite-name
  type: exitcode-stdio-1.0
  hs-source-dirs: test
  main-is: Spec.hs
  build-depends: base >=4.7 \&\& <5, my-haskell-package
  default-language: Haskell2010
```

Here, name specifies the package name, and version specifies the package version in Semantic Versioning format (MAJOR.MINOR.PATCH). The synopsis is a short description, while description provides a more detailed explanation of the package. The category field helps users find packages in a specific domain.

The library section defines the modules exposed in the package, their source directories, and dependencies, while the test-suite section defines the tests for the package. exposed-modules lists the modules that will be available to the users of the package. hs-source-dirs points to the source directory, and default-language sets the Haskell language standard being used.

To build and install a Haskell package, practical Cabal commands are used. Here's how to do it:

```
\$ cabal update
\$ cabal build
\$ cabal install
```

Cabal will first update the package index, build the package by compiling the source files, and then install it for use in Haskell programs.

Additionally, it is important to manage package dependencies. Dependencies are other packages upon which your package relies. Properly specifying dependencies in the build-depends field helps ensure your package works correctly with the appropriate versions of libraries. Wildcard constraints (e.g., >=4.7 && <5) are recommended to allow for compatibility within a range of versions.

Using dependencies, developers can access and integrate existing libraries into their projects. For instance, to use the text library in your package, you'd include it in build-depends:

```
build-depends: base >=4.7 \&\& <5, text >=1.2 \&\& <2
```

The text library provides efficient handling of Unicode text, complementing the String type.

Testing is an integral part of developing robust packages. Including a test-suite in your package configuration ensures your code behaves as expected. Haskell provides several testing frameworks like HUnit and QuickCheck, which can be included as dependencies in the build-depends section.

The package creation and configuration process in Haskell is highly systematic and is facilitated by Cabal. Understanding and employing this mechanism effectively promotes code reusability and sharing within the Haskell ecosystem, enriching the overall functionality available to Haskell developers.

7.8 Cabal: Haskell's Package Manager

Cabal (Common Architecture for Building Applications and Libraries) is the standard package manager and build system for Haskell. It provides the infrastructure to organize and manage Haskell projects, including the handling of dependencies, building, and distribution. Cabal simplifies many aspects of Haskell software development, making it easier to develop, maintain, and deploy packages.

Cabal operates through the command-line tool cabal and utilizes the .cabal file, which contains metadata and configuration for a Haskell project. Key elements managed by Cabal include package dependencies, build settings, and executables. Here, we will detail its usage and configuration by exploring the different facets of Cabal.

Creating a New Project

To create a new Haskell project, use the cabal init command. This command generates the necessary project structure and files, including the .cabal file. A typical invocation looks like this:

```
$ cabal init
```

This command will prompt you to enter various details about the new project, such as the package name, version, author, and license. You can also specify the type of project, whether it's a library, executable, or both. After running this command, you will have a basic project structure as shown below:

```
<project-directory>/
    app/
    src/
    test/
    <project-name>.cabal
    ChangeLog.md
    LICENSE
    README.md
    Setup.hs
```

The .cabal File

The .cabal file is crucial in defining the configuration of the project. Key sections of a .cabal file include:

- name: The name of the package.
- version: The version of the package.
- build-type: Specifies the build methodology, typically Simple.
- library/executable: Defines library modules and executable components.
- dependencies: Lists package dependencies required to build the project.

A simple example of a .cabal file for a library might look like this:

```
name: example
version: 0.1.0.0
build-type: Simple
cabal-version: >= 1.10

library
  exposed-modules: Example
  build-depends: base >=4.7 && <5
  hs-source-dirs: src
  default-language: Haskell2010
```

Building a Project

To build a Haskell project, navigate to the project directory and use the cabal build command. This will compile the source code and place the resulting binaries in a dist-newstyle directory.

```
$ cabal build
```

This command checks for dependencies, compiles the source code, and links everything together to produce the final executable or library.

Dependency Management

Dependencies are specified in the build-depends field of the .cabal file. Cabal uses Hackage, the Haskell package repository, to resolve and fetch these dependencies. To update the list of available packages from Hackage, ensure you have an up-to-date package list by running:

```
$ cabal update
```

Installing Dependencies

To install dependencies, use the cabal install command. During the build process, Cabal will automatically resolve and fetch the necessary dependencies specified in your project's .cabal file.

```
$ cabal install --only-dependencies
```

This command ensures that all dependencies are installed without building the actual project.

Executing Tests

Cabal facilitates the integration of testing frameworks. You can configure test suites in the .cabal file under the test-suite section. After defining your test suite, use the following command to run your tests:

```
$ cabal test
```

A sample test definition in a .cabal file might look like this:

```
test-suite example-test
  type: exitcode-stdio-1.0
  main-is: TestMain.hs
  hs-source-dirs: test
  build-depends: base >=4.7 && <5, example
  default-language: Haskell2010
```

Distribution

To prepare a package for distribution, first clean any existing build artifacts:

```
$ cabal clean
```

Next, create a source distribution:

```
$ cabal sdist
```

This command packages your project into a tarball located in the dist-newstyle/sdist directory, ready for upload to Hackage.

Publishing to Hackage

Before publishing to Hackage, ensure that you have an account and are logged in using cabal. Upload the package by executing:

```
$ cabal upload dist-newstyle/sdist/<package-name-version>.tar.gz
```

Cabal will prompt you to enter your Hackage credentials, and upon successful authentication, it will upload the package to Hackage.

Cabal is an indispensable tool in the Haskell ecosystem, providing comprehensive support for package management, dependency resolution, and distribution. Proper use of Cabal ensures that your Haskell projects are consistent, reproducible, and easily shareable.

7.9 Managing Dependencies

Managing dependencies is a critical aspect of software development in Haskell. Dependencies are external libraries or packages that your project relies on to function. The Haskell ecosystem provides robust tools for managing these dependencies, ensuring that your project remains stable and easily reproducible across different environments. This section will delve into various aspects of dependency management using Cabal and the Haskell Package Archive (Hackage).

Cabal is a powerful and flexible build tool for Haskell that automates the process of specifying, fetching, and installing dependencies. It integrates seamlessly with Hackage, the central repository of Haskell libraries, allowing developers to tap into a vast collection of pre-existing packages.

Cabal projects are typically defined using a .cabal file, which contains metadata about the project such as its name, version, author, and license. Importantly, this file also specifies the project's dependencies.

```
name: example-project
version: 0.1.0.0
synopsis: An example project to demonstrate dependency management.
description: This is a Haskell project that showcases how to manage dependencies using
        Cabal.
license: BSD-3-Clause
license-file: LICENSE
author: Jane Doe
maintainer: jane.doe@example.com
category: Web
```

```
build-type: Simple
cabal-version: >=1.10

library
  hs-source-dirs: src
  exposed-modules: ExampleProject
  build-depends: base >=4.7 && <5, text >=1.2.3 && <1.3
  default-language: Haskell2010
```

The build-depends field is of particular importance, as it lists the libraries that this project depends on. Each dependency is accompanied by a version constraint to ensure compatibility. In this example, the base library is required with a version greater than or equal to 4.7 but less than 5. The text library is required with a version between 1.2.3 and 1.3.

To install dependencies and build the project, the following command is used:

```
$ cabal build
```

This command automatically fetches and installs the specified dependencies from Hackage. Cabal stores these dependencies in a sandboxed environment to avoid conflicts with other projects.

It is good practice to create a cabal.config file to lock the exact versions of dependencies used in the project. This ensures that the same versions are used whenever the project is built, providing consistency and reproducibility.

Here is how to generate the cabal.config file:

```
$ cabal freeze
```

The cabal freeze command generates a cabal.config file containing the exact versions of all dependencies currently installed. This file can be committed to version control, ensuring that all developers working on the project use the same versions.

Dependency resolution in Cabal can sometimes lead to conflicts, especially when multiple libraries require different versions of the same dependency. Cabal resolves such conflicts by selecting a version that satisfies all constraints, if possible. If not, it provides detailed error messages to help diagnose the issue.

Let's consider an example of a dependency conflict:

```
library
  build-depends: base >=4.7 && <5, text >=1.2.3 && <1.3, aeson >=1.4 && <1.5
```

Assume that aeson-1.4.* depends on text-1.2.4, which lies outside the specified range for text. This leads to a conflict that Cabal cannot resolve. To find the exact cause, Cabal will output an error message, and you may need to adjust the version constraints to accommodate compatible versions or consider alternative dependencies that do not have conflicting requirements.

Another critical tool in managing dependencies is stack, which also ensures reproducibility and isolation of dependencies. stack uses a stack.yaml file to specify the resolver and dependencies. The configuration might look something like this:

```
resolver: lts-14.16
packages:
- .
extra-deps:
- text-1.2.4
```

The resolver specifies a consistent set of packages tested to work together, and extra-deps allows you to specify additional dependencies not included in the resolver.

To install and build the project using stack, use the command:

```
$ stack build
```

This command fetches and installs the necessary dependencies into an isolated environment, thus preventing conflicts with other projects.

Proper dependency management ensures that your project builds reliably and behaves consistently across different development environments and deployment platforms. Understanding and utilizing tools like cabal and stack effectively is crucial for maintaining the health and longevity of your Haskell projects.

7.10 Creating and Publishing Packages

Creating a package in Haskell involves several deliberate steps, managed through Cabal, Haskell's build system and package manager. This section will cover the systematic process of creating a Cabal package and subsequently publishing it to Hackage, Haskell's central package archive.

To get started, install the Cabal tool. Assuming you have the Haskell Platform installed, you can update Cabal with the following command:

```
cabal update
```

```
cabal install cabal-install
```

To create a new package structure, use the Cabal command to initialize a new package:

```
cabal init
```

Running cabal init prompts a series of questions to configure your new package. The configuration process generates a .cabal file, typically named after your package. An example of a .cabal file might look as follows:

```
name: mypackage
version: 0.1.0.0
synopsis: Brief description of the package
description: Detailed description of the package.
license: BSD3
license-file: LICENSE
author: Your Name
maintainer: email@example.com
category: Development
build-type: Simple
cabal-version: >=1.10

library
  exposed-modules: MyPackage
  other-modules: MyPackage.Internal
  hs-source-dirs: src
  build-depends: base >=4.7 && <4.9
  default-language: Haskell2010
```

Details in the .cabal file include:

- name: The name of the package. - version: The initial version of the package. - synopsis: A brief one-line summary. - description: A longer description. - license: The license under which the package is released. - author and maintainer: Your name and contact information. - category: The category under which the package falls. - build-type: Usually Simple. - cabal-version: The version of the Cabal specification.

Within the library section:

- exposed-modules: Lists the modules exposed to users. - other-modules: Lists the modules used internally within the library. - hs-source-dirs: Directories containing the Haskell source files. - build-depends: Specifies dependencies on other packages. - default-language: The default language standard.

The directory structure of your package typically includes:

```
mypackage/
  src/
    MyPackage.hs
    MyPackage/
      Internal.hs
  LICENSE
  mypackage.cabal
  README.md
```

The src directory includes the Haskell source files. The LICENSE file includes the license text, and README.md contains information about the package.

To build and test your package locally, use:

```
cabal build
cabal test
```

These commands compile the package and run any included test suites.

Before publishing your package, it is essential to ensure all necessary files are present and the package description is accurate. Validate your package with:

```
cabal check
cabal sdist
```

cabal check performs a set of sanity checks, ensuring that the package conforms to Hackage expectations. cabal sdist creates a source distribution archive of the package, typically a .tar.gz file, found in the dist directory.

To upload the package to Hackage:

```
cabal upload dist/mypackage-0.1.0.0.tar.gz
```

This command uploads the .tar.gz file to Hackage, making it available to the Haskell community. An Hackage account and API key are required for this step.

Maintaining your package involves updating it, fixing bugs, and possibly adding new features. Update the version number in the .cabal file following the Haskell Package Versioning Policy (PVP), which uses three levels of version numbers: breaking changes (major), new features (minor), and bug fixes.

For example, if only internal changes (like fixing typos) are made, increment the last digit: '0.1.0.0' to '0.1.0.1'. If new features or backward-compatible changes are introduced, increment the minor version: '0.1.0.0' to '0.2.0.0'. For backward-incompatible changes, increment the major version: '0.1.0.0' to '1.0.0.0'.

After making updates, repeat the build and testing process, validate with cabal check, and generate a new source distribution with cabal sdist. Then upload the new version using cabal upload.

By carefully creating, maintaining, and publishing packages, you contribute to the Haskell ecosystem, making your work accessible for reuse and further development by the community.

Chapter 8

Input and Output

This chapter discusses handling input and output in Haskell, covering basic I/O operations, user input, and file reading and writing. It explores lazy I/O, working with binary data, exceptions, and error handling. Additionally, it delves into system interactions, advanced I/O concepts, and provides practical examples of I/O operations.

8.1 Introduction to I/O in Haskell

Input and Output (I/O) in Haskell presents a unique paradigm informed by its functional nature. Unlike imperative languages where I/O operations may be interwoven with business logic, Haskell treats these actions as part of its functional framework. Understanding this different approach is fundamental to mastering Haskell.

Haskell's I/O is managed through the IO monad, which encapsulates any side-effect causing operations, ensuring they remain pure from the perspective of the rest of the program. This allows the Haskell compiler to optimize code better without having to account for unpredictable external interactions. The IO type can be simply described as:

```
IO a -- where 'a' is the type of value produced by the I/O action
```

A basic I/O operation in Haskell might be printing a string to the console, using the putStrLn function, which has the type signature:

```
putStrLn :: String -> IO ()
```

This function takes a String and returns an IO action that results in a unit type (). Here's an example of how it can be used within the main function:

```
main :: IO ()
main = do
    putStrLn "Hello, World!"
```

In this example, putStrLn "Hello, World!" is an I/O action that, when executed, prints "Hello, World!" to the standard output. The do notation enables sequencing of multiple I/O actions.

To provide a broader context, consider how Haskell enforces the distinction between pure functions and impure actions. A pure function cannot perform I/O directly; it must return an IO action. For example:

```
pureFunction :: Int -> String
pureFunction x = "Number: " ++ show x

impureFunction :: String -> IO ()
impureFunction str = putStrLn str
```

To bridge pure and impure code, we often see a pattern where a pure function computes the necessary data, and an impure function performs the I/O action. For example:

```
main :: IO ()
main = do
    let msg = pureFunction 42
    impureFunction msg
```

Haskell also supports reading input from users through several functions, notably getLine, which reads a line of input from the standard input:

```
getLine :: IO String
```

Here's a brief example that reads a name from the user and then greets them:

```
main :: IO ()
main = do
    putStrLn "What is your name?"
    name <- getLine
    putStrLn ("Hello, " ++ name ++ "!")
```

In this program, the I/O actions are tied together within a do block. The syntax name <- getLine is used to extract the result from the IO action and bind it to the variable name. This pattern is central to handling I/O in Haskell, where the do notation allows for sequential execution of actions.

Understanding Haskell's approach to I/O through the IO monad is critical. The IO monad is not just a construct for I/O operations; it is part of what ensures the referential transparency and purity of functional programming in Haskell, maintaining a clear separation between pure code and side-effecting actions. This distinction provides both a powerful tool and a model of computation that promotes robust software development. By working with IO monad and do notation, developers are better equipped to manage side effects in a controlled and predictable manner.

8.2 Basic I/O Operations

The essence of input and output (I/O) operations in Haskell revolves around the use of actions that interact with the external environment to read or manipulate data. As a purely functional language, Haskell handles I/O operations differently compared to imperative languages, ensuring that side effects are controlled and managed explicitly.

In Haskell, I/O actions are represented by types IO a, where a is the type of value returned by the action. These actions are constructed and sequenced using specialized functions and the do notation, which provides a readable and natural way to structure I/O operations.

The putStrLn function is one of the most fundamental I/O operations in Haskell. It outputs a string followed by a newline to the standard output (usually the terminal). Below is an example of using putStrLn:

```
main :: IO ()
main = do
  putStrLn "Hello, World!"
```

In this example, the putStrLn function has the type String -> IO (). It takes a String and produces an I/O action that, when executed, will print the string to the console.

For reading input from the user, the getLine function is commonly used. It has the type IO String. When executed, it reads a line of text from standard input and returns it as a String. Here is an example that combines both putStrLn and getLine:

```
main :: IO ()
```

```
main = do
  putStrLn "Enter your name:"
  name <- getLine
  putStrLn ("Hello, " ++ name ++ "!")
```

In this example, getLine reads the user's input, which is then bound to the variable name. The operator <- is used to extract the String from the IO action. The subsequent putStrLn call then constructs a greeting message by concatenating strings using the ++ operator and prints it out.

Haskell also supports more complex I/O operations, such as dealing with files. For reading from and writing to files, the standard library provides several useful functions:

- readFile - Reads the contents of a file into a string. It has the type FilePath -> IO String.
- writeFile - Writes a string to a file, overwriting any existing contents. It has the type FilePath -> String -> IO ().
- appendFile - Appends a string to the end of a file. It has the type FilePath -> String -> IO ().

Here is an example of reading from and writing to files:

```
main :: IO ()
main = do
  contents <- readFile "input.txt"
  putStrLn "Original content:"
  putStrLn contents
  let newContents = "Modified content:\n" ++ contents
  writeFile "output.txt" newContents
  putStrLn "New content written to output.txt."
```

In this example, readFile reads the content of input.txt and binds it to the variable contents. This content is printed out using putStrLn. A new string is constructed by prepending "Modified content:\n" to the original content, which is then written to output.txt using writeFile.

Additionally, Haskell provides functions for interacting with text input/output in a lower-level fashion. Functions like hPutStrLn and hGetLine work with file handles directly, allowing for more fine-grained control over where data is read from or written to. Here's an example using file handles:

```
import System.IO

main :: IO ()
```

```
main = do
  handle <- openFile "input.txt" ReadMode
  contents <- hGetContents handle
  putStrLn "File content:"
  putStrLn contents
  hClose handle
```

In this example, openFile is used to open input.txt in read mode, returning a file handle. The hGetContents function reads from the file handle and binds the content to contents, which is then printed. Finally, the file handle is closed with hClose.

Handling I/O in Haskell can appear different from more traditional languages, but the benefits of maintaining pure functions and explicit side effects provide significant advantages in reliability and maintainability of code. Various utility functions and techniques discussed in subsequent sections will further elaborate on how to effectively manage I/O in Haskell programs.

8.3 Handling User Input

Handling user input in Haskell is straightforward, yet it showcases the elegant and functional nature of the language. User input typically involves reading strings from the console and processing them. This section will cover essential functions and techniques to handle user input efficiently.

To start with, the most basic function to capture user input in Haskell is getLine. This function reads a line from the standard input and returns it as a string.

```
main :: IO ()
main = do
    putStrLn "Please enter your name:"
    name <- getLine
    putStrLn ("Hello, " ++ name ++ "!")
```

In the above example, putStrLn outputs a string to the console without a trailing newline. The getLine function waits for the user to input a line of text and binds the result to the variable name. The putStrLn function then outputs a greeting using the entered name.

When dealing with numeric inputs, the read function is used to convert strings into numeric values.

```
main :: IO ()
main = do
```

```
    putStrLn "Please enter a number:"
    input <- getLine
    let number = read input :: Int
    putStrLn ("The number you entered is: " ++ show number)
```

Here, read input :: Int explicitly converts the input string to an integer. The resulting number is then displayed using show, which converts the integer back to a string for output.

To handle potential errors during the conversion, we use the maybeRead function, which safely attempts to parse the string to the desired numeric type.

```
maybeRead :: Read a => String -> Maybe a
maybeRead s = case reads s of
                [(val, "")] -> Just val
                _ -> Nothing

main :: IO ()
main = do
    putStrLn "Please enter a number:"
    input <- getLine
    case maybeRead input :: Maybe Int of
        Just number -> putStrLn ("The number you entered is: " ++ show number)
        Nothing -> putStrLn "Invalid number entered."
```

In this example, maybeRead attempts to convert the input string to an integer. If the conversion is successful, the entered number is displayed; otherwise, an error message is shown.

For more complex user interactions, such as reading multiple lines, the getContents function is useful. It reads all input until EOF and returns it as a single string.

```
main :: IO ()
main = do
    putStrLn "Enter multiple lines of text (Press Ctrl+D to end):"
    input <- getContents
    putStrLn "You entered:"
    putStrLn input
```

Using getContents, the program continuously reads input until an end-of-file (EOF) character (Ctrl+D) is encountered. This input is then printed in a single block.

Haskell also provides a more advanced mechanism for interaction using the hSetBuffering function from the System.IO module. This function allows us to control how the input and output are buffered.

```
import System.IO

main :: IO ()
main = do
```

```
    hSetBuffering stdin LineBuffering
    putStrLn "Please enter your age:"
    age <- getLine
    putStrLn ("You entered: " ++ age)
```

In this snippet, hSetBuffering stdin LineBuffering sets the buffering mode for the standard input to line buffering. This mode ensures that input is only read after the user presses Enter, rather than character by character.

Finally, dealing with user input in a concurrent environment can be handled using the forkIO function from the Control.Concurrent module.

```
import Control.Concurrent

main :: IO ()
main = do
   forkIO $ inputHandler
   putStrLn "Main thread is running..."
   threadDelay 10000000

inputHandler :: IO ()
inputHandler = do
   putStrLn "Please enter some command:"
   command <- getLine
   putStrLn ("You entered: " ++ command)
   inputHandler
```

In the above example, forkIO is used to create a new thread that runs inputHandler. This handler reads user input in a loop, allowing the main thread to execute other tasks simultaneously. The threadDelay function is used here to prevent the main thread from terminating immediately.

Using these fundamental techniques, Haskell provides robust and flexible ways to handle user input in both simple and complex scenarios.

8.4 Reading and Writing Files

File I/O in Haskell is a fundamental aspect that allows programs to interact with the file system by reading from and writing to files. This section explains the various methods and functions available in Haskell for handling file operations. We will explore essential functions provided by the Prelude and the System.IO module.

To begin with, understanding how to read from a file is crucial. The most straightforward approach is to use the readFile function. This function takes a file path as a string and returns the file contents as a single string. Consider the following example:

```
import System.IO

main :: IO ()
main = do
    contents <- readFile "example.txt"
    putStr contents
```

In this example, the readFile function reads the content of example.txt and stores it in the contents variable. The putStr function then prints the contents to the console. The operation is performed within the IO Monad, ensuring proper handling of side effects.

For writing to a file, Haskell provides the writeFile function. This function takes a file path and a string to write to that file. Here is an example:

```
import System.IO

main :: IO ()
main = do
    let content = "Hello, World!"
    writeFile "output.txt" content
```

In this case, writeFile creates or overwrites output.txt with the string "Hello, World!". The write operation also takes place within the IO Monad.

To append data to an existing file, we utilize the appendFile function. This function operates similarly to writeFile, but instead of overwriting the file, it appends the provided string to the file's existing contents:

```
import System.IO

main :: IO ()
main = do
    let additionalContent = "\nAppended line."
    appendFile "output.txt" additionalContent
```

This appends the string "\nAppended line." to output.txt, ensuring that previous content remains intact.

For more sophisticated file operations, Haskell's System.IO module provides handles, which give more control over I/O processes. To open a file for reading or writing using handles, the openFile function is utilized. The file can be opened in various modes, such as ReadMode, WriteMode, AppendMode, and ReadWriteMode.

Here is an example demonstrating the use of file handles for reading:

```
import System.IO

main :: IO ()
main = do
```

```
    handle <- openFile "example.txt" ReadMode
    contents <- hGetContents handle
    putStr contents
    hClose handle
```

The openFile function opens example.txt in ReadMode, returning a file handle. The hGetContents function reads the file contents using the handle, and putStr prints it. Finally, hClose ensures that the file handle is properly closed.

Writing to a file using handles follows a similar pattern:

```
import System.IO

main :: IO ()
main = do
    handle <- openFile "output.txt" WriteMode
    hPutStr handle "This is written using handle."
    hClose handle
```

In this scenario, openFile opens output.txt in WriteMode. The hPutStr function writes to the file via the handle, and hClose closes the handle afterward.

For scenarios where random access to a file's content is necessary, Haskell provides functions like hSeek, hTell, and hIsEOF. The hSeek function lets you move to a specific position within a file, while hTell returns the current position, and hIsEOF checks whether the end of the file has been reached.

Consider this example demonstrating random access:

```
import System.IO

main :: IO ()
main = do
    handle <- openFile "output.txt" ReadWriteMode
    hPutStr handle "Writing at the start."
    hSeek handle AbsoluteSeek 0
    hPutStr handle "Overwrite start."
    hClose handle
```

Here, the file output.txt is opened in ReadWriteMode. The hPutStr function writes "Writing at the start." to the beginning of the file. The hSeek function then moves the file pointer back to the start, and hPutStr overwrites the beginning of the file with "Overwrite start."

Reading and writing binary data involves using similar techniques but requires functions like hGetBuf and hPutBuf instead of their string counterparts. Handles are also used extensively in binary I/O operations.

The above code samples and methods illustrate fundamental file I/O operations in Haskell. Understanding these basics is paramount for performing more advanced file manipulations and integrating file I/O seamlessly within larger Haskell projects.

8.5 Lazy I/O

Haskell's lazy evaluation model extends to input and output operations, introducing a concept known as lazy I/O. Laziness in I/O allows the reading of input data to be deferred until it's actually needed, which can lead to efficient memory usage and improved performance in certain scenarios. This approach, however, introduces complexity and potential pitfalls that need careful consideration.

Lazy I/O in Haskell is primarily facilitated by the functions readFile, writeFile, and appendFile. These functions enable deferred reading and writing of file contents, meaning the file is not read into memory all at once, but rather as the program processes it.

The following example demonstrates how readFile operates lazily:

```
main :: IO ()
main = do
  contents <- readFile "example.txt"
  putStrLn (take 100 contents)
```

In this example, readFile "example.txt" does not immediately read the entire file into memory. Instead, it returns a lazy String that will read the file contents as necessary. The take 100 contents expression extracts the first 100 characters, causing readFile to only read as much of the file as needed to satisfy this demand.

Despite these benefits, lazy I/O can complicate resource management, particularly with file handles. Because the file is read lazily, the file handle may remain open for an indeterminate period, which can lead to resource exhaustion if many files are opened simultaneously. This issue, commonly referred to as "the lazy I/O problem," necessitates careful handling to avoid leaking file handles.

To illustrate this problem, consider the following:

```
import System.IO

main :: IO ()
main = do
  contents <- readFile "example.txt"
  putStrLn "File has been read"
```

```
putStrLn (take 100 contents)
-- Subsequent code that does not use 'contents'
```

Even after the program outputs "File has been read," the file handle remains open because the contents have not been fully consumed. If the program opens many files in this manner, it quickly exhausts available file handles.

To mitigate this, Haskell provides more control over resource management through functions like withFile. The function withFile ensures the file handle is properly managed and closed after use. Here's how withFile can be used to manage lazy I/O:

```
import System.IO

main :: IO ()
main = withFile "example.txt" ReadMode (\handle -> do
  contents <- hGetContents handle
  putStrLn (take 100 contents))
```

In this code, withFile takes three arguments: the file path, the mode in which to open the file (ReadMode, WriteMode, etc.), and a function that operates on the file handle. Once the function completes, withFile ensures the file handle is closed, even if an error occurs.

Lazy I/O can also be compared with strict I/O operations using functions such as hGetContents and hPutStr. Here is an example illustrating strict reading using hGetContents:

```
import System.IO

main :: IO ()
main = do
  handle <- openFile "example.txt" ReadMode
  contents <- hGetContents handle
  putStrLn (take 100 contents)
  hClose handle
```

In this example, hGetContents initiates a lazy read, but the explicit hClose handle ensures the file handle is closed immediately after reading the required contents, avoiding potential file handle leaks.

While lazy I/O can provide performance benefits by handling large files without loading them entirely into memory, it must be balanced against the complexity of managing resources effectively. In scenarios where resource management is critical, strict I/O or controlled lazy I/O through functions like withFile is recommended.

The concept of lazy I/O extends beyond files to other data streams, including network operations and inter-process communication. Whether dealing with files, sockets, or other streams, understanding and managing the laziness of Haskell's I/O operations is crucial for writing efficient and safe programs.

8.6 Working with Binary Data

In Haskell, binary data manipulation is essential when working with various applications involving file encoding, network protocols, or any form of non-textual data exchange. While Haskell provides robust support for text-based I/O, handling binary data requires a nuanced understanding of the language's capabilities in terms of performance and correctness.

To work effectively with binary data in Haskell, one must leverage specialized libraries and functions designed to facilitate operations like encoding, decoding, reading from and writing to binary streams.

ByteStrings

The 'Data.ByteString' module is central to binary data handling in Haskell. It provides efficient operations on sequences of bytes. 'ByteString' comes in two main variants: strict and lazy.

- Data.ByteString.Strict deals with strict bytestrings ('ByteString'). Strict bytestrings are more memory efficient for smaller data as they are represented as contiguous arrays of bytes.

- Data.ByteString.Lazy provides lazy bytestrings ('LazyByteString'). These are useful for handling large data streams as they are implemented as lists of strict bytestring chunks, facilitating efficient data processing without exhausting memory resources.

```
import qualified Data.ByteString as B
import qualified Data.ByteString.Lazy as LB
```

Reading and Writing Binary Data

Reading binary data from a file involves using the 'B.readFile' or 'LB.readFile' functions, which read the contents of a file into a 'ByteString' or 'LazyByteString', respectively.

```
-- Reading an entire file into a strict ByteString
readStrictFile :: FilePath -> IO B.ByteString
readStrictFile path = B.readFile path
```

```
-- Reading an entire file into a lazy ByteString
readLazyFile :: FilePath -> IO LB.ByteString
```

```
readLazyFile path = LB.readFile path
```

Writing binary data back to the file system can be performed using 'B.writeFile' or 'LB.writeFile'.

```
-- Writing a strict ByteString to a file
writeStrictFile :: FilePath -> B.ByteString -> IO ()
writeStrictFile path content = B.writeFile path content
```

```
-- Writing a lazy ByteString to a file
writeLazyFile :: FilePath -> LB.ByteString -> IO ()
writeLazyFile path content = LB.writeFile path content
```

Binary Serialization

Serialization is the process of converting data structures into a binary format suitable for storage or transmission. The 'cereal' package provides a straightforward means of serialization. Using the 'Data.Serialize' module, one can easily serialize and deserialize data structures.

```
import qualified Data.Serialize as S
```

To serialize a data structure, it must be an instance of the 'Serialize' typeclass. Let's define a simple data structure and implement serialization for it.

```
data Person = Person {
    name :: String,
    age :: Int
} deriving (Show, Generic)

instance S.Serialize Person
```

Now, you can serialize and deserialize instances of 'Person'.

```
serializePerson :: Person -> B.ByteString
serializePerson person = S.encode person

deserializePerson :: B.ByteString -> Either String Person
deserializePerson byteString = S.decode byteString
```

Interacting with Network Byte Streams

Networking often involves handling binary data over streams. The 'Network.Socket.ByteString' module allows sending and receiving 'ByteString' data over network sockets.

```
import qualified Network.Socket as NS
import qualified Network.Socket.ByteString as NBS
```

To interact with network streams, create a socket, connect to a host, and use 'NBS.send' and 'NBS.recv' for transmission and reception.

```
sendData :: NS.Socket -> B.ByteString -> IO Int
sendData sock content = NBS.send sock content

receiveData :: NS.Socket -> IO B.ByteString
receiveData sock = NBS.recv sock 4096 -- Receiving up to 4096 bytes
```

Binary Data Processing

Processing binary data often involves parsing or constructing binary formats. The 'attoparsec' library offers powerful combinators to parse 'ByteString' efficiently.

```
import qualified Data.ByteString.Char8 as BC
import qualified Data.Attoparsec.ByteString as A
```

Example: Parsing a simple binary format where a string is prefixed with its length.

```
-- An Attoparsec parser for length-prefixed strings
stringParser :: A.Parser String
stringParser = do
    len <- A.anyWord8 -- Read length prefix (one byte)
    BC.unpack <$> A.take (fromIntegral len)
```

In this parsing example, 'A.anyWord8' reads a single byte representing the length of the subsequent string, and 'A.take' extracts the string based on this length. The result is then unpacked into a standard Haskell 'String'.

Using these techniques, Haskell programmers can handle complex binary data manipulation tasks efficiently and effectively, leveraging the language's powerful type system and abstractions for both performance and correctness considerations.

8.7 Exceptions and Error Handling

Handling exceptions and errors is crucial in building robust Haskell programs, particularly in I/O operations where many unforeseen issues may arise, such as missing files or invalid input. This section delves into the mechanisms Haskell provides for exception handling and error management, enhancing the reliability and stability of your applications.

The Control.Exception module offers the core functionality for dealing with exceptions in Haskell. To employ these features, begin by importing the necessary module:

```
import Control.Exception
```

Control.Exception provides several key components, including the Exception type class, predefined exception types, and various functions for throwing, catching, and handling exceptions.

- throwIO: This function throws an exception in the IO monad. It ensures that the exception is thrown in a predictable manner, respecting the sequencing of I/O operations.
- try: This function catches exceptions and returns an Either type, allowing both success and failure scenarios to be handled.
- catch: This function catches an exception and allows for the definition of a handler to deal with it.
- finally: This function ensures that a computation is run even if an exception occurs, often used for cleanup operations.

Throwing Exceptions

Throwing exceptions deliberately allows for signaling unforeseen issues effectively. The throwIO function throws an exception in the IO monad:

```
throwIO (userError "This is an error!")
```

The userError function constructs an IOError from a string, but custom exceptions can also be defined for more specific error handling.

Catching Exceptions

To catch and handle exceptions, the catch function can be used. Its type signature is as follows:

```
catch :: Exception e => IO a -> (e -> IO a) -> IO a
```

This indicates that catch takes an IO action and an exception handler function, returning a new IO action.

```
import Control.Exception

main :: IO ()
main = do
  result <- try (readFile "nonexistent_file.txt") :: IO (Either IOError String)
  case result of
    Left ex -> putStrLn $ "Caught exception: " ++ show ex
    Right content -> putStrLn content
```

In this example, try captures any IOError exceptions that occur during file reading and returns an Either type. The Left constructor signifies an error, and the Right constructor contains the file content if successful.

Handle and Finally

The handle function is a convenience wrapper around catch, which flips the order of arguments:

```
handle :: Exception e => (e -> IO a) -> IO a -> IO a
```

An example using handle:

```
main :: IO ()
main = handle handler readFileAction
  where
    handler :: IOError -> IO ()
    handler e = putStrLn $ "Error occurred: " ++ show e
    readFileAction = do
      content <- readFile "nonexistent_file.txt"
      putStrLn content
```

The finally function ensures that a subsequent computation is executed regardless of whether an exception is thrown. It is commonly used for cleanup actions:

```
main :: IO ()
main = do
  handle <- openFile "somefile.txt" ReadMode
  finally (hGetContents handle >>= putStrLn)
          (hClose handle)
```

This code snippet ensures that the file handle is closed, even if reading the file or printing its contents causes an exception.

Custom Exceptions

Defining custom exception types allows for more nuanced error handling. Custom exceptions must be instances of the Exception type class, which usually involves deriving from Show and Typeable:

```
{-# LANGUAGE DeriveDataTypeable #-}

import Control.Exception
import Data.Typeable

data MyException = MyException String
  deriving (Show, Typeable)

instance Exception MyException
```

With this custom exception, you can now throw and catch it using the same functions:

```
main :: IO ()
main = do
  result <- try (throwIO (MyException "Something went wrong")) :: IO (Either
        MyException ())
  case result of
    Left ex -> putStrLn $ "Caught MyException: " ++ show ex
    Right _ -> return ()
```

Best Practices

Apply these best practices to ensure effective exception handling in Haskell:

- **Specificity**: Catch specific exceptions where possible to avoid inadvertently catching unrelated errors.
- **Resources**: Always release resources using finally or bracket to prevent resource leaks.
- **Logging**: Log exceptions to facilitate debugging and monitoring.
- **User-friendly Messages**: Provide informative error messages to improve user experience or debugging.

Developing an understanding of exception handling patterns in Haskell enhances the reliability and maintainability of your code, particularly in the context of I/O operations where errors are common. Every I/O action should be carefully managed to handle potential failures gracefully, ensuring the robustness of Haskell applications.

8.8 Interacting with the System

Interacting with the system is a crucial aspect of advanced I/O operations in Haskell. This section covers system interaction through environment variables, executing external commands, and managing processes. Understanding these concepts enables developers to build more dynamic and flexible applications that can respond to and control the environment they run in.

Environment variables store configuration settings and system information that programs can access and modify. In Haskell, the System.Environment module provides functions to handle environment variables.

import System.Environment

To retrieve the value of an environment variable, use the getEnv function. This function requires you to pass the variable name as an argument and returns the value wrapped in the IO monad.

getEnv :: String -> IO String

For example, to retrieve the value of the HOME environment variable:

```
main :: IO ()
main = do
    homeDir <- getEnv "HOME"
    putStrLn $ "Your home directory is: " ++ homeDir
```

To list all environment variables available in the current session, use the getEnvironment function:

getEnvironment :: IO [(String, String)]

The function returns a list of key-value pairs representing the environment variables and their values.

```
main :: IO ()
main = do
    envVars <- getEnvironment
    mapM_ (putStrLn . show) envVars
```

You can also set or modify environment variables using the setEnv function:

setEnv :: String -> String -> IO ()

The first argument specifies the variable name, and the second argument specifies its new value. If the environment variable does not already exist, setEnv will create it.

```
main :: IO ()
main = do
    setEnv "MY_VAR" "Haskell"
    varValue <- getEnv "MY_VAR"
    putStrLn $ "MY_VAR is set to: " ++ varValue
```

The System.Process module offers another level of system interaction by allowing Haskell programs to execute external system commands and manage system processes. This module provides functions such as callCommand, createProcess, and readProcess.

To execute a shell command and discard its output, use callCommand:

callCommand :: String -> IO ()

```
main :: IO ()
main = do
    callCommand "echo 'Hello from Haskell!'"
```

For more complex process management, createProcess provides detailed control over how the process is executed:

createProcess :: CreateProcess -> IO (Maybe Handle, Maybe Handle, Maybe Hand

CreateProcess is a data structure that allows you to specify various options such as the command to run, arguments, environment variables, and standard input/output streams. Here is how you can use createProcess:

```
import System.Process
import System.IO

main :: IO ()
main = do
    (_, Just hout, _, _) <- createProcess (proc "ls" ["-l"]) { std_out = CreatePipe }
    output <- hGetContents hout
    putStrLn $ "Process output: " ++ output
```

readProcess is suitable for running an external command and capturing its output as a string:

readProcess :: FilePath -> [String] -> String -> IO String

```
main :: IO ()
main = do
    result <- readProcess "date" [] ""
    putStrLn $ "Current date and time: " ++ result
```

Managing processes involves not only executing commands but also handling process termination and signal management. The terminateProcess function sends a termination signal to a running process:

terminateProcess :: ProcessHandle -> IO ()

This function is useful when you need to safely stop a running process.

```
main :: IO ()
main = do
    (_, _, _, ph) <- createProcess (proc "sleep" ["10"])
    putStrLn "Sleeping for 10 seconds..."
    threadDelay 2000000
    terminateProcess ph
    putStrLn "Process terminated after 2 seconds."
```

To wait for a process to complete and obtain its exit code, use the waitForProcess function:

$$\text{waitForProcess :: ProcessHandle -> IO ExitCode}$$

```
main :: IO ()
main = do
    (_, _, _, ph) <- createProcess (proc "sleep" ["2"])
    putStrLn "Waiting for process to complete..."
    exitCode <- waitForProcess ph
    putStrLn $ "Process exited with code: " ++ show exitCode
```

System interaction capabilities enhance the robustness and flexibility of Haskell applications, allowing them to adapt dynamically to their operating environment and extend their functionality through external processes and commands. By mastering these techniques, developers can create more powerful and adaptable programs that integrate seamlessly with their system environment.

8.9 Advanced I/O Concepts

Advanced I/O operations in Haskell build upon fundamental concepts to handle more complex requirements, such as concurrent I/O, event-driven programming, and sophisticated resource management. This section focuses on these advanced techniques, offering a comprehensive exploration to equip you with the proficiency needed for handling real-world challenges.

Concurrent I/O

Haskell supports concurrent I/O operations, which allow multiple I/O actions to progress independently. The Control.Concurrent module provides the necessary tools, such as forkIO and MVar, to facilitate this. Here's an example of how to perform concurrent I/O using forkIO:

```
import Control.Concurrent
import Control.Monad (replicateM_)
```

```
main :: IO ()
main = do
  tid1 <- forkIO $ replicateM_ 5 $ putStrLn "Thread 1"
  tid2 <- forkIO $ replicateM_ 5 $ putStrLn "Thread 2"
  putStrLn "Main thread waiting"
  threadDelay 1000000
```

In this example, forkIO creates two threads that run concurrently, each executing a given I/O action. The threadDelay function holds the main thread, allowing the concurrent threads to print their messages.

Event-Driven I/O

Event-driven programming is another advanced I/O concept, where I/O operations are driven by events such as user input or network messages. The Control.Concurrent.Chan module provides a way to handle events using channels. Here's how to set up an event-driven I/O system using channels:

```
import Control.Concurrent
import Control.Concurrent.Chan

main :: IO ()
main = do
  eventChan <- newChan
  forkIO $ eventProducer eventChan
  eventConsumer eventChan

eventProducer :: Chan String -> IO ()
eventProducer chan = do
  writeChan chan "Event 1"
  threadDelay 500000
  writeChan chan "Event 2"

eventConsumer :: Chan String -> IO ()
eventConsumer chan = forever $ do
  event <- readChan chan
  putStrLn $ "Received: " ++ event
```

In this example, eventProducer generates events and writes them to the channel, while eventConsumer reads events from the channel and processes them. The forever function keeps the consumer running indefinitely.

Resource Management with Bracket

Proper resource management is crucial in advanced I/O operations to ensure resources are acquired and released correctly. The bracket function from the Control.Exception module helps manage resources safely. Here's an example of using bracket for resource management:

```
import Control.Exception (bracket)
import System.IO
```

```
main :: IO ()
main = bracket
  (openFile "example.txt" ReadMode)
  (hClose)
  (\handle -> do
      contents <- hGetContents handle
      putStrLn contents)
```

In this example, bracket ensures that the file handle is closed properly after the action, even if an exception occurs. The bracket function takes three arguments: a resource acquisition function, a release function, and an action to perform with the resource.

Asynchronous I/O

Asynchronous I/O operations allow you to overlap computation with I/O, improving efficiency. The async library provides the async function, which allows you to perform I/O operations asynchronously. Here's how to use it:

```
import Control.Concurrent.Async

main :: IO ()
main = do
  a <- async $ do
    threadDelay 1000000
    putStrLn "Finished work in async"
  putStrLn "Waiting for async to complete"
  wait a
```

In this example, async runs the given I/O operation concurrently, and wait waits for the asynchronous action to complete. This allows the main program to continue executing without blocking on the I/O operation.

Interfacing with Foreign Functions

When advanced I/O operations require interaction with external libraries or system calls, you can employ the Foreign Function Interface (FFI) in Haskell. The Foreign module provides mechanisms to call C functions from Haskell. Here's an example of calling a simple C function from Haskell:

```
-- C code saved in example.c
#include <stdio.h>

void printMessage() {
  printf("Hello from C\n");
}

-- Haskell code
{-# LANGUAGE ForeignFunctionInterface #-}

import Foreign.C
```

```
foreign import ccall "printMessage" c_printMessage :: IO ()

main :: IO ()
main = c_printMessage
```

In this two-part example, the first part is a C function defined in example.c, and the second part is the Haskell code that calls this C function. Using the foreign import ccall keyword, we declare the Haskell binding to the C function.

Efficient I/O with conduit

For scenarios involving the streaming of large amounts of data, the conduit library provides an efficient abstraction. Here's a simple example of how to use conduit for streaming I/O:

```
import Data.Conduit
import qualified Data.Conduit.Combinators as C
import System.IO

main :: IO ()
main = runConduitRes $
  C.sourceFile "input.txt" .|
  C.mapM_C (liftIO . putStrLn . ("Line: " ++))
```

In this example, sourceFile creates a source that reads data from a file, and mapM_C applies a given action to each line read from the file. The liftIO function is used to lift the putStrLn action into the conduit pipeline.

These advanced I/O techniques expand the range of possibilities for handling complex tasks in Haskell, providing the tools necessary for effective and efficient resource management, concurrency, and integration with external systems.

8.10 Practical I/O Examples

In the preceding sections, we have explored various aspects of input and output operations in Haskell, including basic I/O, user input, file handling, and advanced I/O concepts. This section aims to provide comprehensive examples that illustrate the practical application of these concepts.

To start, let's consider a simple example of reading user input, performing a computation, and displaying the result.

```
main :: IO ()
```

```
main = do
    putStrLn "Enter the first number:"
    firstNumInput <- getLine
    putStrLn "Enter the second number:"
    secondNumInput <- getLine
    let firstNum = read firstNumInput :: Int
    let secondNum = read secondNumInput :: Int
    let sumResult = firstNum + secondNum
    putStrLn ("The sum is: " ++ show sumResult)
```

In this example, getLine is used to capture user input from the terminal. The inputs are read as Strings and converted to Ints using the read function. The sum of the numbers is calculated and displayed to the user with putStrLn.

Next, we will explore a more complex example involving file operations. The following Haskell program reads from a file called input.txt, processes the content, and writes the output to a file called output.txt.

```
import System.IO

main :: IO ()
main = do
    handle <- openFile "input.txt" ReadMode
    contents <- hGetContents handle
    let fileLines = lines contents
    let processedLines = map processLine fileLines
    writeFile "output.txt" (unlines processedLines)
    hClose handle

processLine :: String -> String
processLine = reverse
```

In this program, the openFile function opens input.txt in read mode, and hGetContents reads the entire content of the file as a String. The content is split into lines using the lines function. Each line is then processed by the processLine function, which simply reverses the characters in the line. The processed lines are combined back into a single String using unlines, and the result is written to output.txt using writeFile. Finally, the file handle is closed with hClose.

Handling binary data is essential when dealing with non-text files such as images or executables. Here's a practical example demonstrating how to read and write binary data in Haskell:

```
import qualified Data.ByteString as BS

main :: IO ()
main = do
    -- Read binary data from file
    binaryData <- BS.readFile "binaryInput.dat"

    -- Process the binary data
    let processedData = processBinaryData binaryData
```

```
    -- Write binary data to file
    BS.writeFile "binaryOutput.dat" processedData

processBinaryData :: BS.ByteString -> BS.ByteString
processBinaryData = BS.map (\byte -> byte + 1)
```

In this example, the Data.ByteString module is used to read and write binary data. The BS.readFile function reads the entire content of binaryInput.dat as a ByteString, and BS.writeFile writes the processed ByteString to binaryOutput.dat. The processBinaryData function demonstrates a simple processing task by incrementing each byte in the ByteString.

Exception handling is crucial for robust I/O operations. The following example showcases how to handle exceptions that may occur during file operations:

```
import System.IO
import Control.Exception

main :: IO ()
main = do
    result <- try (readFile "nonExistentFile.txt") :: IO (Either IOException String)
    case result of
        Left ex -> putStrLn $ "Caught exception: " ++ show ex
        Right contents -> putStrLn contents
```

Here, the try function is used to catch any IOException that occurs when attempting to read a non-existent file. The result is an Either type, where Left represents an exception, and Right holds the file contents if the operation is successful. The program appropriately handles both cases by either displaying an error message or the file contents.

Interactive programs often require interacting with the system. The following example demonstrates how to run a system command and capture its output:

```
import System.Process

main :: IO ()
main = do
    (exitCode, stdout, stderr) <- readProcessWithExitCode "ls" ["-l", "/"] ""
    putStrLn "Standard Output:"
    putStrLn stdout
    putStrLn "Standard Error:"
    putStrLn stderr
    putStrLn ("Exit Code: " ++ show exitCode)
```

The readProcessWithExitCode function runs the ls -l / command, capturing both its standard output and error streams, along with the exit code. The program prints these outputs to the terminal, providing useful information about the command execution result.

This set of examples demonstrates practical input and output operations in Haskell, encapsulating user interaction, file processing, binary data handling, exception management, and system interaction. Incorporating these techniques equips developers with the necessary tools to handle real-world I/O requirements effectively.

Chapter 9

Monads and Functors

This chapter explains the concepts of functors, applicative functors, and monads in Haskell, including their laws and usage. It discusses common monads, using monads for I/O operations, and explores monad transformers. The chapter also covers functional programming with monads and monadic composition.

9.1 Introduction to Functors

The *functor* is a core concept in Haskell that provides a way to apply a function to values wrapped in a context, such as a list or Maybe type. In Haskell, functors are categorized as types that can be mapped over. The Functor typeclass is defined in the Prelude as follows:

```
class Functor f where
    fmap :: (a -> b) -> f a -> f b
```

The Functor typeclass consists of a single fundamental method, fmap, which applies a function (a -> b) to a value of type f a to obtain a value of type f b. This capability is significant because it allows generalization over the operation of mapping functions across various data structures.

The syntax of fmap can be broken down as follows:

- (a -> b): a function that takes a value of type a and returns a value of type b.
- f a: a functor containing values of type a.

- f b: the result of applying the function to the functor, which contains values of type b.

To understand the essence of functors, consider a common example involving the Maybe type. The Maybe type is defined as:

```
data Maybe a = Nothing | Just a
```

The Maybe type can be made an instance of the Functor typeclass:

```
instance Functor Maybe where
    fmap _ Nothing = Nothing
    fmap f (Just x) = Just (f x)
```

In this instance, fmap applies the function f to the contents of Just x, leaving Nothing unaffected. For example:

```
fmap (+ 1) (Just 2)
```

This expression evaluates to Just 3. If we apply fmap to Nothing:

```
fmap (+ 1) Nothing
```

This expression evaluates to Nothing, maintaining the structure of the functor without altering its underlying value.

Similarly, lists in Haskell are also functors. The instance of Functor for lists is defined as:

```
instance Functor [] where
    fmap = map
```

The fmap function for lists leverages the map function, thus applying a given function across all elements in a list. For example:

```
fmap (* 2) [1, 2, 3]
```

This expression evaluates to $[2, 4, 6]$. The application of fmap is not limited to simple data structures; it extends to more complex constructs such as trees, sequences, and even user-defined types.

To better harness the power of functors, one needs to understand how the Functor laws ensure consistent and predictable behavior. The two fundamental laws of functors are:

- Identity Law: fmap id = id
- Composition Law: fmap (f . g) = fmap f . fmap g

The Identity Law states that mapping the identity function, id, over a functor should produce the same functor without any alteration. This can be illustrated with lists:

```
fmap id [1, 2, 3]
```

This returns $[1, 2, 3]$, complying with the identity law. The Composition Law ensures that mapping the composition of two functions $(f \,.\, g)$ over a functor is the same as mapping g over the functor and then mapping f over the result. This can be demonstrated:

```
fmap (negate . (* 2)) [1, 2, 3]
```

Which is equivalent to:

```
fmap negate (fmap (* 2) [1, 2, 3])
```

Both expressions result in $[-2, -4, -6]$, adhering to the composition law.

Understanding the fmap function and the properties of functors facilitates a deeper comprehension of functional programming's capabilities in Haskell. Functors provide a basis for more advanced abstractions like applicative functors and monads, which are explored in subsequent sections of this book. By adhering to the functor laws, developers can ensure their abstract data types behave reliably and predictably when mapped over with functions.

9.2 Functor Laws

In Haskell, functors are a type class that defines a mapping over or transformation of a structure without altering the structure itself. Formally, a functor is an instance of the Functor type class which requires the implementation of the fmap function. Functor laws are a set of rules that every functor implementation must obey to ensure consistent behavior.

The Functor type class is defined as follows:

```
class Functor f where
    fmap :: (a -> b) -> f a -> f b
```

fmap applies a function to each element inside the functor. For a type f to be a valid instance of the Functor type class, it must obey two fundamental laws: the identity law and the composition law. These laws ensure that the functor behaves predictively and sensibly.

Identity Law

The identity law states that if you map the identity function id over a functor, the functor that you get back should be the same as the original functor. Formally, for a functor f, this law can be expressed as:

$$\text{fmap id} = \text{id}$$

Let's break down this law to understand what it implies. The identity function, id, is defined as:

```
id :: a -> a
id x = x
```

This function simply returns its argument. Applying the identity law to a functor means that:

fmap id <functor> = <functor>

For example, consider the list functor. According to the identity law:

```
fmap id [1, 2, 3] = [1, 2, 3]
```

Showcasing that mapping the identity function over a list returns the original list.

Composition Law

The composition law states that composing two functions and then mapping the resulting function over a functor should be the same as first mapping one function over the functor and then mapping the second function over the result. Formally, for a functor f, this law can be written as:

$$\text{fmap (f . g)} = \text{fmap f . fmap g}$$

Where . denotes function composition. This law ensures that the order of applying functions is preserved whether we map a composed function or map each function in sequence.

In Haskell, function composition is defined by:

```
(.) :: (b -> c) -> (a -> b) -> (a -> c)
f . g = \x -> f (g x)
```

Let's illustrate this with a concrete example using lists again. Suppose we have two functions, f and g, such that:

```
f :: Int -> Int
f x = x + 1

g :: Int -> Int
g x = x * 2
```

According to the composition law, the following should hold:

```
fmap (f . g) [1, 2, 3] == fmap f (fmap g [1, 2, 3])
```

Evaluating both sides:

```
fmap (f . g) [1, 2, 3]
= fmap (\x -> f (g x)) [1, 2, 3]
= fmap (\x -> (x + 1) ((x * 2)) [1, 2, 3]
= fmap (\x -> x * 2 + 1) [1, 2, 3]
= [3, 5, 7]

fmap f (fmap g [1, 2, 3])
= fmap f [2, 4, 6]
= fmap (\x -> x + 1) [2, 4, 6]
= [3, 5, 7]
```

Thus, fmap (f . g) [1, 2, 3] equals fmap f (fmap g [1, 2, 3] confirming that both sides produce the list [3, 5, 7].

Adherence to these functor laws is critical for maintaining the integrity of operations involving functors, ensuring that functions can be reliably composed and applied within the context of the functor structure.

9.3 Introduction to Applicative Functors

In Haskell, an *applicative functor* extends the idea of a functor by enabling the application of functions encapsulated within a context (or computational context) to values that are similarly encapsulated. Applicative functors provide intermediate abstraction between functors and monads, offering greater expressivity than functors while being simpler than monads.

The primary type class for applicative functors is defined as Applicative, found in the Control.Applicative module. The Applicative class is defined as follows:

```
class Functor f => Applicative f where
    pure :: a -> f a
    (<*>) :: f (a -> b) -> f a -> f b
```

pure is a function that takes a value and embeds it into the applicative functor context. Essentially, it places the value inside a minimal default context. The (<*>), often pronounced "ap", is the application operator which takes a functor containing a function and another functor, and applies the function to the value inside the second functor.

To illustrate, consider the following example where we use a list as an applicative functor:

```
instance Applicative [] where
    pure x = [x]
    fs <*> xs = [f x | f <- fs, x <- xs]
```

Here, pure x returns a singleton list containing x. The application operator (<*>) uses list comprehension to apply each function in the list of functions fs to each value in the list xs, resulting in a list of the outcomes.

When dealing with applicative functors, several laws must be upheld to maintain consistency and reliability of operations. These laws are:

- **Identity:** Applying the pure id to an applicative functor should produce the same functor:

```
pure id <*> v = v
```

- **Composition:** The composition of functions within the applicative functor context should equals to the application of their composed outside:

```
pure (.) <*> u <*> v <*> w = u <*> (v <*> w)
```

- **Homomorphism:** Applying a pure function to a pure value using the application operator should behave the same as applying the function to the value directly and then embedding the result in the applicative functor:

```
pure f <*> pure x = pure (f x)
```

- **Interchange:** Applying a functor that encapsulates a function to a pure value should behave the same as applying the function to the value:

```
u <*> pure y = pure ($ y) <*> u
```

With these laws, applicative functors maintain the structure and provide predictable interactions, ensuring reliable compositionality.

In practice, applicative functors allow us to manage multiple independent effects and combine them neatly. Consider the following example which demonstrates the application of a binary function within the context of the Maybe applicative functor:

```
instance Applicative Maybe where
    pure = Just
    Nothing <*> _ = Nothing
    (Just f) <*> something = fmap f something

add :: Maybe Int -> Maybe Int -> Maybe Int
add x y = pure (+) <*> x <*> y

-- Example usage
add (Just 3) (Just 5) -- Just 8
add (Just 3) Nothing -- Nothing
```

In this example, pure is used to lift the addition operation into the Maybe context. The application operator $(<*>)$ then applies the lifted addition operation to the values inside the Maybe context. If either operand is Nothing, the result is Nothing, effectively short-circuiting the computation.

Through these mechanisms, applicative functors provide a robust framework for manipulating and combining values in computational contexts, extending the power and utility of functors in functional programming.

9.4 Applicative Functor Laws

Applicative functors in Haskell extend the functionality of functors by allowing for functions embedded within a context (such as a computational context, list, or any other container) to be applied to values within another context. To ensure the correctness and consistency of their behavior, applicative functors abide by four essential laws:

- Identity
- Composition
- Homomorphism
- Interchange

Each of these laws provides a fundamental property that applicative functors must satisfy. We shall now explore these laws in detail.

Identity Law: This law states that applying the pure identity function to a value should yield the same result as applying the identity function directly to the value within an applicative context. Formally, this is expressed as:

$$\text{pure id} <*> \text{v} = \text{v}$$

Here, the pure function lifts the identity function id into an applicative context, and <*> is the applicative function application operator. For example, consider the following implementation in Haskell:

```
pure id <*> Just 5
```

The output will be:

```
Just 5
```

Composition Law: The composition law enforces the composition of functions within the applicative context to resemble ordinary function composition when applied to values. This law is expressed as:

$$\text{pure (.)} <*> \text{u} <*> \text{v} <*> \text{w} = \text{u} <*> (\text{v} <*> \text{w})$$

This law involves three applicative functors u, v, and w, and the function composition operator (.). The operator <*> enables the application of contexts. To see this in practice, consider:

```
f = pure (.) <*> Just (+2) <*> Just (*3) <*> Just 5
```

The output will be:

```
Just ((+2) . (*3)) 5
Just 17
```

Homomorphism Law: This law ensures that applying a function to a value using the applicative context is equivalent to applying the function directly to the value and then lifting it into the applicative context. This can be expressed as:

$$\text{pure f} <*> \text{pure x} = \text{pure (f x)}$$

Here, both the function f and value x are lifted into the applicative context with pure. For instance:

```
pure (+2) <*> pure 3
```

This will produce:

```
pure (3 + 2)
Just 5
```

Interchange Law: The interchange law states that applying a function within a context to a value within a context is the same as first applying the function to the value outside of any context and then lifting the result back into the context. This law is formulated as:

$$u <*> pure\ y = pure\ (f \text{ -> } f\ y) <*> u$$

Where u is an applicative functor containing a function, and y is a pure value. Consider:

```
Just (+2) <*> pure 5
```

This adheres to the interchange law and provides:

```
pure (\f -> f 5) <*> Just (+2)
Just 7
```

Verification of these laws ensures that our implementations of applicative functors behave predictably and consistently, providing a robustness fundamental to functional programming principles in Haskell. Here, we have systematically demonstrated how each of these laws operates within Haskell, reflecting their critical importance in the context of applicative functors.

9.5 Introduction to Monads

Monads are a fundamental concept in Haskell that provide a framework for managing side effects, encapsulating computation contexts, and defining sequences of operations. Understanding monads is crucial for leveraging Haskell's powerful and expressive capabilities to manage state, handle errors, and perform I/O operations in a purely functional manner.

A monad is defined by the Monad type class, which consists of three essential components: the return function, the »= (bind) operator, and the » (then) operator. The Monad type class is declared as follows:

```
class Applicative m => Monad (m :: * -> *) where
    (>>=) :: m a -> (a -> m b) -> m b
    (>>) :: m a -> m b -> m b
    return :: a -> m a
    fail :: String -> m a
    fail s = error s
```

The Monad class requires that any monad must also be an instance of the Applicative class. This is because all monads are applicative functors, but not all applicative functors are monads. The primary functions and their roles include:

- return: Embeds a value into the monadic context. It is sometimes referred to as the pure function in the Applicative type class.
- »= (bind): Chains two monadic operations by taking a value from within a monad, applying a function that returns another monad, and flattening the result into a single monad.
- »: Sequences two monadic actions where the result of the first action is discarded.
- fail: Provides a way to handle failure within the context of a monad, although its usage is discouraged in favor of more explicit error handling mechanisms.

To illustrate the concept of monads, consider the Maybe monad, which encapsulates computations that might fail. The Maybe monad is defined as:

```
instance Monad Maybe where
    return = Just
    Nothing >>= _ = Nothing
    Just x >>= f = f x
    fail _ = Nothing
```

In the Maybe monad:

- return wraps a value in the Just constructor.
- »= applies a function to the value inside Just, propagating Nothing if present.

Here's an example of using the Maybe monad to chain computations that might fail:

```
safeDiv :: Int -> Int -> Maybe Int
safeDiv _ 0 = Nothing
safeDiv x y = Just (x `div` y)

-- Chain safe divisions
result :: Maybe Int
result =
    return 20 >>= \a ->
    return 4 >>= \b ->
    safeDiv a b >>= \c ->
    safeDiv c 2
```

The result will be Just 2 if all divisions are successful, and Nothing if any division by zero occurs.

Monads also provide syntactic sugar via do notation, which makes chained operations more comprehensible and manageable. The previous example can be rewritten using do notation as follows:

```
result :: Maybe Int
result = do
    a <- return 20
    b <- return 4
    c <- safeDiv a b
    safeDiv c 2
```

The do notation simplifies the chaining process and enhances code readability, providing a sequential style of writing monadic operations while retaining the purely functional nature of Haskell.

Consider another common monad, the IO monad, which manages input and output operations. The IO monad encapsulates side effects, ensuring that I/O actions are safely integrated into Haskell's functional paradigm. An example of using the IO monad to read from the console and print a message is as follows:

```
main :: IO ()
main = do
    putStrLn "Enter a number:"
    input <- getLine
    let number = read input :: Int
    putStrLn ("You entered: " ++ show number)
```

In this example, the do notation sequences the I/O actions, ensuring the proper order of execution while keeping the code clear and concise. The putStrLn function outputs a string to the console, while getLine reads a line of input from the user. The read function converts the input string to an integer, and show converts the integer back to a string for display.

Understanding monads and their role in Haskell enables programmers to structure complex computations in a modular and reusable manner. With monads, side effects and context-dependent operations become manageable, enhancing both code maintainability and clarity.

9.6 Monad Laws

Monads in Haskell are defined by three primary operations: return, »= (bind), and ». These operations must adhere to certain laws to ensure consistent behavior. These laws, known as the Monad Laws, guarantee that monads behave predictably when used within functional programming.

The three fundamental monad laws are:

- **Left identity**
- **Right identity**
- **Associativity**

Left Identity

The left identity law states that if you take a value, put it in a default context with return, and then apply a function to it using »=, it is identical to just applying the function to the value. Formally, this can be expressed as:

$$\text{return a} \gg= \text{f} \equiv \text{f a}$$

This law can be illustrated in Haskell as follows:

```
return a >>= f == f a
```

For example, for the Maybe monad:

```
return 3 >>= (\x -> Just (x + 1)) -- This should be identical to the result of (\x ->
     Just (x + 1)) 3
Just 3 >>= (\x -> Just (x + 1)) -- This results in Just 4
```

```
Just 4
```

Thus, return 3 »= (\x -> Just (x + 1)) produces Just 4, just as (\x -> Just (x + 1)) 3 does.

Right Identity

The right identity law states that if you have a monadic value and you use »= to feed it to return, the result is the original monadic value. Formally, this is written as:

$$\text{m} \gg= \text{return} \equiv \text{m}$$

In Haskell, it can be illustrated with the following expression:

```
m >>= return == m
```

For example, using the List monad:

```
[1, 2, 3] >>= return -- This should return [1, 2, 3]
```

```
[1, 2, 3]
```

Thus, $[1, 2, 3] \gg= \text{return}$ still results in $[1, 2, 3]$, satisfying the right identity law.

Associativity

The associativity law states that when you have a chain of monadic operations, the order in which you perform the operations should not matter. Formally, this law can be expressed as:

$$(\text{m} \gg= \text{f}) \gg= \text{g} \equiv \text{m} \gg= (\backslash\text{x -> f x} \gg= \text{g})$$

In Haskell, this means that:

```
(m >>= f) >>= g == m >>= (\x -> f x >>= g)
```

For a concrete example, consider the List monad:

```
[1, 2] >>= (\x -> [x, x+1]) >>= (\y -> [y, y*2])
-- This should be equivalent to:
[1, 2] >>= (\x -> (\y -> [y, y*2]) =<< [x, x+1])
```

Let's compute both sides:

```
-- Left-hand side:
[1, 2] >>= (\x -> [x, x+1]) >>= (\y -> [y, y*2])
[1, 2, 2, 3] >>= (\y -> [y, y*2])
[1, 2, 2, 3, 2, 4, 3, 6]

-- Right-hand side:
[1, 2] >>= (\x -> (\y -> [y, y*2]) =<< [x, x+1])
[1, 2] >>= (\x -> (\y -> [y, y*2]) x + 1)
```

```
[1, 2] >>= (\y -> [y, y*2])
[1, 2, 2, 3, 2, 4, 3, 6]
```

The results from both methods are:

```
[1, 2, 2, 3, 2, 4, 3, 6]
```

These elements exemplify the associative property in practice.

Observing the Monad laws is crucial because they guarantee that monads can be composed and manipulated predictably. This predictability is fundamental to reliable and understandable functional programming.

9.7 Common Monads in Haskell

In Haskell, monads provide a powerful way to handle computations along with side effects in a purely functional manner. Understanding common monads and their usage is crucial for mastering functional programming in Haskell. This section provides an in-depth examination of several widely used monads: the Maybe monad, the Either monad, the List monad, the IO monad, and the State monad.

The Maybe Monad

The Maybe monad is used to represent computations that might fail. It is particularly useful for dealing with optional values. The Maybe type is defined as:

```
data Maybe a = Nothing | Just a
```

Here is how Maybe is made into a monad:

```
instance Monad Maybe where
    return = Just
    Nothing >>= _ = Nothing
    Just x >>= f = f x
```

The return function wraps a value into a Just. The bind operation (»=) applies a function to a Just value, and propagates a Nothing without applying the function.

Example usage of Maybe monad:

```
safeDivide :: Double -> Double -> Maybe Double
safeDivide _ 0 = Nothing
safeDivide x y = Just (x / y)
```

```
result :: Maybe Double
result = safeDivide 10 2 >>= \x -> safeDivide x 5
```

result will be Just 1.0, demonstrating how Maybe captures the possibility of failure.

The Either Monad

The Either monad is useful for computations that can return a value or an error. It is defined as:

```
data Either a b = Left a | Right b
```

To make Either e a monad:

```
instance Monad (Either e) where
    return = Right
    Left l >>= _ = Left l
    Right r >>= f = f r
```

In this monad, Left is used for error values and Right for successful computations.

Example:

```
safeDivide :: Double -> Double -> Either String Double
safeDivide _ 0 = Left "Division by zero"
safeDivide x y = Right (x / y)

result :: Either String Double
result = safeDivide 10 2 >>= \x -> safeDivide x 5
```

result will be Right 1.0, while a division by zero would yield Left "Division by zero".

The List Monad

The List monad encapsulates nondeterministic computations, where a computation can result in multiple values. The List type is defined as:

```
instance Monad [] where
    return x = [x]
    xs >>= f = concat (map f xs)
```

In this instance, return creates a single-element list, and »= (bind) applies a function to each element of the list, concatenating the results.

Example:

```
pairs :: [a] -> [b] -> [(a, b)]
pairs xs ys = xs >>= \x -> ys >>= \y -> return (x, y)
```

For pairs [1,2] ["a","b"], the result will be [(1,"a"), (1,"b"), (2,"a"), (2,"b")].

The IO Monad

The IO monad allows Haskell programs to perform input and output operations while maintaining purity in the functional paradigm. It is defined as:

```
newtype IO a = ...
```

Haskell's IO monad wraps side-effecting operations, ensuring that side effects are explicitly managed. Binding operations in IO are seamless due to syntactic sugar provided by Haskell, usually seen through the do notation.

Example:

```
main :: IO ()
main = do
    putStrLn "Enter a number: "
    input <- getLine
    let number = read input :: Int
    putStrLn ("You entered: " ++ show number)
```

Running main will ask the user to input a number and display the entered value.

The State Monad

The State monad encapsulates stateful computations. It allows functions to access and modify a shared state. The state monad is defined as:

```
newtype State s a = State { runState :: s -> (a, s) }

instance Monad (State s) where
    return a = State $ \s -> (a, s)
    (State h) >>= f = State $ \s ->
        let (a, newState) = h(s)
            (State g) = f(a)
        in g(newState)
```

The state monad allows chaining stateful computations easily.

Example:

```
type Stack = [Int]

pop :: State Stack Int
pop = State $ \(x:xs) -> (x, xs)

push :: Int -> State Stack ()
push a = State $ \xs -> ((), a:xs)
```

```
stackManip :: State Stack Int
stackManip = do
    push 3
    pop
    pop

result = runState stackManip [5, 8, 2]
```

Here, result will be (8, [2]), demonstrating stack manipulation using the State monad.

Understanding and utilizing these common monads effectively enhances one's ability to write robust, expressive, and maintainable Haskell code. By leveraging the power of these monads, complex patterns of computation can be expressed succinctly and clearly.

9.8 Using Monads for I/O

In Haskell, input/output (I/O) operations are handled using the IO monad, which encapsulates side effects and maintains purity within the functional programming paradigm. The IO monad is a concrete example of how monads can be used to sequence computations involving side effects, such as reading from or writing to the terminal or files. This section provides a detailed examination of the IO monad, its usage, and associated functions.

Basic I/O Operations

The foundation of I/O operations in Haskell lies in actions that denote computations to be performed by the runtime. These actions are represented by values of type IO a, where a is the type of the result produced by the action. The core functions for performing basic I/O operations include putStr, putStrLn, getLine, and print.

```
main :: IO ()
main = do
    putStrLn "Enter your name:"
    name <- getLine
    putStrLn ("Hello, " ++ name ++ "!")
```

In this example, the main function, which is of type IO (), performs a sequence of actions: it first prints a prompt using putStrLn, then reads a line of input from the user using getLine, and finally prints a greeting.

putStr and putStrLn functions are defined as follows:

```
putStr :: String -> IO ()
putStr = ...
```

```
putStrLn :: String -> IO ()
putStrLn s = putStr (s ++ "\n")
```

Function putStrLn adds a newline character to the string before printing, which differentiates it from putStr.

getLine is used to read a line of input from the standard input:

```
getLine :: IO String
getLine = ...
```

The print function converts a value to a string using the Show typeclass and then prints it:

```
print :: Show a => a -> IO ()
print x = putStrLn (show x)
```

Sequencing and Monadic Bind

The sequencing of I/O operations is accomplished using the » and »= operators. The » operator sequences actions, discarding any intermediate results:

```
(>>) :: IO a -> IO b -> IO b
a >> b = a >>= \_ -> b
```

The »= operator (monadic bind) is crucial for chaining actions and passing results:

```
(>>=) :: IO a -> (a -> IO b) -> IO b
```

Using »=, we can rewrite the main function as:

```
main :: IO ()
main = putStrLn "Enter your name:" >> getLine >>= \name -> putStrLn ("Hello, "
    ++ name ++ "!")
```

Reading and Writing to Files

Haskell provides functions for file I/O, which are encapsulated within the IO monad. The readFile function reads the contents of a file into a lazy String:

```
readFile :: FilePath -> IO String
```

The writeFile function writes a String to a file, overwriting the file if it exists:

```
writeFile :: FilePath -> String -> IO ()
```

The following example demonstrates reading and writing files:

```
main :: IO ()
main = do
    contents <- readFile "input.txt"
    writeFile "output.txt" (processData contents)

processData :: String -> String
processData = map toUpper
```

In this example, we read the contents of input.txt, process the data using processData, and write the result to output.txt.

Exception Handling in I/O

The IO monad supports exception handling through the Control.Exception module, which provides functions such as catch and try to manage exceptions arising from I/O actions.

Using catch to handle an exception:

```
import Control.Exception (catch, IOException)

main :: IO ()
main = do
    contents <- catch (readFile "input.txt") handler
    putStrLn contents

handler :: IOException -> IO String
handler ex = return ("Error: " ++ show ex)
```

The catch function takes an I/O action and an exception handler. If the action throws an IOException, the handler provides a fallback value.

Combining I/O with Other Monads

The IO monad can be combined with other monads using the liftM function from the Control.Monad module. This is particularly useful when working with computations in monad transformers.

Demonstration with the MaybeT monad transformer:

```
import Control.Monad.Trans.Maybe
import Control.Monad.IO.Class (liftIO)

main :: IO ()
main = do
    result <- runMaybeT $ do
        liftIO $ putStrLn "Enter a number:"
        input <- liftIO getLine
        let number = readMaybe input :: Maybe Int
        MaybeT $ return number
    case result of
        Nothing -> putStrLn "Invalid input"
        Just n -> putStrLn ("You entered: " ++ show n)
```

In this example, we use MaybeT to perform I/O while handling possible failure in parsing the input.

Understanding and effectively using monads for I/O operations in Haskell ensures that side effects are managed in a controlled and predictable manner. The use of monadic constructs allows for clear and concise sequencing of I/O actions, preserving the functional purity of Haskell programs.

9.9 Monad Transformers

Monad transformers provide a method to combine the functionalities of multiple monads into a single composite monad. This is particularly useful in Haskell, where functions often need to work within a particular monadic context. Monad transformers address the issue of monad stacking, allowing the programmer to use multiple monadic effects simultaneously while retaining the ability to compose these effects in a straightforward manner.

A monad transformer t for a monad m is itself a monad, often written as t m a, where a is the type parameter. A typical monad transformer will carry the structure and behavior of its respective monad while being parameterized by another underlying monad.

MonadTrans is a type class defined in the Control.Monad.Trans module, and is the primary interface for monad transformers. It provides the lift function, which is used to lift a computation from the base monad to the transformed monad.

```
class MonadTrans t where
    lift :: Monad m => m a -> t m a
```

To illustrate monad transformers, let us consider how they can be used with the Maybe monad, which provides a context for computations that might fail, and the IO monad, which deals with input and output operations.

The MaybeT transformer is used to combine these monadic effects. The following example demonstrates how to stack the Maybe monad over the IO monad:

```
import Control.Monad.Trans.Maybe
import Control.Monad.Trans.Class
import Control.Monad.IO.Class

getInput :: MaybeT IO String
```

```
getInput = liftIO getLine

processInput :: String -> MaybeT IO String
processInput input = if null input
                     then MaybeT (return Nothing)
                     else return ("Processed: " ++ input)

runMaybeTExample :: IO ()
runMaybeTExample = do
    result <- runMaybeT $ do
             input <- getInput
             processInput input
    case result of
        Nothing -> putStrLn "No input provided."
        Just output -> putStrLn output
```

The getInput function is lifted into the MaybeT IO monad using the liftIO function from the Control.Monad.IO.Class module. The processInput function processes the input string and uses the MaybeT constructor to handle potential Nothing values.

When it comes to implementing monad transformers, it is crucial to understand their laws and behavior. Monad transformers must obey the monad laws: left identity, right identity, and associativity.

- **Left Identity:** return a »= k should be equivalent to k a.
- **Right Identity:** m »= return should be equivalent to m.
- **Associativity:** (m »= k) »= h should be equivalent to m »= (\x -> k x »= h).

When working with transformer stacks, it is also possible to lift auxiliary functions through multiple layers of transformers. This is done using the lift . lift idiom. For example, if we need to lift a computation through two layers of monad transformers:

```
import Control.Monad.Trans.Reader
import Control.Monad.Trans.State

type Config = String

computation :: StateT Int (ReaderT Config IO) String
computation = do
    lift . lift $ putStrLn "Enter a number:"
    numStr <- lift . lift $ getLine
    let num = read numStr :: Int
    modify (+ num)
    state <- get
    return $ "New state: " ++ show state

runComputation :: Config -> IO ()
runComputation config = do
    let computation' = runReaderT (runStateT computation 0) config
```

```
    result <- computation'
    print result
```

In the computation function, StateT is layered over ReaderT, which is further layered over IO. The lift . lift syntax is used to lift putStrLn and getLine through both transformer layers to reach the base IO monad.

Lastly, when using monad transformers, the types of computations often need to be carefully managed, particularly with respect to the diverse type signatures and transformer stack. This requires familiarity with the lift, MonadTrans functions, and the utility of specific transformers such as MaybeT, StateT, ReaderT, and ExceptT.

Understanding monad transformers and their application facilitates complex functional programming patterns in Haskell, enabling developers to more effectively manage side effects and monadic contexts within their code.

9.10 Functional Programming with Monads

Understanding how to leverage monads in functional programming is crucial to mastering Haskell. Monads provide a powerful and elegant approach to handling side effects, chaining computations, managing state, error handling, and more, all within a purely functional paradigm. By structuring programs using monads, we can ensure code remains succinct, modular, and expressive.

To see how this works in practice, consider the Maybe Monad, which is used to represent computations that may fail. The Maybe type encapsulates an optional value. It can either contain a value of type a, represented as Just a, or it might be absent, represented as Nothing.

```
data Maybe a = Nothing | Just a
```

When working with Maybe, monads allow us to chain computations that may fail without having to explicitly handle each case. This is done using the >>= (bind) operator and the return function. The return function for Maybe simply lifts a value into the Maybe context:

```
instance Monad Maybe where
    return = Just

    Nothing >>= _ = Nothing
    Just x >>= f = f x
```

Here, Nothing »= _ = Nothing bypasses the subsequent computation because the computation is defined in context where it might have failed. The Just x »= f = f x pattern ensures that if the computation succeeds (i.e., Just x), the next function f can be applied to the extracted value x.

Consider the following illustrative example, which does a series of computations that may fail. This function chains multiple Maybe operations to safely compute the final result.

```
safeDivide :: Double -> Double -> Maybe Double
safeDivide _ 0 = Nothing
safeDivide x y = Just (x / y)

chainComputations :: Double -> Double -> Double -> Maybe Double
chainComputations a b c =
    safeDivide a b >>= \res1 ->
    safeDivide res1 c >>= \res2 ->
    return res2
```

In this example, the function chainComputations takes three numbers and performs two division operations. If any division results in a divide-by-zero error, the entire chain will gracefully fail and produce Nothing.

Another useful monad is the Either Monad, which is commonly used for computations that can result in an error. The Either type encapsulates a computation that might return a value of type a (Right a) or an error of type e (Left e).

```
data Either e a = Left e | Right a
```

The Either Monad leverages the same bind operator to propagate errors through a sequence of computations. Here's its instance declaration:

```
instance Monad (Either e) where
    return = Right

    Left e >>= _ = Left e
    Right x >>= f = f x
```

To illustrate, consider a scenario where we need to perform a sequence of operations that could fail, each potentially returning an error message.

```
validatePositive :: Double -> Either String Double
validatePositive x
    | x >= 0 = Right x
    | otherwise = Left "Negative number"

safeRoot :: Double -> Either String Double
safeRoot x
```

```
    | x >= 0 = Right (sqrt x)
    | otherwise = Left "Cannot take root of negative number"

processNumber :: Double -> Either String Double
processNumber x =
    validatePositive x >>= \validNum ->
    safeRoot validNum >>= \sqrtNum ->
    Right (sqrtNum * 2)
```

In this example, processNumber first validates that the input is positive. If it is not, it returns an appropriate error message wrapped in Left. If the input is valid, it proceeds to compute the square root safely. Finally, the result is doubled and returned in the Right context.

Monads also provide a standardized way to deal with stateful computations within the State Monad. The State Monad encapsulates computations that manipulate state. It provides state handling without explicitly passing state through functions.

Here is an implementation of the State Monad in Haskell:

```
newtype State s a = State { runState :: s -> (a, s) }

instance Monad (State s) where
    return x = State $ \s -> (x, s)

    (State h) >>= f = State $ \s ->
        let (a, newState) = h(s)
            (State g) = f a
        in g newState
```

An example use case is a simple stateful counter:

```
increment :: State Int Int
increment = State $ \s -> (s, s + 1)

doubleIncrement :: State Int Int
doubleIncrement = do
    increment
    increment

runCounter :: State Int Int -> Int -> (Int, Int)
runCounter st = runState st
```

In this example, increment is a stateful computation that returns the current state and increments it by one. doubleIncrement uses the do notation to sequentially increment the state twice. The utility function runCounter runs a stateful computation with an initial state and returns the final state along with the result.

The use of monads in functional programming extends beyond these examples. Monads help manage different computation contexts in a clean and composable way. Whether it is handling failure with

Maybe, errors with Either, or state with the State Monad, monads allow the combination of complex operations while preserving the functional paradigm's purity.

9.11 Monadic Composition

Monadic composition in Haskell is an integral concept that facilitates chaining together multiple monadic operations in a coherent and maintainable manner. In functional programming, monads provide a standardized way to handle side effects, sequence computations, and manage code complexity. Monadic composition allows developers to encapsulate and sequence these computations in a clean and declarative manner.

To illustrate monadic composition, consider the »= operator (often pronounced as "bind"), which is central to the Monad type class. This operator takes a monadic value and a function that maps a normal value to a monadic value, sequencing the operations by passing the result of the first computation as the input to the next. The »= operator is defined as:

```
(>>=) :: Monad m => m a -> (a -> m b) -> m b
```

To understand this better, let's explore its usage through a simple example involving the Maybe monad, which encapsulates an optional value.

Consider the following chained computation, where we have two functions, f and g, which both return a Maybe value:

```
f :: Int -> Maybe Int
f x = if x > 0 then Just (x + 1) else Nothing

g :: Int -> Maybe Int
g y = if y < 10 then Just (y * 2) else Nothing
```

We can compose these two functions using the »= operator to create a new function that combines their effects:

```
h :: Int -> Maybe Int
h z = f z >>= g
```

Here, h is a function that takes an integer z, applies f to it, and then applies g to the result if f z is Just a. If f z is Nothing, the entire computation yields Nothing.

We can also use the do notation, which is syntactic sugar to make monadic composition more readable and imperative in style. The same function h can be rewritten as:

```
h :: Int -> Maybe Int
h z = do
    a <- f z
    g a
```

The do block allows us to write sequential code that appears imperative but is purely functional under the hood. Each line within the do block represents a monadic action whose result can be used in subsequent actions.

Let's extend this concept to the IO monad, commonly used for input-output operations. Consider the following example involving reading from standard input and processing the input with monadic composition:

```
import System.IO

main :: IO ()
main = do
    putStrLn "Enter a number:"
    input <- getLine
    let number = read input :: Int
    result <- process number
    case result of
        Just value -> putStrLn ("Result: " ++ show value)
        Nothing -> putStrLn "Invalid input."

process :: Int -> IO (Maybe Int)
process n = return (f n >>= g)
```

Here, process takes an integer n, applies f and g using >>=, and returns the result wrapped in the IO monad. The function main demonstrates reading from the standard input, applying process, and printing the result.

Monadic composition is not limited to Maybe and IO monads. It can be applied to any monad, including custom monads or those provided by libraries. For example, the List monad can be used to represent nondeterministic computations, where each element in the list represents a possible result. Consider the following example using the List monad:

```
import Control.Monad (guard)

combinations :: [Int] -> [Int] -> [(Int, Int)]
combinations xs ys = do
    x <- xs
    y <- ys
    guard (x + y > 10)
    return (x, y)
```

In this example, combinations takes two lists of integers, xs and ys, and produces a list of pairs (x, y) such that the sum of x and y is greater than 10. The guard function is used to filter out pairs that do not satisfy this condition. The do notation makes it easy to express the list comprehensions involving filtering and mapping.

Furthermore, the monadic composition can be generalized using the MonadPlus type class, which extends Monad with additional operations for monads that also support the concept of a zero element and an associative binary operation. The mzero and mplus functions are defined as follows:

```
class Monad m => MonadPlus m where
    mzero :: m a
    mplus :: m a -> m a -> m a
```

In the context of the List monad, mzero is the empty list [] and mplus is list concatenation (++). This allows for powerful monadic compositions, particularly useful in parsing and other combinatorial logic.

Through these examples, it becomes evident that monadic composition provides a versatile mechanism to handle complex functional programming patterns involving sequential and conditional operations. In essence, it forms the backbone of effective and expressive Haskell programs, enabling clear and concise code that adheres to functional programming paradigms.

Chapter 10

Advanced Data Structures

This chapter explores advanced data structures in Haskell, including trees and tree traversals, binary search trees, and balanced trees such as AVL and Red-Black trees. It covers graph algorithms, heaps, priority queues, and hash tables. The chapter also examines lazy and persistent data structures, demonstrating their use in practical Haskell programming.

10.1 Introduction to Advanced Data Structures

Advanced data structures play a crucial role in efficient algorithm design and implementation in Haskell. These structures not only improve the performance of operations but also open up new possibilities for complex problem-solving. This section will delve into the fundamental concepts that set the stage for understanding more sophisticated data structures explored in the subsequent sections.

Data structures can be broadly categorized into linear and non-linear types. Linear data structures, such as arrays and lists, follow a sequential order, while non-linear data structures, such as trees and graphs, do not. As we venture into the realm of advanced data structures, we prioritize performance and functionality, emphasizing structures that can handle dynamic and complex data efficiently.

Trees are hierarchical data structures that represent relationships in a parent-child paradigm. There are several types of trees, such as binary trees, AVL trees, and Red-Black trees, each optimized for specific operations like insertion, deletion, and searching. A binary tree, for example, allows each node to have at most two children. A tree's traversal mechanisms, namely in-order, pre-order, and post-order traversals, define the sequence in which the nodes are visited. Consider the following Haskell representation of a simple binary tree:

```
data Tree a = Empty | Node a (Tree a) (Tree a)
    deriving (Show, Eq)
```

To traverse this tree in an in-order fashion, one must visit the left subtree, the root node, and then the right subtree. Here is an implementation of an in-order traversal:

```
inOrder :: Tree a -> [a]
inOrder Empty = []
inOrder (Node value left right) =
    inOrder left ++ [value] ++ inOrder right
```

Another essential class of advanced data structures is balanced trees. Balanced trees maintain additional properties to ensure that the tree remains balanced, thereby guaranteeing more predictable operational performance. AVL and Red-Black trees are common examples that ensure the balance through different mechanisms such as rotations.

Graphs are more general structures consisting of nodes (vertices) connected by edges. They are pivotal in representing and solving problems involving networked data. Graph algorithms like Depth First Search (DFS) and Breadth First Search (BFS) allow efficient exploration of nodes and are fundamental for applications such as finding paths and detecting cycles.

Heaps and priority queues are specialized tree-based data structures that manage a dynamically changing dataset to always allow quick access to the minimum or maximum element. For example, a binary heap supports efficient extract-min operation crucial for algorithms like Dijkstra's shortest path algorithm. Here is a rudimentary implementation of a min-heap property check in Haskell:

```
isMinHeap :: (Ord a) => [a] -> Bool
isMinHeap [] = True
isMinHeap [x] = True
isMinHeap (parent:children) =
    all (>= parent) children && isMinHeap (tail children)
```

Hash tables offer near constant time complexity for inserts, deletes, and lookups using a hash function to distribute keys evenly. This minimizes the chances of collisions and maintains an average-case constant time complexity. The Haskell language provides the Data.Map and Data.HashMap modules as efficient implementations.

Lazy data structures leverage Haskell's non-strict evaluation model to compute elements only when needed. This approach enables the handling of potentially infinite data structures and enhances performance for applications needing demand-driven computations:

```
lazyList :: [Int]
lazyList = [1..]
```

Persistent data structures retain their previous versions when modified, ensuring immutability and enabling functionalities like undo operations or concurrent access without locks. These traits are especially compatible with functional programming paradigms and are extensively used in Haskell programming.

Advanced data structures such as these go beyond the basic capabilities of arrays and lists, providing efficient solutions for a wide array of computational problems. As we progress through this chapter, we will delve deeper into each advanced data structure, exploring their implementations, use cases, and performance considerations in Haskell.

10.2 Trees and Tree Traversals

A tree is a widely utilized data structure that simulates a hierarchical tree structure with a set of nodes and edges. Each node contains a value or a condition and references to child nodes. Trees are instrumental in various applications such as representing hierarchical data, facilitating efficient searching and sorting, and supporting structured data representation.

In Haskell, trees can be defined using algebraic data types. Consider the simple definition of a binary tree:

```
data Tree a = Empty
            | Node a (Tree a) (Tree a)
            deriving (Show, Eq)
```

In this definition, Tree is a parameterized type, where a stands for the type of elements stored in the tree. A tree is either Empty, representing an empty tree, or a Node containing a value of type a and two subtrees.

Tree Traversals

Traversing a tree involves visiting all the nodes in a specific order. The primary tree traversal methods are:

- Pre-order traversal
- In-order traversal
- Post-order traversal
- Level-order traversal

Pre-order Traversal: This traversal method visits the root node first, followed by the left subtree, and then the right subtree. In Haskell, pre-order traversal can be implemented as follows:

```
preOrder :: Tree a -> [a]
preOrder Empty = []
preOrder (Node x left right) = [x] ++ preOrder left ++ preOrder right
```

Here, preOrder is a function that takes a Tree and returns a list of elements. For an Empty tree, it returns an empty list. For a Node, it constructs the result by visiting the node's value x first, followed by the values obtained from the left and right subtrees.

In-order Traversal: In this method, the left subtree is visited first, followed by the root node, and finally the right subtree. The Haskell implementation is:

```
inOrder :: Tree a -> [a]
inOrder Empty = []
inOrder (Node x left right) = inOrder left ++ [x] ++ inOrder right
```

Post-order Traversal: This traversal visits the left subtree first, followed by the right subtree, and then the root node. The Haskell implementation is:

```
postOrder :: Tree a -> [a]
postOrder Empty = []
postOrder (Node x left right) = postOrder left ++ postOrder right ++ [x]
```

Level-order Traversal: Also known as breadth-first traversal, it visits nodes level by level from top to bottom. This requires a queue data structure to keep track of nodes at the current level. Here is a possible implementation, using a list as a queue:

```
import Data.List (foldl')
```

```
levelOrder :: Tree a -> [a]
levelOrder root = bfs [root]
  where
    bfs [] = []
    bfs xs = map nodeValue xs ++ bfs (concatMap nodeChildren xs)

    nodeValue (Node x _ _) = x
    nodeValue Empty = error "Empty node in level order traversal"

    nodeChildren (Node _ left right) = filter isNotEmpty [left, right]
    nodeChildren Empty = error "Empty node in level order traversal"

    isNotEmpty Empty = False
    isNotEmpty _ = True
```

In this implementation, bfs is a helper function performing breadth-first search using a queue of nodes. It extracts node values and their children at each level.

It is essential to understand how these traversals behave for different tree structures and applications. Pre-order traversal is valuable for prefix notation expressions, in-order traversal is often used with binary search trees to retrieve sorted values, post-order traversal is helpful for evaluating postfix expressions, and level-order traversal is useful in various algorithms like breadth-first search in graph theory.

Proficiency with tree traversals in Haskell enables the implementation of complex tree-based algorithms and fosters a deeper grasp of hierarchical data structures. Leveraging Haskell's functional capabilities ensures concise and expressive traversal implementations.

10.3 Binary Search Trees

Binary Search Trees (BSTs) are a type of data structure that maintain sorted order among elements, allowing efficient insertion, deletion, and lookup operations. In a BST, each node stores a key and has two subtrees: the left subtree contains nodes with keys less than the node's key, and the right subtree contains nodes with keys greater than the node's key. This property ensures that BSTs facilitate operations such as search, minimum, maximum, predecessor, successor, insertion, and deletion in logarithmic time on average.

To implement a BST in Haskell, we first define the data type for the binary search tree:

```
data BST a = Empty
           | Node a (BST a) (BST a)
           deriving (Show, Eq)
```

This type definition specifies that a BST is either Empty or a Node containing a value of type a, along with left and right subtrees, which are also BSTs.

Insertion The insertion function ensures that the tree remains a BST by recursively placing the new element in the correct subtree.

```
insert :: (Ord a) => a -> BST a -> BST a
insert x Empty = Node x Empty Empty
insert x (Node y left right)
    | x < y = Node y (insert x left) right
    | x > y = Node y left (insert x right)
    | otherwise = Node y left right
```

This insert function takes an element x and a BST, and returns a new BST with x inserted. If the tree is empty, it creates a new node. If x is less than y, it inserts x into the left subtree; if greater, into the right subtree. If x is equal to y, it means that the element is already present, hence no changes are made.

Searching The search operation checks whether a given element exists in the tree.

```
search :: (Ord a) => a -> BST a -> Bool
search _ Empty = False
search x (Node y left right)
    | x < y = search x left
    | x > y = search x right
    | otherwise = True
```

The search function takes an element x and a BST, returning True if the element is found, and False otherwise. It performs a recursive traversal depending on whether x is less than, greater than, or equal to the current node's value.

Minimum and Maximum To find the minimum element, traverse the left subtree until the end. Conversely, to find the maximum element, traverse the right subtree until the end.

```
findMin :: BST a -> Maybe a
findMin Empty = Nothing
findMin (Node x Empty _) = Just x
findMin (Node _ left _) = findMin left

findMax :: BST a -> Maybe a
findMax Empty = Nothing
findMax (Node x _ Empty) = Just x
findMax (Node _ _ right) = findMax right
```

These functions return Maybe a type to handle the case when the tree is empty. If the tree is empty, they return Nothing; otherwise, they recursively traverse the appropriate subtree and return Just the minimum or maximum value found.

Deletion The deletion operation is more complex due to three possible scenarios: 1. The node to be deleted is a leaf. 2. The node to be deleted has one child. 3. The node to be deleted has two children.

```
delete :: (Ord a) => a -> BST a -> BST a
delete _ Empty = Empty
delete x (Node y left right)
    | x < y = Node y (delete x left) right
    | x > y = Node y left (delete x right)
    | otherwise = case (left, right) of
                    (Empty, Empty) -> Empty
                    (Empty, _) -> right
                    (_, Empty) -> left
                    _ -> let (Just minRight) = findMin right
                         in Node minRight left (delete minRight right)
```

This delete function removes an element x from the BST. It first recursively traverses the tree to find the node to delete. If the node is found: - If it is a leaf, remove it directly. - If it has one child, replace it with that child. - If it has two children, find the minimum element in the right subtree, replace the node's value with this minimum, and recursively delete this minimum from the right subtree.

The provided Haskell implementations handle core BST operations. By maintaining the BST properties, we ensure efficient performance for dynamic set operations. The next section will delve into balanced trees, which leverage additional operations to maintain balanced height and thus guarantee logarithmic time complexity for all operations, even in the worst case.

10.4 Balanced Trees (AVL, Red-Black)

Balanced trees are crucial structures in computer science, ensuring that operations such as insertion, deletion, and search are performed efficiently. Two primary types of balanced trees are AVL trees and Red-Black trees. These trees maintain a balanced height, preventing the worst-case time complexities associated with unbalanced trees.

AVL Trees

An AVL tree is a height-balanced binary search tree. Named after its inventors Adelson-Velsky and Landis, an AVL tree guarantees that the difference in heights between the left and right subtrees of any node (the balance factor) is at most one.

The essential operations in an AVL tree include rotations, which are required to maintain its balance. There are four types of rotations:

- Right Rotation (RR)
- Left Rotation (LL)
- Left-Right Rotation (LR)
- Right-Left Rotation (RL)

Right Rotation (RR)

```
data AVLTree a = Empty | Node a (AVLTree a) (AVLTree a) Int

height :: AVLTree a -> Int
height Empty = 0
height (Node _ _ _ h) = h

singleRightRotate :: AVLTree a -> AVLTree a
singleRightRotate (Node x (Node y T1 T2) T3) =
    Node y T1 (Node x T2 T3)
```

This rotation adjusts the balance when the left child of the left subtree becomes unbalanced.

Left Rotation (LL)

```
singleLeftRotate :: AVLTree a -> AVLTree a
singleLeftRotate (Node x T1 (Node y T2 T3)) =
    Node y (Node x T1 T2) T3
```

This rotation is the mirror operation of the right rotation, used when the right child of the right subtree is unbalanced.

Left-Right Rotation (LR)

```
leftRightRotate :: AVLTree a -> AVLTree a
leftRightRotate (Node x T1 (Node y T2 T3)) =
    singleRightRotate (Node x T1 (singleLeftRotate (Node y T2 T3)))
```

This rotation corrects the balance when the right child of the left subtree is causing the imbalance.

Right-Left Rotation (RL)

```
rightLeftRotate :: AVLTree a -> AVLTree a
rightLeftRotate (Node x T1 (Node y T2 T3)) =
    singleLeftRotate (Node x (singleRightRotate T1) T2)
```

This rotation addresses imbalances where the left child of the right subtree causes problems.

The implementation of these rotations ensures that an AVL tree remains balanced during insertion and deletion operations.

Red-Black Trees

A Red-Black tree is a balanced binary search tree with an additional color attribute for each node, which can either be red or black. The fundamental properties of Red-Black trees are:

- Every node is either red or black.
- The root is always black.
- Red nodes cannot have red children (no two red nodes can be adjacent).
- Every path from a node to its descendant leaves has the same number of black nodes.

These properties ensure that the longest path from the root to a leaf is at most twice as long as the shortest path, which maintains balance and ensures efficient operations.

Insertion and deletion in Red-Black trees involve a series of rotations and color changes to preserve their properties. The essential operations include:

- Insertion
- Fixing Insertions (Recoloring and Rotations)
- Deletion
- Fixing Deletions (Recoloring and Rotations)

Insertion

```
data Color = Red | Black
data RBTree a = E | N Color (RBTree a) a (RBTree a)

insert :: Ord a => a -> RBTree a -> RBTree a
insert x s = makeBlack (ins s)
  where
    ins E = N Red E x E
    ins (N color a y b)
      | x < y = balance color (ins a) y b
      | x > y = balance color a y (ins b)
      | otherwise = N color a y b

    makeBlack (N _ a y b) = N Black a y b
```

The balance function ensures that the tree retains its Red-Black properties after insertion:

```
balance :: Color -> RBTree a -> a -> RBTree a -> RBTree a
balance Black (N Red (N Red a x b) y c) z d = N Red (N Black a x b) y (N Black c z
    d)
balance Black (N Red a x (N Red b y c)) z d = N Red (N Black a x b) y (N Black c z
    d)
balance Black a x (N Red (N Red b y c) z d) = N Red (N Black a x b) y (N Black c z
    d)
balance Black a x (N Red b y (N Red c z d)) = N Red (N Black a x b) y (N Black c z
    d)
balance color a x b = N color a x b
```

The balance function applies the required rotations and color changes to fix any violations of the Red-Black properties.

Understanding and implementing AVL and Red-Black trees in Haskell enhances the ability to handle balanced data structures, ensuring optimal performance for dynamic datasets requiring frequent updates.

10.5 Graphs and Graph Algorithms

Graphs represent a collection of interconnected nodes or vertices where edges connect pairs of vertices. In Haskell, graphs can be modeled using various data structures, enabling efficient traversal and manipulation. This section delves into the representation of graphs, graph traversal algorithms, and the application of these algorithms in Haskell.

A graph G is defined as $G = (V, E)$ where V is a set of vertices, and E is a set of edges connecting these vertices. Graphs can be directed or undirected, reflecting whether edges have a direction or not. Additionally, graphs can be weighted, where edges have associated weights, or unweighted, where all edges are considered to have the same weight.

In Haskell, one common way to represent a graph is through adjacency lists. An adjacency list represents a graph as a list of nodes, each node having a list of adjacent nodes. Here is a simple type definition for an undirected graph using adjacency lists:

```
type Vertex = Int
type Graph = [(Vertex, [Vertex])]
```

Vertex is represented as an Int, and Graph is a list of tuples where each tuple contains a Vertex and a list of adjacent vertices. For instance, the graph:

```
A -- B
| / |
C -- D
```

can be represented in Haskell as follows:

```haskell
graphExample :: Graph
graphExample = [(1, [2, 3]), (2, [1, 3, 4]), (3, [1, 2, 4]), (4, [2, 3])]
```

To traverse a graph, we can use algorithms such as Depth-First Search (DFS) and Breadth-First Search (BFS). DFS explores as far as possible along a branch before backtracking. BFS explores all neighbors of a vertex before moving to the next level. Here is a DFS implementation in Haskell:

```haskell
import qualified Data.Set as Set

dfs :: Graph -> Vertex -> [Vertex]
dfs graph start = dfs' Set.empty [start]
  where
    dfs' visited [] = []
    dfs' visited (x:xs)
      | Set.member x visited = dfs' visited xs
      | otherwise = x : dfs' newVisited newStack
      where
        newVisited = Set.insert x visited
        neighbors = case lookup x graph of
                      Just ns -> ns
                      Nothing -> []
        newStack = neighbors ++ xs
```

In this implementation, dfs takes a graph and a starting vertex, then recursively visits each vertex. The visited set keeps track of visited nodes to prevent cycles. For BFS, the algorithm uses a queue (FIFO) instead of a stack (LIFO):

```haskell
import qualified Data.Sequence as Seq
import qualified Data.Foldable as F

bfs :: Graph -> Vertex -> [Vertex]
bfs graph start = bfs' Set.empty (Seq.singleton start)
  where
    bfs' visited Seq.Empty = []
    bfs' visited (x Seq.:<| xs)
      | Set.member x visited = bfs' visited xs
      | otherwise = x : bfs' newVisited newQueue
      where
        newVisited = Set.insert x visited
        neighbors = case lookup x graph of
                      Just ns -> ns
                      Nothing -> []
        newQueue = xs Seq.>< Seq.fromList neighbors
```

Graph algorithms often require finding the shortest path between nodes. Dijkstra's algorithm efficiently finds the shortest path in a weighted graph using a priority queue:

```
import qualified Data.Map as Map
import qualified Data.PSQueue as PSQ

dijkstra :: Graph -> Vertex -> Map.Map Vertex Int
dijkstra graph start = dijkstra' initialQueue Map.empty
  where
    initialQueue = PSQ.insert start 0 PSQ.empty
    dijkstra' pq distances
      | PSQ.null pq = distances
      | otherwise = dijkstra' newQueue newDistances
      where
        Just (u PSQ.:-> d, pq') = PSQ.minView pq
        neighbors = case lookup u graph of
                      Just ns -> ns
                      Nothing -> []
        newDistances = foldl' updateDistance distances neighbors
        newQueue = foldl' (updateQueue d) pq' neighbors

        updateDistance m v = Map.insertWith min v (d + weight u v) m
        updateQueue d pq v = PSQ.insertWith min v (d + weight u v) pq

    weight _ _ = 1 -- Assuming all edges have weight 1 for simplicity
```

This implementation of Dijkstra's algorithm assumes all edges have a weight of 1, simplifying the example. The priority queue (PSQ) ensures that the vertex with the smallest known distance is processed next.

Graphs can also be represented using adjacency matrices and the edge list representation. Adjacency matrices are typically used for dense graphs, where we can use a 2D array to store edge weights. Here's an example of an adjacency matrix for the same graph:

```
type GraphMatrix = Array (Vertex, Vertex) Int

graphMatrixExample :: GraphMatrix
graphMatrixExample = array ((1,1), (4,4)) [((i,j), edge i j) | i <- [1..4], j <- [1..4]]
  where
    edge 1 2 = 1
    edge 1 3 = 1
    edge 2 1 = 1
    edge 2 3 = 1
    edge 2 4 = 1
    edge 3 1 = 1
    edge 3 2 = 1
    edge 3 4 = 1
    edge 4 2 = 1
    edge 4 3 = 1
    edge _ _ = 0
```

Given the extensive range of graph algorithms and representations, it is essential to select the most appropriate for the problem at hand, ensuring both efficiency and clarity in implementation. Haskell provides powerful abstractions and libraries such as containers for maps and sets and PSQueue for priority queues, facilitating the construction of complex graph algorithms.

10.6 Heaps and Priority Queues

Heaps are a specialized tree-based data structure that satisfy the heap property. For a binary heap, this implies that for every parent node p with children $c1$ and $c2$, the property $p <= c1$ and $p <= c2$ must hold if it is a min-heap, or $p >= c1$ and $p >= c2$ must hold if it is a max-heap. Heaps are critical for efficiently implementing priority queues where elements with higher priority are dequeued before elements with lower priority.

In Haskell, heaps can be realized using various structures, such as arrays or custom tree structures. We will focus on binary heaps and their applications in priority queues. To demonstrate implementation in Haskell, we need to understand both the structure and the operations that maintain the heap property.

Heap Data Structure

The most common way to represent a binary heap is by using a binary tree, but an array-based implementation is also frequent due to its space and cache efficiency. The following is the binary tree definition for a heap in Haskell:

```
data Heap a = Empty | Node a (Heap a) (Heap a) deriving (Show, Eq)
```

The above type definition can represent a binary tree where each $Node$ contains an element and references to left and right subtrees. For convenience, an empty heap is represented by $Empty$.

Insertion in a Heap

Insertion involves adding an element while maintaining the heap property. This is achieved by placing the new element at the bottom-most, right-most position and then allowing it to "bubble up" to its correct position.

Here is the insertion function in Haskell:

```
insert :: (Ord a) => a -> Heap a -> Heap a
insert x Empty = Node x Empty Empty
insert x (Node v l r)
  | height l <= height r = bubbleUp (Node v (insert x l) r)
  | otherwise = bubbleUp (Node v l (insert x r))

bubbleUp :: (Ord a) => Heap a -> Heap a
bubbleUp (Node x Empty _) = Node x Empty Empty
bubbleUp (Node x (Node y ll lr) r)
  | x > y = Node y (bubbleUp (Node x ll lr)) r
  | otherwise = Node x (Node y ll lr) r
bubbleUp (Node x l (Node y rl rr))
```

```
  | x > y = Node y l (bubbleUp (Node x rl rr))
  | otherwise = Node x l (Node y rl rr)
```

This algorithm inserts an element and ensures the heap property by allowing the element to ascend to its correct position.

Deletion from a Heap

Removing the minimum (or maximum) element from a heap, often referred to as extract-min or extract-max, involves removing the root node and then maintaining the heap property. The process includes replacing the root with the last element and then "bubbling down" this element.

The deletion function is as follows:

```
deleteMin :: (Ord a) => Heap a -> Heap a
deleteMin Empty = Empty
deleteMin (Node _ Empty Empty) = Empty
deleteMin (Node _ l Empty) = l
deleteMin (Node _ Empty r) = r
deleteMin (Node _ l r) = bubbleDown (Node lastElem l' r')
  where
    (lastElem, l', r') = removeLast (l, r)

bubbleDown :: (Ord a) => Heap a -> Heap a
bubbleDown (Node x Empty _) = Node x Empty Empty
bubbleDown (Node x l@(Node y _ _) r@(Node z _ _))
  | x <= min y z = Node x l r
  | y <= z = Node y (bubbleDown (Node x (leftChild l) (rightChild l))) r
  | otherwise = Node z l (bubbleDown (Node x (leftChild r) (rightChild r)))
bubbleDown (Node x (Node y _ _) Empty)
  | x > y = Node y (bubbleDown (Node x Empty Empty)) Empty
  | otherwise = Node x (Node y Empty Empty)

removeLast :: (Ord a) => (Heap a, Heap a) -> (a, Heap a, Heap a)
removeLast (Empty, Empty) = error "removeLast called on empty heaps"
removeLast (Node x Empty Empty, r) = (x, Empty, r)
removeLast (l, Empty) = (x, l', Empty)
  where
    (x, l', Empty) = removeLast l
removeLast (Node x l r, rightmostHeap)
  | height l > height r = (lastElem, Node x l newRight, newRightmostHeap)
  | otherwise = (lastElem, Node x newLeft r, newRightmostHeap)
  where
    (lastElem, newLeft, newRightmostHeap) = removeLast r
```

Priority Queues Using Heaps

Priority queues can utilize heaps to efficiently manage elements based on priority. A priority queue's primary operations include enqueue to insert elements and dequeue to remove the highest priority element.

enqueue operation follows the same insertion process as in heaps, while dequeue corresponds to the extraction of the minimum (or maximum) element.

The following defines a priority queue using heaps:

```
data PriorityQueue a = PQ (Heap a) deriving (Show, Eq)

enqueue :: (Ord a) => a -> PriorityQueue a -> PriorityQueue a
enqueue x (PQ h) = PQ (insert x h)

dequeue :: (Ord a) => PriorityQueue a -> (Maybe a, PriorityQueue a)
dequeue (PQ Empty) = (Nothing, PQ Empty)
dequeue (PQ (Node x l r)) = (Just x, PQ (deleteMin (Node x l r)))
```

Heaps provide an efficient way to manage priority queues, with insertion and deletion operations both achieving $O(\log n)$ complexity due to the height of the tree being logarithmic in relation to the number of elements. This efficiency is crucial in applications requiring dynamic priority management such as task scheduling and graph algorithms like Dijkstra's shortest path algorithm.

10.7 Hash Tables

Hash tables are an efficient data structure for storing and retrieving key-value pairs. They offer average-case constant time complexity for both insertion and lookup operations, making them an excellent choice for implementing associative arrays.

A hash table consists of an array of buckets. Each bucket can contain zero or more key-value pairs. A hash function is used to compute an index into the array of buckets, from which the desired value can be found.

HashTable operations are typically defined by three primary methods:

- insert: Adds a new key-value pair to the hash table.
- lookup: Retrieves the value associated with a given key.
- delete: Removes a key-value pair from the hash table.

Structure and Implementation

In Haskell, a hash table can be implemented using the Data.HashTable module. The fundamental operations insert, lookup, and delete are provided. Below is an example of how to create and manipulate a hash table in Haskell:

```
import qualified Data.HashTable.IO as H

type HashTable k v = H.BasicHashTable k v

main :: IO ()
main = do
    ht <- H.new :: IO (HashTable Int String)

    -- Insert key-value pairs
    H.insert ht 1 "Haskell"
    H.insert ht 2 "Programming"

    -- Lookup value for a given key
    result <- H.lookup ht 1
    case result of
        Just value -> putStrLn value -- Output: "Haskell"
        Nothing -> putStrLn "Key not found"

    -- Delete a key-value pair
    H.delete ht 1

    -- Try to lookup a deleted key
    result <- H.lookup ht 1
    case result of
        Just value -> putStrLn value
        Nothing -> putStrLn "Key not found" -- Output: "Key not found"
```

This example illustrates the core operations on a hash table in Haskell:

1. H.new initializes a new, empty hash table.
2. H.insert adds key-value pairs to the hash table.
3. H.lookup retrieves values based on keys.
4. H.delete removes key-value pairs from the hash table.

The Data.HashTable.IO library in Haskell implements mutable hash tables in the IO monad, facilitating in-place updates and deletions. Alternative libraries, such as Data.HashMap.Strict from the unordered-containers package, offer immutable hash tables suitable for pure functional programming. Below is a brief example using Data.HashMap.Strict:

```
import qualified Data.HashMap.Strict as HM

type HashMap k v = HM.HashMap k v

main :: IO ()
main = do
    let hm = HM.insert 1 "Haskell" HM.empty
        hm' = HM.insert 2 "Programming" hm

    -- Lookup value for a given key
    case HM.lookup 1 hm' of
```

```
    Just value -> putStrLn value -- Output: "Haskell"
    Nothing -> putStrLn "Key not found"

-- Delete a key-value pair
let hm'' = HM.delete 1 hm'

-- Try to lookup a deleted key
case HM.lookup 1 hm'' of
    Just value -> putStrLn value
    Nothing -> putStrLn "Key not found" -- Output: "Key not found"
```

In this example, the hash map is built and manipulated in a purely functional manner, without using the IO monad. Immutability ensures that each modification results in a new version of the hash map, preserving the original one.

Hash Function

The efficiency of a hash table largely depends on the quality of its hash function. A good hash function should distribute keys uniformly across the buckets to minimize collisions. In Haskell, common hash functions are provided by the hashable library. The Hashable type class specifies a function hash that computes the hash value of an object:

```
import Data.Hashable

instance Hashable MyType where
    hashWithSalt salt myValue = ...
```

The hashWithSalt function allows customizing the hash function by incorporating a salt value. This can help in preventing hash table poisoning attacks, where an adversary deliberately causes many collisions.

Collision Resolution

When two keys hash to the same index, a collision occurs. Hash tables typically handle collisions using one of two methods:

- Chaining: Each bucket points to a list of key-value pairs, and collisions are handled by appending the new key-value pair to the list.
- Open Addressing: All elements are stored in the array itself, and collisions are resolved by probing alternative slots in the array.

Haskell Data.HashTable.IO employs chaining. When implementing hash tables with chaining, the performance can degrade if many collisions occur, transforming the time complexity from O(1) to O(n). Thus, maintaining a low load factor (the ratio of the number of elements to the number of buckets) is imperative.

Example of a Custom Hash Table

For educational purposes, here's a simple custom hash table implementation in Haskell using associations and chaining for collision resolution:

```
import Data.List (find)
import Data.Maybe (isJust, fromMaybe)

data HashTable k v = HashTable [[(k, v)]] Int

hashFunction :: Int -> Int -> Int
hashFunction size key = key `mod` size

emptyHashTable :: Int -> HashTable k v
emptyHashTable size = HashTable (replicate size []) size

insert :: (Eq k) => HashTable k v -> k -> v -> HashTable k v
insert (HashTable buckets size) key value =
    let hashIndex = hashFunction size (hash key)
        newBucket = (key, value) : filter ((/= key) . fst) (buckets !! hashIndex)
        newBuckets = take hashIndex buckets ++ [newBucket] ++ drop (hashIndex +
            1) buckets
    in HashTable newBuckets size

lookup :: (Eq k) => HashTable k v -> k -> Maybe v
lookup (HashTable buckets size) key =
    let hashIndex = hashFunction size (hash key)
    in fmap snd . find ((== key) . fst) $ buckets !! hashIndex

delete :: (Eq k) => HashTable k v -> k -> HashTable k v
delete (HashTable buckets size) key =
    let hashIndex = hashFunction size (hash key)
        newBucket = filter ((/= key) . fst) (buckets !! hashIndex)
        newBuckets = take hashIndex buckets ++ [newBucket] ++ drop (hashIndex +
            1) buckets
    in HashTable newBuckets size
```

This simple hash table implementation provides a basic foundation for understanding underlying principles.

10.8 Lazy Data Structures

Haskell, as a lazy evaluation language, provides unique capabilities for defining and working with lazy data structures. These data structures offer significant advantages, such as the ability to handle potentially infinite data structures and improved efficiency by deferring computations until absolutely necessary. In this section, we will delve into the intricacies of lazy data structures, their implementation in Haskell, and their practical applications.

Understanding Laziness in Haskell: In Haskell, laziness refers to the delayed computation of expressions until their values are actually needed. This is achieved through the use of thunks, which are unevaluated expressions that store the necessary information to compute the value when it is required. The lazy evaluation strategy can be particularly advantageous in constructing data structures that deal with infinite or large amounts of data where immediate computation might be impractical or unnecessary.

Lazy Lists: One of the most fundamental examples of lazy data structures in Haskell is the lazy list. Lazy lists allow the representation of potentially infinite sequences without causing evaluation problems. Consider the following Haskell code to define an infinite list of natural numbers:

```
nats :: [Integer]
nats = [0..]
```

In this example, nats is a lazy list that starts from 0 and enumerates all natural numbers. The range syntax [0..] creates an infinite list, leveraging Haskell's lazy evaluation to generate list elements on demand. Accessing an element or a finite portion of this list forces the evaluation of only the required segment.

Streams: A stream is an abstraction similar to lazy lists, often used in functional programming to handle sequences of data wherein elements are computed as they are accessed. In Haskell, streams can be represented as follows:

```
data Stream a = Cons a (Stream a)

streamFrom :: Integer -> Stream Integer
streamFrom n = Cons n (streamFrom (n + 1))

takeStream :: Int -> Stream a -> [a]
takeStream 0 _ = []
takeStream n (Cons x rest) = x : takeStream (n-1) rest
```

In the above definitions, Stream is a custom data type where each element Cons contains a value and a reference to the next element in the stream. The function streamFrom generates an infinite stream of integers starting from a given number. The function takeStream extracts a finite list of elements from a stream, again leveraging Haskell's lazy evaluation properties.

Lazy Trees: Trees can also be lazily evaluated, which allows for operations on trees containing infinite structures or deferred computations. For example, consider a simple lazy binary tree:

```
data Tree a = Leaf | Node a (Tree a) (Tree a)

treeFrom :: Integer -> Tree Integer
treeFrom n = Node n (treeFrom (2 * n)) (treeFrom (2 * n + 1))

takeTree :: Int -> Tree a -> Tree a
takeTree 0 _ = Leaf
takeTree n Leaf = Leaf
takeTree n (Node x left right) = Node x (takeTree (n-1) left) (takeTree (n-1) right)
```

Here, Tree is a data structure where each Node contains a value and two subtrees (left and right). The function treeFrom generates an infinite binary tree where each node's children are generated by multiplying the parent value by 2 and 2 plus 1, respectively. The function takeTree retrieves a finite portion of the tree up to a certain depth.

Practical Applications: Lazy data structures are widely used in scenarios where deferred computations are beneficial. Examples include handling large datasets, implementing efficient incremental algorithms, and constructing pipelines for stream processing. They facilitate operations on potentially infinite data series without exhausting computational resources prematurely.

Consider this use case for handling large data files:

```
processFile :: FilePath -> IO ()
processFile path = do
    content <- readFile path
    let linesList = lines content
    mapM_ putStrLn (take 10 linesList)
```

In this code, readFile reads a file lazily, meaning the content is read and processed on demand instead of loading the entire file into memory at once. This approach is particularly effective for large files, enabling the program to remain responsive and memory-efficient.

By harnessing the power of lazy evaluation, Haskell programmers can build data structures that elegantly and efficiently handle complex and large-scale problems, offering unique advantages over strict evaluation counterparts.

10.9 Persistent Data Structures

Persistent data structures are fundamental in the realm of functional programming, providing immutability and ensuring that previous versions of data remain accessible even after modifications. In Haskell, the persistent nature of data structures aligns seamlessly with the language's purity and referential transparency.

In traditional imperative programming, data structures are typically ephemeral, meaning that once modified, the previous state is lost unless explicitly copied. In contrast, persistent data structures leverage immutability and share unchanged parts between different versions, optimizing both memory usage and efficiency.

To illustrate the concept, consider a simple example of a persistent list. Modifying this list does not result in the original list being overwritten. Instead, a new list is created, sharing common elements with the original.

```
data List a = Nil | Cons a (List a)

-- Example of modifying a persistent list
let originalList = Cons 1 (Cons 2 Nil)
let modifiedList = Cons 0 originalList
```

In the above code, originalList remains unchanged even after modifiedList is created. Both lists share the common structure corresponding to Cons 1 (Cons 2 Nil).

Persistent data structures commonly used in Haskell include:

- Data.Map: A persistent implementation of ordered maps (dictionaries).
- Data.Set: A persistent set data structure.
- Data.Sequence: A persistent sequence data structure.
- Data.Vector: Mutable and immutable vectors.

Efficient Persistent Data Structures

Efficiency is a critical consideration in the design of persistent data structures. Purely functional data structures must balance the cost of immutability with performance. A classic efficient persistent data structure is the purely functional queue:

```
module PersistentQueue (
    Queue,
    empty,
    snoc,
    head,
    tail
) where

data Queue a = Queue [a] [a]
```

```
empty :: Queue a
empty = Queue [] []

snoc :: Queue a -> a -> Queue a
snoc (Queue front back) x = Queue front (x : back)

head :: Queue a -> a
head (Queue [] []) = error "empty queue"
head (Queue [] back) = Prelude.head (reverse back)
head (Queue (x:_) _) = x

tail :: Queue a -> Queue a
tail (Queue [] []) = error "empty queue"
tail (Queue [] back) = Queue (Prelude.tail (reverse back)) []
tail (Queue (_:xs) back) = Queue xs back
```

The Queue data structure uses two lists to represent the front and back of the queue, allowing amortized $O(1)$ operations for enqueue (snoc) and dequeue (tail).

Persistent Arrays and Hash Arrays Mapped Tries

Efficient persistent arrays are more challenging due to the need for random access and update operations. The Hash Array Mapped Trie (HAMT) is an advanced data structure that provides efficient persistent hash maps and sets.

The HAMT uses a hash array mapped trie to store key-value pairs and efficiently handles collision using a combination of hashing and array indexing. This data structure is defined as follows:

```
import Data.Bits (shiftR)
import qualified Data.Array as A

data HAMT k v = Empty
              | Leaf k v
              | Node (A.Array Int (HAMT k v))

hash :: k -> Int
hash = -- implementation of your hash function here

insert :: (Eq k) => k -> v -> HAMT k v -> HAMT k v
insert key value Empty = Leaf key value
insert key value (Leaf k v)
    | key == k = Leaf key value
    | otherwise = -- collision handling
insert key value (Node arr) = -- node insertion logic
```

The HAMT structure balances space and time efficiency, allowing for near-constant time performance for insertion, deletion, and lookup operations.

Applications of Persistent Data Structures

Persistent data structures are invaluable in functional reactive programming (FRP), where the immutability and ability to maintain previous versions of data are critical. They are also used extensively in version control systems, undo mechanisms, and anywhere historical data tracking is essential.

```
import Data.Map (Map)
import qualified Data.Map as Map

type VersionedMap k v = [Map k v]

insertVersion :: (Ord k) => k -> v -> VersionedMap k v -> VersionedMap k v
insertVersion key value versions =
    let newVersion = Map.insert key value (head versions)
    in newVersion : versions
```

In the code snippet above, modifications to a VersionedMap create a new version incorporating the changes while retaining all previous versions intact, thus facilitating rollback and historical data analysis.

The principles and practices of persistent data structures are crucial in leveraging Haskell's functional programming advantages, enhancing both code reliability and data integrity.

10.10 Using Advanced Data Structures in Haskell

Advanced data structures play an essential role in optimizing performance and managing complexity in Haskell programs. In this section, we will examine practical applications of advanced data structures introduced earlier in the chapter: trees, graphs, heaps, hash tables, as well as lazy and persistent data structures. We will illustrate their integration and use in Haskell through coherent code examples.

Given the functional nature of Haskell, most data structures are immutable, and operations on them return new structures while preserving the original versions. This immutability simplifies reasoning about code and avoids concurrency issues inherent in mutable state.

Binary Search Trees: Consider a scenario where we need to maintain a dynamic set of integers in sorted order to enable quick look-ups and insertions. A Binary Search Tree (BST) suffices for this purpose.

```
data BST a = Empty
           | Node (BST a) a (BST a)
           deriving (Show, Eq)

insert :: (Ord a) => a -> BST a -> BST a
```

```
insert x Empty = Node Empty x Empty
insert x (Node left v right)
    | x < v = Node (insert x left) v right
    | x > v = Node left v (insert x right)
    | otherwise = Node left v right

search :: (Ord a) => a -> BST a -> Bool
search x Empty = False
search x (Node left v right)
    | x < v = search x left
    | x > v = search x right
    | otherwise = True
```

This Haskell implementation of a BST provides an efficient way to insert elements and search for elements, with an average-case time complexity of $O(\log n)$ for both operations.

AVL Trees: To avoid the degradation of the time complexity to $O(n)$ in the worst case, where the tree becomes unbalanced, we use AVL Trees. AVL trees maintain a balance factor for each node and perform rotations to keep the tree balanced during insertions and deletions.

```
data AVL a = Empty
           | Node (AVL a) a (AVL a) Int
           deriving (Show, Eq)

height :: AVL a -> Int
height Empty = 0
height (Node _ _ _ h) = h

balanceFactor :: AVL a -> Int
balanceFactor Empty = 0
balanceFactor (Node left _ right _) = height left - height right

rotateLeft :: AVL a -> AVL a
rotateLeft (Node left v (Node rightLeft rightValue rightRight rightHeight) height) =
    Node (Node left v rightLeft (height-1)) rightValue rightRight (height-1)

rotateRight :: AVL a -> AVL a
rotateRight (Node (Node leftLeft leftValue leftRight leftHeight) v right height) =
    Node leftLeft leftValue (Node leftRight v right (height-1)) (height-1)

balance :: AVL a -> AVL a
balance node@(Node left v right h)
    | bf > 1 && balanceFactor left >= 0 = rotateRight node
    | bf > 1 = rotateRight (Node (rotateLeft left) v right h)
    | bf < -1 && balanceFactor right <= 0 = rotateLeft node
    | bf < -1 = rotateLeft (Node left v (rotateRight right) h)
    | otherwise = node
    where bf = balanceFactor node

avlInsert :: (Ord a) => a -> AVL a -> AVL a
avlInsert x Empty = Node Empty x Empty 1
avlInsert x (Node left v right h)
    | x < v = balance $ Node (avlInsert x left) v right (1 + max (height left) (height
        right))
    | x > v = balance $ Node left v (avlInsert x right) (1 + max (height left) (height
        right))
    | otherwise = Node left v right h
```

The above code snippets demonstrate the insertion and balancing operations of an AVL Tree. AVL Trees ensure that the height difference between left and right subtrees is at most one, maintaining the $O(\log n)$ complexity for insertion, deletion, and search operations.

Hash Tables: Hash Tables provide an efficient way to store key-value pairs with average-case time complexities of $O(1)$ for insertion, deletion, and search operations. Haskell's Data.HashTable module offers efficient hash table manipulations.

```
import qualified Data.HashTable.IO as H

type HashTable k v = H.BasicHashTable k v

hashTableOps :: IO ()
hashTableOps = do
   ht <- H.new :: IO (HashTable Int String)
   H.insert ht 1 "Haskell"
   H.insert ht 2 "Functional"
   H.insert ht 3 "Programming"

   v1 <- H.lookup ht 1
   v2 <- H.lookup ht 2
   v3 <- H.lookup ht 3

   print v1
   print v2
   print v3
```

In this example, the Data.HashTable.IO module creates a hash table and performs basic operations like insertion and lookup. The results demonstrate the effective use of hash tables for quick access and manipulation of key-value pairs.

Heaps and Priority Queues: Heaps are used to implement priority queues in Haskell efficiently. Priority queues require efficient access to the minimum (or maximum) element.

```
import qualified Data.Heap as Heap

priorityQueueOps :: IO ()
priorityQueueOps = do
    let pq = Heap.empty :: Heap.MinHeap Int
    let pq1 = Heap.insert 5 pq
    let pq2 = Heap.insert 3 pq1
    let pq3 = Heap.insert 10 pq2

    let minElem = Heap.minimum pq3
    let pq4 = Heap.deleteMin pq3

    print minElem
    print $ Heap.toList pq4
```

In this example, we use Data.Heap to demonstrate the basic operations on a min-heap, including element insertion, finding the minimum element, and deletion of the minimum element. The resulting priority queue facilitates efficient priority-based processing.

Graphs: Graph algorithms are fundamental in solving problems like shortest paths, network flows, and connectivity. Haskell's Data.Graph module supports graph representation and manipulation.

```
import qualified Data.Graph as Graph

graphOps :: IO ()
graphOps = do
    let edges = [(1, 2), (2, 3), (3, 1), (3, 4)]
    let (graph, nodeFromVertex, vertexFromKey) = Graph.graphFromEdges [((), 1, [2]),
            ((), 2, [3]), ((), 3, [1, 4])]

    let neighbors = Graph.neighbors graph (vertexFromKey 1)

    print neighbors
```

The example above illustrates constructing and manipulating a directed graph using the Data.Graph module, emphasizing edge definitions and retrieval of neighboring vertices.

Lazy and Persistent Data Structures: Haskell advocates lazy evaluation, allowing deferred computations for performance benefits.

```
data Stream a = Cons a (Stream a)

streamFrom :: Int -> Stream Int
streamFrom n = Cons n (streamFrom (n + 1))

takeStream :: Int -> Stream a -> [a]
takeStream 0 _ = []
takeStream n (Cons x xs) = x : takeStream (n - 1) xs

exampleStream :: [Int]
exampleStream = takeStream 10 (streamFrom 0)
```

This example defines a lazy Stream data structure, generating an infinite sequence of integers starting from a given number. The takeStream function extracts a finite list from this infinite stream, demonstrating lazy evaluation's power in managing potentially infinite data.

Using advanced data structures in Haskell allows the seamless integration of efficient algorithms in a functional programming paradigm, leveraging immutability and lazy evaluation to ensure robust, maintainable, and performant code. These data structures unlock a vast array of possibilities for optimizing and solving complex computational problems within the Haskell ecosystem.

Made in the USA
Monee, IL
05 November 2026

67911526R00148